It's Not Personal

In order to be confirmed to a lifetime appointment on the federal bench, all district and circuit court nominees must appear before the Senate Judiciary Committee for a confirmation hearing. Despite their relatively low profile, these lower court judges make up 99 percent of permanent federal judgeships and decide cases that relate to a wide variety of policy areas. To uncover why senators hold confirmation hearings for lower federal court nominees and the value of these proceedings more generally, the authors analyzed transcripts for all district and circuit court confirmation hearings between 1993 and 2012, the largest systematic analysis of lower court confirmation hearings to date. The book finds that the time-consuming practice of confirmation hearings for district and circuit court nominees provides an important venue for senators to advocate on behalf of their policy preferences and bolster their chances of being re-elected. The wide variation in lower court nominees' experiences before the Judiciary Committee exists because senators pursue these goals in different ways, depending on the level of controversy surrounding a nominee. Ultimately, the findings inform a (re)assessment of the role hearings play in ensuring quality judges, providing advice and consent, and advancing the democratic values of transparency and accountability.

Logan Dancey is Associate Professor of Government at Wesleyan University. **Kjersten R. Nelson** is Associate Professor of Political Science at North Dakota State University. **Eve M. Ringsmuth** is Associate Professor of Political Science at Oklahoma State University.

LEGISLATIVE POLITICS & POLICY MAKING

Series Editors

Janet M. Box-Steffensmeier, Vernal Riffe Professor of Political Science, The Ohio State University

David Canon, Professor of Political Science, University of Wisconsin, Madison

RECENT TITLES IN THE SERIES:

Losing to Win: Why Congressional Majorities Play Politics Instead of Make Laws
JEREMY GELMAN

It's Not Personal: Politics and Policy in Lower Court Confirmation Hearings
LOGAN DANCEY, KJERSTEN R. NELSON, AND EVE M. RINGSMUTH

On Parliamentary War: Partisan Conflict and Procedural Change in the U.S. Senate
JAMES I. WALLNER

The Jeffords Switch: Changing Majority Status and Causal Processes in the U.S. Senate
CHRIS DEN HARTOG AND NATHAN W. MONROE

The Committee: A Study of Policy, Power, Politics, and Obama's Historic Legislative Agenda on Capitol Hill
BRYAN W. MARSHALL AND BRUCE C. WOLPE

The Whips: Building Party Coalitions in Congress
C. LAWRENCE EVANS

Indecision in American Legislatures
JEFFREY J. HARDEN AND JUSTIN H. KIRKLAND

Electoral Incentives in Congress
JAMIE L. CARSON AND JOEL SIEVERT

Gendered Vulnerability: How Women Work Harder to Stay in Office
JEFFREY LAZARUS AND AMY STEIGERWALT

Politics over Process: Partisan Conflict and Post-Passage Processes in the U.S. Congress
HONG MIN PARK, STEVEN S. SMITH, AND RYAN J. VANDER WIELEN

The Rise of the Representative: Lawmakers and Constituents in Colonial America
PEVERILL SQUIRE

Implementing Term Limits: The Case of the Michigan Legislature
MARJORIE SARBAUGH-THOMPSON AND LYKE THOMPSON

For a complete list of titles in this series, please see www.press.umich.edu.

IT'S NOT PERSONAL

Politics and Policy in Lower Court Confirmation Hearings

Logan Dancey, Kjersten R. Nelson, and Eve M. Ringsmuth

University of Michigan Press
Ann Arbor

eni, Carly Mayes, and Erik Meyers for their research assistance. A special thanks to Emma Solomon for the time she spent enthusiastically and skillfully coding transcripts for our intercoder reliability analyses. Emma helped advance the project in many other ways as both a research assistant and a collaborator.

We also wish to thank the editors and staff at the University of Michigan Press, especially Danielle Coty, Elizabeth Demers, and Kevin Rennells. The feedback from anonymous reviewers improved the book in numerous ways, and we are grateful for the time and energy they invested in reading and commenting on the manuscript.

For personal support and never-ending patience, Kjersten thanks Ryan Nagle; Sue Wolf Nelson and Barry Nelson; and colleague/friends Nick Bauroth, Sarah Boonstoppel, Steve Briggs, A. J. Myer, and Dan Pemstein. For the occasional (welcome) distraction and sources of perspective, all her thanks and love to Signe, Cormac, and Eamonn. And, of course, she gives thanks to the two best coauthors a person could ask for.

For her love and support in all facets of life, Logan offers his thanks to Laura Baum. He would also like to acknowledge the support of Marcia Dancey, George Dancey, Carmen Daskalos, his colleagues in the Government Department at Wesleyan, and the lunchtime crew at the Daniel Family Commons. Finally, for the daily joys they bring, he offers a special thanks to Maya and Owen.

For his unfailing love and support of her and this project despite things always taking longer than she'd hoped, Eve thanks her husband, Simon. She would also like to acknowledge the long-standing encouragement provided by Marybeth and Maurice Champion-Garthe, John and Heather Van Sice, John and Sue Ringsmuth, Peter and Kristena Rudloff, Andrea Adams, Sarah Prior, Keira Craig, Beth Ringsmuth Stolpman, and the Lee 0/1 Bears. Finally, she is especially grateful for the love of Isaac and Jonah, who continuously provide humbling and inspiring perspective.

As we were finalizing this manuscript to be printed, we learned of the passing of our friends, Aaron Rapport and Joyce Heckman. Aaron and Joyce were a Minnesota graduate school power couple. Aaron was a colleague of ours in the political science graduate program, and his sharp wit, generosity, and biting humor made graduate school decidedly more pleasant for all of us. We came to know Joyce through Aaron; she was concurrently working on her PhD in apparel design and feminist studies. We quickly came to appreciate her intellect, kindness, and humor. We are deeply grateful for our friendship with Joyce and Aaron and for the time we shared with them.

Contents

Digital materials related to this title can be found on the Fulcrum platform via the following citable URL: https://doi.org/10.3998/mpub.10020712

Tables and Figures

Tables

Figures

ONE

Introduction

Despite receiving a "well qualified" rating from the American Bar Association, President Obama's Ninth Circuit nominee Goodwin Liu appeared before the Senate Judiciary Committee twice. During his two confirmation hearings, he was asked more than 150 questions by 14 members of the Judiciary Committee, even though Democrats controlled both the White House and the Senate during the hearings. These questions tended to be rigorous too. For example, many senators interrogated Liu about previous writings, in particular asking him to defend his philosophy of constitutional fidelity. Others focused on his behavior during the process, suggesting that he had not been completely forthcoming in materials provided to the committee. This type of in-depth and tailored questioning by multiple committee members suggests that senators used the hearings as an opportunity to scrutinize Liu regarding his fitness to occupy a seat on the federal bench.

In contrast, when Samuel Alito faced the Judiciary Committee for his confirmation hearing to become a judge on the U.S. Court of Appeals for the Third Circuit, only two senators participated, one Republican and one Democrat. The senators posed a meager four questions collectively even though the Senate was controlled by Democrats and Alito had been nominated by Republican President George H. W. Bush. Alito's circuit court hearing featured positive comments from the two members of the committee in attendance and playful banter with Alito's then four-year-old son. The questions posed were routine, not particularly challenging, and did not require Alito to wade into any controversial territory. For example, though he was a member of the president's opposition party, Senator Kennedy (D-MA) asked innocuous questions such as, "If you are confirmed, will you be able to see both sides of the claims against the Government?" and, "Based on your experience [in the Office of the Solicitor General], what qualities do you believe are most important for an appellate Judge?" The types of questions asked and the overall tone of Liu's and Alito's hearings signal that significant variation exists in how senators approach confirmation hearings for lower court nominees.

This leads to the core question of the book: *Why do senators hold confirmation hearings for lower federal court nominees, and what is the value of these hearings in the larger advice and consent process?* One obvious answer to this question is that senators hold confirmation hearings to vet individual nominees. These proceedings provide an opportunity for senators to scrutinize the president's nominees, and if used in this manner the hearings could help position senators to make informed decisions that ensure only those who are fit to serve are confirmed to positions on the federal bench. Goodwin Liu's in-depth hearings fit this explanation. We find, however, that most hearings do not resemble Liu's. The majority of lower court confirmation hearings are akin to Alito's experience before the Judiciary Committee when he was a circuit court nominee. In such hearings, nominees are asked a modest number of questions by only a few senators. Notably, this relatively light public scrutiny of nominees has endured even as the contentiousness of the broader confirmation process has increased (Bell 2002a; Scherer 2005; Binder and Maltzman 2009; Steigerwalt 2010; Tobias 2016). Our analyses show that members of the Judiciary Committee rarely use these proceedings to closely scrutinize lower court nominees on their individual merits. As we discuss in chapter 2, nominees endure a significant vetting process before they get to the hearing stage; once there, and in the absence of attendant controversy, committee members tend to assume the nominee is "acceptable" and move quickly through the hearing and confirmation (Scherer, Bartels, and Steigerwalt 2008).

If senators do not hold confirmation hearings primarily for the purpose of scrutinizing individual nominees, why do these hearings endure? Further, why do these proceedings continue to occupy so much of the Judiciary Committee's scarce time? Ultimately, we argue that senators use these hearings to advance both electoral and policy goals. The wide variation in lower court nominees' experiences before the Judiciary Committee exists because senators pursue these goals in different ways, depending on the level of controversy surrounding a nominee. As the cases of Liu and Alito demonstrate, there are two types of confirmation hearings: relatively routine hearings for typical nominees and more contentious, better-attended hearings for controversial nominees.

A Platform for Advancing Electoral and Policy Goals

Building on the work of Fenno (1973), we view members of Congress as pursuing multiple goals, with re-election and good public policy chief among them. Hearings are thus designed with both policy and electoral goals of the members in mind. Importantly, we also argue that there is variation in how senators use confirmation hearings to advance these goals. Namely, senators seek policy and electoral benefits in different ways in hearings for a small but important subset of controversial nominees—like Goodwin Liu—compared to hearings for more typical nominees.

Electoral Goals

The use of confirmation hearings to advance senators' electoral goals is most apparent at the high-profile, contentious hearings for controversial nominees. These hearings often resemble Supreme Court confirmation hearings, with nominees fielding hundreds of questions on topics ranging from their past writings to their current judicial philosophy and views on salient cases. Scholars have shown how interest groups play an important role in identifying controversial nominees and mobilizing support for or opposition to their confirmations (Scherer 2005; Scherer, Bartels, and Steigerwalt 2008; Steigerwalt 2010). For senators who want to "score points" with these interest groups as a way of gaining electoral support (Scherer 2005), the hearings offer a public venue for criticizing or defending a nominee. Additionally, given that members of the Judiciary Committee are more ideologically extreme and tend to represent "safe" districts (see Lewis 2014 and chapter 2), publicly criticizing or defending a nominee will also likely play well with their voters.

At hearings for noncontroversial nominees, the lack of involvement by interest groups and constituencies supporting or opposing the nominee makes it unlikely that members see much electoral benefit from their questioning of nominees. That does not preclude senators from participating in hearings in other ways that might further their electoral goals. In particular, when nominees from a senator's state appear before the committee, senators can use introductory remarks as a way of highlighting their role in identifying and advocating for nominees from their state. In so doing, senators cultivate an "impression of influence" (Grimmer, Westwood, and Messing 2014) in the process of selecting and confirming high quality judicial nominees, which is something about which they can boast to constituents. As we show in chapter 6, senators from both parties make frequent use of such opportunities, regardless of whether or not they sit on the Judiciary Committee.

We supplement our coding of the transcripts with interviews of key players in the confirmation process, including current and former staffers on the Senate Judiciary Committee, interest group staffers, and two former senators who served on the Judiciary Committee: Jon Kyl (R-AZ) and Ted Kaufman (D-DE). The interviews, which are described in more detail in appendix A, provide insight into how different actors view the hearings and their role in the larger advice and consent process.[1] As a result, we are able to speak to both broad trends in the way hearings are conducted as well as to individualized accounts of how key actors approach the hearings.

Ultimately, by investigating our core question from a variety of perspectives, our examination of lower court confirmation hearings provides an account of why senators hold confirmation hearings for lower court nominees. The analyses also allow us to assess the value of these proceedings within the advice and consent process more broadly and to speak to recent critiques of and calls for reforming the hearings.

Outline of the Book

In the next chapter, we begin our assessment of the role confirmation hearings play by providing an overview of their place in the sequence of events that make up the larger confirmation process. In addition, we detail the process by which the Senate Judiciary Committee considers nominations, with an emphasis on who gets a hearing and how the hearings operate. We also take stock of who serves (and has served) on the Judiciary Committee and what committee composition might indicate about the manner in which confirmation hearings are conducted. Then, in chapter 3, we discuss the differences between hearings for controversial and noncontroversial nominees—a distinction we use throughout the book—and provide justification for that classification. Noncontroversial nominees make up the bulk of lower court nominees, so their hearings furnish an understanding of how a typical hearing will unfold. Controversial nominees, on the other hand, receive a disproportionate share of resources and attention from committee members but also from other senators, interest groups, the media, and citizens. Thus, while these are a small segment of nominees, it is vital to understand how controversy changes the nature of the hearings. In chapter 3, we also introduce the hearing data and discuss how the hearing transcripts were coded, and we offer some initial aggregate analyses of the data. These analyses largely provide evidence for a lack of a clear upward or downward trend over time for key metrics, such as the number and types of questions asked, despite the changing context around them. Importantly, though, we identify Congress-to-Congress variation in the content of confirmation hearings, which is linked to changes in the political context. This then is the springboard for the empirical analyses that follow.

In the remainder of the book, we analyze district and circuit court confirmation hearings for both noncontroversial and controversial nominees to assess the incentives for senators to engage in these proceedings. Are senators motivated by a desire to individually vet each judicial nominee? Or are committee senators more motivated by policy and electoral goals? Chapter 4 begins a systematic investigation of these questions by examining variation in the extent to which senators participate in hearings for individual nominees. The analyses in this chapter provide the first evidence that typical hearings are not a site for individual vetting of judicial nominees; instead, senators are more motivated to participate based on political and institutional factors.

Chapter 5 focuses on how senators on the Judiciary Committee use the hearings as a venue for engaging in larger policy battles irrespective of the individual nominees a president selects. This chapter provides further evidence, in the case of noncontroversial nominees, that senators do not use the hearings to vet individual nominees. By analyzing the likelihood of receiving questions in three broad categories—qualifications of the nominee, issue area questions, and questions about the nominee's judicial philosophy—we find that Judiciary Committee members increase the number of questions related to policy during periods of broader conflict and when the nominee would fill a position that could affect the policy decisions made by a given court. Through an analysis of four long-serving senators' questions, we also show how individual committee members use the hearings to raise topics of particular concern to the senator. In sum, the evidence presented in chapter 5 suggests that confirmation hearings reflect senators' responses to larger political and institutional forces and their desire to influence the direction of policy.

Chapter 6 examines how confirmation hearings may serve to further senators' electoral goals, both for the members of the Judiciary Committee *and* the wider Senate. Senators not on the committee have the opportunity to introduce nominees from their own state at the beginning of confirmation hearings. We find evidence that senators use introductory remarks as a platform for credit claiming—a key activity used to procure electoral benefits (Mayhew 1974)—as they tout their role in the judicial selection and confirmation process. For committee members, the potential for electoral benefits is low for typical nominees' hearings. When controversy surrounds a nominee, however, this alters the calculus for committee members. The higher salience associated with these hearings both incentivizes attempts to "score points" with attentive interest groups who can help mobilize votes for allied senators (Scherer 2005) and provides opportunities to vet nominees that senators may see as too ideologically extreme for the bench.

In chapter 7 we focus our attention on these controversial nominees. We further develop our argument that the incentives for senators to participate in confirmation hearings change in important ways when controversial nominees are involved. We submit that the involvement of national interest groups in the confirmation processes for controversial nominees creates a national, ideologically driven, and partisan audience that stands in stark contrast to the low profile of typical confirmation hearings. This audience, we argue, motivates senators to engage in much more intensive, individualized scrutiny of nominees in order to advance senators' policy and electoral goals. Overall, the evidence we present in this chapter confirms that these hearings are not simply longer versions of noncontroversial nominees' hearings. Instead, committee members use hearings for controversial nominees to rigorously scrutinize the previous behaviors, writings, and decisions of nominees by focusing more on issue-based questions and questioning nominees in highly individualized ways.

In the final chapter, we reconsider the value of confirmation hearings in the advice and consent process in light of the core findings presented throughout the book. In an era of declining confirmation rates and increasingly contentious battles over staffing the federal courts, scholars and practitioners have advanced a variety of reform proposals (e.g., Binder and Maltzman 2009; Galston 2012; Tobias 2016). The hearings themselves have come under criticism, with Circuit Court Judge John Walker referring to hearings as "political theater" that "trivializes" the process (Walker 2012) and others calling for the elimination of hearings altogether at the district court level (Shenkman 2012). Although our results suggest that eliminating hearings would have minimal impact on the scrutiny most individual nominees receive, our findings offer a nuanced take on what would be lost in the absence of hearings. Most notably, these hearings serve (or have the potential to serve) a unique role in fostering a public, interbranch dialogue over the direction of the federal courts and public policy more generally, and they also function as an important safety net in the rare instances when significant questions are raised about a nominee's fitness for the bench. We therefore conclude with an assessment of the role hearings play in ensuring quality judges, providing advice and consent, and advancing the democratic values of transparency and accountability.

TWO

Confirmation Hearings

Who Conducts Them, Who Gets One, and How They Work

When then Judge Sonia Sotomayor appeared before the Senate Judiciary Committee for her confirmation hearing to become a U.S. Supreme Court justice, the members of the committee asked her approximately 700 questions (Farganis and Wedeking 2014). This was a markedly different experience compared to when she appeared before this body for her earlier confirmation hearings. At her district court hearing, only the presiding senator, Sen. Ted Kennedy (D-MA), posed any questions, and he limited his interaction with Sotomayor to six questions. Likewise, while her circuit court confirmation hearing included questioning by more members of the committee, four total, the bulk of the committee chose not to participate in the proceedings. Sotomayor's three hearings before the committee looked quite different from one another and suggest that the most visible type of confirmation hearings—those for Supreme Court nominees—are distinct from the hearings examined in this book. Part of the differences between hearings for judicial nominees at various levels may be tied to the different roles district courts, courts of appeals, and the Supreme Court play within the federal judiciary. We begin with a brief discussion of the function of district courts and courts of appeals in the federal judiciary. Then we will turn our attention to the primary purpose of this chapter, which is to provide an overview of how district and circuit court confirmation hearings are conducted while detailing how hearings fit into the larger advice and consent process.

next meeting (Steigerwalt 2010, 73). While this by itself is a short-term tactic, when committee members join forces and each in turn requests the postponement of a vote or members ask for a postponement right before a recess, it can result in significant delays (Steigerwalt 2010, 73). In sum, the authority to determine whether and when a nominee receives a confirmation hearing and a committee vote is a powerful tool of the Judiciary Committee or—more pragmatically—the chair of the Judiciary Committee and the majority party.

The Judiciary Committee's role in the confirmation of federal judges was not always so pivotal. In the next section, we explore the history of judicial confirmation hearings for lower court judgeships and the rise of the committee's influence on this critical step of the confirmation process.

Judicial Confirmation Hearings in a Historical Context

While the Senate created the Judiciary Committee in 1816 (Collins and Ringhand 2013, 34), the committee did not immediately take on its current role as a major stop in the journey of a lower court nomination. For example, during President Monroe's administration (1817–1825), only 1 out of 21 lower court nominees was referred to the Judiciary Committee (Sollenberger 2011, 104). Instead, it was customary for the Senate as a whole to consider these nominations unless the nominee was unfamiliar, or if questions arose (Sollenberger 2011). As the size of the federal bench increased and the responsibilities of the Senate grew, it became impractical for the entire Senate to consider judicial nominations without the help of the Judiciary Committee (Sollenberger 2011). As a result, in 1868 the Senate began automatically referring judicial nominations to the Judiciary Committee (Collins and Ringhand 2013, 34).[10] This change set the stage for the Judiciary Committee to assert the influence in the judicial confirmation process that we see today.

Though confirmation hearings conducted by the Judiciary Committee have been a regular fixture in the confirmation process for lower court nominations for several decades, this was not always the case. Between the middle 1950s and late 1970s, hearings were conducted by an "ad hoc subcommittee" rather than by the full Judiciary Committee (Eastland 1962, 364; Sollenberger 2011, 120). In other words, only a subset of the Judiciary Committee was assigned to conduct a particular confirmation hearing. More recently, the hearings are no longer delegated to a subcommittee. Instead, they are handled as part of the full Judiciary Committee's responsibilities, though it is still most common for only a handful of senators to attend each hearing.

While no Senate or Judiciary Committee rule formally requires confirmation hearings, it is now standard practice that a hearing is a necessary but not sufficient condition for confirmation as a federal judge. Since 1977, all nominees who were reported out of the Judiciary Committee in some fashion have first testified at a confirmation hearing (Sollenberger 2011). Additionally, at his or her discretion, the chair may convene more than one hearing for a nominee, which, at a minimum, delays the progress of the nomination. Though we have seen this tactic employed in recent years (e.g., President G. W. Bush's D.C. Circuit nominee Brett Kavanaugh and President Obama's Seventh Circuit nominee David Hamilton), this is not a new phenomenon, as Reagan's nominee to the Federal Circuit, Sherman Unger, was subjected to five separate hearings in 1983 (Sollenberger 2011). Thus, as noted above, by controlling which nominees are scheduled for a confirmation hearing and when, the Judiciary Committee chair wields considerable power in the contemporary advice and consent process.

The Gatekeeping Role of the Judiciary Committee

As discussed above, the Judiciary Committee has the power to kill a judicial nomination. A lack of action on the part of the committee prevents a nomination from moving forward and blocks a confirmation vote by the full Senate. Given the committee's authority over the necessary steps of a confirmation hearing and a vote reporting the nomination out of committee, by opting not to do either of these things, the committee can prevent a nominee from being confirmed. Thus, our investigation of confirmation hearings necessarily excludes the Judiciary Committee's interactions, or lack thereof, with nominees who do not receive a hearing. Systematically denying confirmation hearings, whether due to nominee-specific factors, contextual factors, or a combination of the two, could provide an important backdrop for the Judiciary Committee's behavior during confirmation hearings.

For example, senators may be less likely to hold a confirmation hearing for nominees with lower levels of qualifications. If individuals about whom senators have serious concerns regarding credentials are effectively weeded out prior to the hearing stage, it would be unsurprising if members of the Judiciary Committee ask very few questions about qualifications during confirmation hearings. Such a finding may then be interpreted not as a lack of emphasis on qualifications by the Judiciary Committee, but rather as an indication that these types of concerns are addressed via other mechanisms. Before we proceed with our investigation of why senators hold confirmation hearings and the value of these proceedings within the larger confirmation process, it is important to consider the extent to which and circumstances under which the Judiciary Committee chooses not to hold a hearing for a nominee. We address this in two ways: first, by examining whether a nominee receives a hearing within the Congress in which he or she was first nominated, and second, by examining whether a nominee receives a hearing within the first Congress in which he or she was nominated or *any subsequent Congress* within the same presidential administration.[11]

We first assembled a database of all district and circuit court nominees between 1993 and 2012, a time frame that encompasses the Clinton and George W. Bush presidencies and the first term of the Obama presidency. This period includes approximately 1,000 district and circuit court nominees, 435 of whom were nominated by Clinton, 371 of whom were nominated by Bush, and 215 of whom were nominated by Obama. It also features a mix of presidential party, divided and unified government, and party of the Senate majority.

Across the ten Congresses occurring between 1993 and 2012, 85 percent of district court nominees received a hearing within the first Congress in which they were nominated, while only 75 percent of circuit nominees did (the difference is statistically significant, $p < 0.01$).[12] This suggests that senators treat circuit court positions and nominees differently than their trial court counterparts. Importantly, the vast majority of both district court (93 percent) and circuit court nominees (84 percent) receive a hearing at some point in the nomination process, though circuit nominees are again disadvantaged (the difference is statistically significant, $p < 0.01$). Whether a nominee receives a hearing is not constant across congressional sessions, however. Two Congresses—the 106th (1999–2000) and 110th (2007–2008)—stand out due to a high proportion of nominees who never received a hearing. In fact, over half of the circuit court nominees in these two Congresses never received a hearing. Further, these two Congresses account for 60 percent of the nominees for whom the Judiciary Committee declined to grant a hearing. This can almost certainly be explained by the fact that the 106th and 110th Congresses were the final Congress during the Clinton and Bush presidencies, respectively. Nominees are less likely to be confirmed during presidential election years (Martinek, Kemper, and Van Winkle 2002; Binder and Maltzman 2009; Steigerwalt 2010), and, not surprisingly, they are also less likely to ever receive a hearing.[13] Moreover, given that these are the final years of the presidents' terms, they did not have a chance to renominate these individuals, thereby leading to higher no-hearing rates.

To further unpack why a subset of nominees are not allowed to proceed to the hearing phase of the confirmation process, we examined both whether a nominee received a hearing during the Congress in which he or she was first nominated and whether a nominee received a hearing within the first Congress in which he or she was nominated or *any subsequent Congress* within the same presidential administration as a function of several factors. In doing so, we account for key nominee characteristics (ABA rating, sex of the nominee, race of the nominee, and whether the nominee has at least one home-state senator from the president's opposition party); whether the nomination occurred during divided government, the last Congress of a presidential administration, or during the Obama, Clinton, or Bush administrations; as well as for the number of calendar days between the specific nominee's first nomination and the end of the two-year congressional session (see appendix table A2.1 for these models).[14]

Two factors related to the Senate's opportunity to confirm a nominee stand out as consistent predictors of who receives a hearing across all models: whether the first nomination is made during the last Congress of a presidential administration and the number of calendar days left in the two-year congressional session. First, even after controlling for other factors, being nominated during the final Congress of a presidential administration is associated with a nominee being less likely to ever face a hearing. With all other variables in the model held at their median or mode, a district court nominee has a 97 percent chance of having a hearing at some point if nominated before the final Congress of an administration, but only an 85 percent chance if nominated in the final Congress of a presidential administration (the difference is statistically significant, $p < 0.1$). This effect is substantially larger for circuit court nominees, who have a 92 percent chance of being granted a hearing at some point if nominated prior to the final Congress of a presidential administration, but only a 36 percent chance if nominated during the final Congress (the difference is statistically significant, $p < 0.01$).

Second, the amount of time remaining in the Congress in which a nominee was first nominated also shapes the likelihood that the Judiciary Committee will hold a hearing for a given nominee. Though the overall probability of receiving a hearing remains high, district court nominees nominated early in a Congress are slightly more likely to receive a hearing than those nominated with considerably less time remaining. Again, this change is more pronounced for circuit court nominees, who have a 97 percent chance of being summoned for a hearing when nominated near the beginning of a Congress (i.e., with 643 days remaining; 90th percentile), whereas those nominated toward the end of a Congress (i.e., with 190 days remaining; 10th percentile) have a 78 percent chance of appearing before the Judiciary Committee for a hearing (the difference is statistically significant, $p < 0.10$).

A few other factors are also predictive of which nominees receive a hearing. To start, the Judiciary Committee is more likely to grant a confirmation hearing to district court nominees with higher ABA ratings (both within the first Congress and within the presidential administration more broadly), which suggests that such ratings do matter in the confirmation process.[15] Further, the models indicate that Clinton's nominees, both district and circuit, were more likely to receive a hearing than Bush's during the first Congress in which they were nominated. Finally, divided government during the first Congress in which a nomination is put forward also reduces the likelihood that a circuit court nominee will be granted a hearing during that same Congress.

Taken together, these findings indicate that the timing of a nomination plays a major role in the likelihood that the committee will grant a nominee a hearing. This suggests that the large proportion of nominees who receive a hearing are likely representative of the broader pool of nominees as a whole. While we find that district court nominees who have a hearing are slightly more qualified according to the ABA, this is tempered by the fact that 93 percent of district court nominees receive a hearing at some point.

With the exception of circuit court nominees whose names were put forward in the final Congress of a presidential administration, the likelihood of receiving a hearing at some point is quite favorable. This provides important context as we proceed with our analysis of our core question of the book: Why do senators hold confirmation hearings for lower federal court nominees, and what is the value of these hearings in the larger advice and consent process?

Procedures and Logistics of the Hearing Phase

Before a hearing is held, Judiciary Committee staff members gather detailed information about nominees. Committee staff members conduct their own reconnaissance, though there are many sources to which they can turn. Since the late 1970s, all nominees complete the committee's "Questionnaire for Judicial Nominees" prior to any action by the Judiciary Committee (Sollenberger 2011). This questionnaire is a mix of lists (e.g., employment history, education, important cases the nominee has worked on, financial disclosures) and narratives (for example, describing how the nominee will resolve any potential conflicts of interest and describing the nature of the nominee's legal career). It is long and thorough; one staffer we interviewed referred to it as "monstrous." There is a high degree of respect afforded the questionnaire, with serious expectations for full disclosure and mechanisms for nominees to add to the questionnaire if they discover they (inadvertently) left out relevant information (Rutkus 2016, 19–20). The committee may also receive information from the White House (which has its own questionnaire for potential nominees), the Department of Justice, and the Federal Bureau of Investigation, though the nature of these documents is different than the investigation submitted to the White House (Rutkus 2016, 20).

Additional information on the nominee also comes from the American Bar Association (ABA). The ABA's Standing Committee on the Federal Judiciary issues ratings for all judicial nominees, categorizing the nominees as "well qualified," "qualified," or "not qualified." The Standing Committee can issue unanimous or split decisions, though if a majority of the committee rates the nominee as "well qualified" or "qualified," there is no further information regarding the Standing Committee's process or conclusion. If the nominee receives a majority "not qualified" rating, then the Standing Committee will provide additional written information as to their reasoning no more than 48 hours before the hearing (Rutkus 2016, 21). The chair of the Standing Committee will also testify at the nominee's hearing in instances of a "not qualified" rating but does not routinely testify, as is the practice for hearings for Supreme Court nominees (Sollenberger 2011).

Interest groups will also begin gathering information at this point. Interest groups do not have the resources to thoroughly vet every nominee as the committee and administration can, so they focus their efforts on those who appear to pose the largest threat to their ideology or specific issue. One former committee staff member noted that "you can't paint interest groups [with] one brush," but the larger umbrella groups were a constant presence. Importantly, all this research is happening at the same time, making it hard to pinpoint where controversy originates in the rare cases where there is controversy. Sen. Jon Kyl's recollection of controversy is that . . .

> it all sort of occurred at the same time. In other words, if a nominee were going to be controversial it was manifested pretty quickly. . . . If there was no controversy about a nominee, the fact that one or the other happened to come out for or against him didn't make a whole lot of difference; but if you had kind of a weak nominee, a nominee that was politically controversial and then you had a whole bunch of interest groups coming out against besides, that was just more weight on the scale.

Finally, the nominee's home-state senators may provide information about the nominee through the blue slip process. All home-state senators—regardless of party affiliation—are given the opportunity to weigh in with their assessments of nominees from their home states. Home-state senators who do not return the blue slip, or return it with a negative assessment, can stall or kill a nominee's chance to have a hearing and, subsequently, be confirmed (Rutkus 2016, 11).

With all these avenues of information, individual members of the Judiciary Committee make two decisions: whether they will attend a given nominee's hearing and, if so, what they will ask the nominee. Most often, senators will decide not to attend, but when they do, the procedure will be familiar. The presiding chair will call the hearing to order; the presiding chair may be the chair of the committee but more often is the chair's designee or, in Senator Kyl's estimation, a junior member of the committee who "drew the short straw." Committee rules only require a quorum of one, though there is typically a representative from the minority party as well (Rutkus 2016, 23). The presiding chair might make a short introduction then give the floor to the nominee's home-state senators; the vast majority of the time, at least one home-state senator is present, and often both are. Other officials from the nominee's home state might also make statements of support at this time, such as a senior member of the House (Rutkus 2016, 22). At this point, the questioning from the present committee members begins and might range from no questions for a nominee—which was the experience of nine nominees in our dataset—to 402 questions fielded by Brett Kavanaugh as a nominee to the D.C. Circuit.

Committee members may ask nominees to follow up with written answers to additional questions; it is understood that these requested responses must be submitted before the committee will vote on the nomination. Finally, once questioning is done, there is the opportunity—though rarely taken—for other witnesses to testify for or against the nominee. The most common situation where this testimony takes place is when the nominee has received a majority "not qualified" rating from the ABA. More often, the committee receives written testimony from supporters or opponents of nominees (Rutkus 2016, 24). The committee schedules a separate meeting to vote on how to report the nominee to the full chamber.

Given that most individuals' reference point for judicial confirmation hearings is a Supreme Court nomination, these hearings are notably different in several key ways. First, the room is emptier. As we show in later chapters, the average hearing draws a small number of senators, and media and public attention is obviously lower at district and circuit court hearings than at hearings for the Supreme Court. Second, while the room overall is typically emptier than a Supreme Court confirmation hearing, the nominee table will be fuller. Nominees are generally scheduled for hearings in panels; this means several district court nominees will face the committee at the same time with, perhaps, one circuit court nominee included. Sometimes, the circuit court nominee is technically part of a separate panel, though the hearings run concurrently.

In a typical hearing, then, a senator might ask one question and have all the nominees in attendance answer in turn. Committee members have significant discretion in terms of what questions they might ask, though most commonly they do not ask many. The median district court nominee faces 5 questions, while the median circuit court nominee fields 11 questions. A typical nominee is done with his or her committee interaction after this single hearing, though a small proportion of nominees (generally controversial ones) are called back for an additional hearing. Given the lower number of senators involved and questions asked, hearings for lower court nominees are consistently significantly shorter than those of Supreme Court nominees, which routinely span multiple days (Farganis and Wedeking 2014).

Finally, with respect to procedure, the Judiciary Committee does not routinely hold a closed-door session to discuss any investigative charges for lower court nominees as they do for Supreme Court nominees (Sollenberger 2011). Further, lower court nominees do not typically meet individually with members of the Judiciary Committee and Senate leadership for courtesy calls as their Supreme Court counterparts do (Sollenberger 2011).[16]

We have established the Senate Judiciary Committee's authority over confirmation hearings and the central role of the committee in the confirmation process more generally. Given our interest in understanding senators' motivations for engaging in and continuing the practice of confirmation hearings, in what follows we consider the composition of the Judiciary Committee and what the composition of the committee may tell us about what senators hope to gain from confirmation hearings.

Who Serves on the Judiciary Committee and Why?

Senator participation in judicial confirmation hearings is not solely reserved for members of the Judiciary Committee, as home-state senators frequently attend hearings to introduce nominees. Although we explore home-state senator participation in chapter 6, the bulk of our analyses in the book focus on the question-and-answer portion of the hearings. The questions posed during this aspect of the hearings come from the senators who serve on the Judiciary Committee. To better understand what senators hope to gain from the question-and-answer portion of the hearing, then, requires some understanding of who serves on the Judiciary Committee and why.

Research on committee composition in Congress starts from the premise that members of Congress use their committee assignments to further certain goals. In the seminal work on the topic, Fenno (1973) argues that members are primarily motivated by re-election, good public policy, and power inside the chamber, with certain committees better equipped to advance certain goals. Members may thus seek out certain committees due to policy or electoral goals, although scholars note that members often have a mix of goals they can pursue simultaneously (Fenno 1973; Smith and Deering 1984; Frisch and Kelly 2004; Grimmer 2013; Bernhard and Sulkin 2018).

If committees are divided into those that serve re-election goals and those that serve policy goals, the Judiciary Committee fits most comfortably into the policy category. The classic re-election (or constituency) committee is one that focuses on issues of "low national salience, high local salience, low conflict, and a narrow jurisdiction," while policy-oriented committees often involve conflict over salient issues (Smith and Deering 1984, 87–88). Senators who want to curry favor with constituents focus on noncontroversial issues with tangible benefits, while those who want to contribute to policy debates may see conflict over an issue as evidence of its importance (Smith and Deering 1984, 87). The Judiciary Committee often considers high-profile "culture war" issues such as abortion and gay marriage (Lewis 2014) that are "salient and steeped in conflict" (Evans 1997, 7). Because of this, scholars typically classify the Senate Judiciary Committee as a policy committee (Smith and Deering 1984; Munger and Torrent 1993; Frisch and Kelly 2006). In the words of Sen. Ted Kaufman, "You deal with all the kind of hot button issues on the Judiciary Committee—confirmation process or not."

A background in law is one potential marker of a senator's interest in

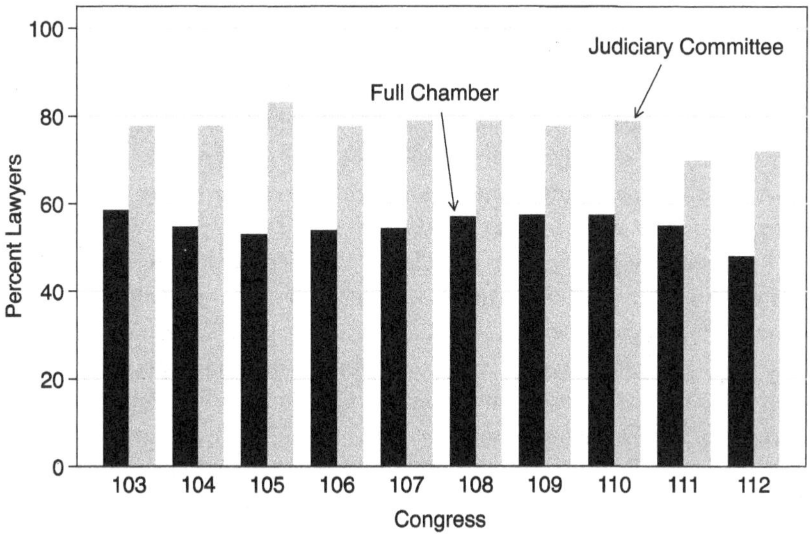

Fig. 2.1. Percentage of Senators with Previous Occupation in Law; Full Chamber vs. Judiciary Committee (1993–2012)

the policy content of the Judiciary Committee. Indeed, research shows lawyers are consistently more likely to both request (Bullock 1985) and serve (Lewis 2014) on the Judiciary Committee. According to Senator Kyl, "If you're a real lawyer, it's an interesting place to be because we really did deal with real law sometimes—complicated things: patent law and antitrust law and so on." Consistent with the findings of previous research, lawyers are overrepresented on the Judiciary Committee in every Congress in our timespan. From the 103rd (1993–94) through 112th (2011–12), the percentage of the chamber whose previous occupation is listed as law falls between 48 percent and 58 percent, with a mean of 55 percent. In these same Congresses, law is listed on average as the previous occupation of 77 percent of the Judiciary Committee membership (see fig. 2.1).[17]

In addition to having a substantive interest in the work of the Judiciary Committee, senators who serve on the committee may have greater electoral freedom to pursue their policy interests. Senators on the committee tend to represent states with a greater share of copartisans, meaning citizens aligned with their senator's party. In an era of increasingly partisan voting by the electorate (Bartels 2000; Sievert and McKee 2018), a high share of copartisans is a marker of electoral security. Using same-party presidential vote share as a measure of copartisans (see Grimmer 2013), in every Congress in our timespan, senators on the Judiciary Committee represented a greater percentage of copartisans on average than senators not on the committee. This difference is statistically significant in the 108th–112th Congresses (2003–2012) at the $p < 0.10$ level. The differences are smaller and not statistically significant in the 103rd–107th Congresses (1993–2002), although the mean same-party presidential vote share is greater for committee members in all five of these Congresses.[18]

Another way to consider the electoral differences between Judiciary Committee members and the wider chamber is to consider situations where a senator represents a state that the other party's presidential candidate won. Especially in the later Congresses in our timespan, it is rare for such a senator to serve on the Judiciary Committee. For example, at the start of the last Congress in our time span (2011–2012), 25 out of 100 senators represented states that the other party's presidential candidate won in 2008, but only one of these senators (Chuck Grassley of Iowa) served on the 18-member Judiciary Committee. By way of comparison, 10 such senators served on the 18-member Homeland Security and Governmental Affairs Committee.[19]

Although senators on the committee may have greater freedom to pursue their policy goals as a result of the electoral context of their state, the decision to engage with the salient, conflictual issues on the Judiciary Committee need not necessarily be divorced from members' electoral goals. Position taking, after all, is typically considered an electoral strategy (Mayhew 1974). In the more polarized and nationalized political climate of recent years (Jacobson 2015; Abramowitz and Webster 2016), constituents may be especially likely to prioritize representation on important national issues (Lapinski et al. 2016). As Bernhard and Sulkin (2018, 18) argue, "Most of what legislators do does not approximate a forced dichotomous choice wherein one option promotes reelection prospects and the other harms them. More often, the decision is about *which* re-election oriented behaviors to pursue" (18). Such an argument is consistent with research that shows senators who represent more copartisans tend to engage in more position taking in their press releases (Grimmer 2013).

The focus of the Judiciary Committee's jurisdiction on "culture war" issues may also attract or deter senators based on the religious demographics of their state. Noting that issues of abortion, gay marriage, and religious liberties are often decided in the federal courts, Lewis (2014) argues that the proportion of Christian conservatives in a state may be related to a senator's interest in serving on the committee. In an analysis of committee composition post-1981, he finds that Republicans from states with more Christian conservatives are more likely to serve on the Judiciary Committee, while Democrats are less likely to serve on the committee as the proportion of Christian conservatives in their states increases. Lewis (2014, 180) concludes, "All in all, through the Christian Right era, the Judiciary Committee seems to have become a place where conservative Christian interests and polarized partisans wage war." This conflict can help serve the electoral goals of some senators, while imperiling those of others.

The senators for whom it is electorally advantageous to take positions on controversial issues tend to come from the ideological extremes of their party, making the Judiciary Committee particularly polarized. Figure 2.2 shows the average NOMINATE score of both parties in the chamber as a whole and among Judiciary Committee senators. For all Congresses from the 103rd to 112th, the average Democrat on the Judiciary Committee was more liberal than the average Senate Democrat. Since 2003, the average Republican on the committee has been more conservative than the average Senate Republican. Since the 105th Congress, the committee has been the first, second, or third most polarized committee in the Senate (out of 16) based on the distance between the average Democrat's and average Republican's NOMINATE scores.[20] The committee roster in recent years has also included such notable conservatives as Ted Cruz (R-TX) and Mike Lee (R-UT) and liberals like Kamala Harris (D-CA) and Cory Booker (D-NJ).[21]

Finally, for one subgroup in particular, the clash of (presumed) policy and electoral goals—or perhaps just the complex electoral terrain associated with gender and party identities—causes Republican women senators to actively avoid serving on the Judiciary Committee. Swers (2013, 2016) finds that even conservative Republican woman senators with legal backgrounds, such as Sen. Elizabeth Dole (R-NC), have refused membership on the committee due to the prominence of the abortion issue for the committee. This is borne out by the membership of the committee over the course of our dataset—while there are four women Democrats who served on the committee at some point during the course of our dataset,[22] there are no women Republican members of the Judiciary Committee during our time frame.

In sum, senators appear drawn to the Judiciary Committee due to a mix of policy and electoral goals. As Senator Kyl noted, senators with a background in law see the committee as an opportunity to engage with legal issues. The committee is also a place to debate high-salience, controversial policy topics, whether during confirmation hearings or while the commit-

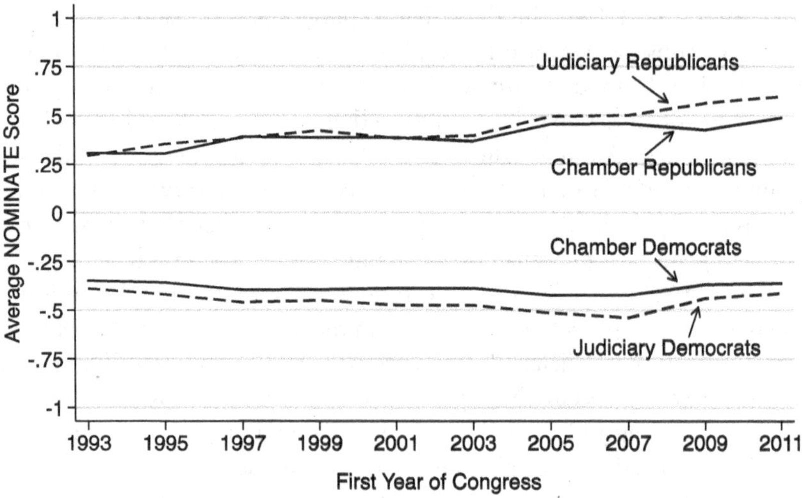

Fig. 2.2. Average NOMINATE Scores by Party; Judiciary Committee vs. Chamber Average; Depicts ideology of senators from −1 (liberal) to 1 (conservative)
Source: Vital Statistics on Congress; Lewis et al. 2019

tee conducts other business. For certain senators, a desire to engage in such debates could result from a policy interest in the topics being discussed, an electoral motivation, or both.

The membership profile of the committee in recent years—relative ideological extremity, legal expertise, and those whose electoral context allows (or even encourages) them to prioritize polarizing and partisan issues—suggests that senators view the Judiciary Committee as an institutional position from which they can pursue their policy and electoral goals. In the following chapters of the book, we argue that confirmation hearings in particular offer an important opportunity to work toward these goals.

Conclusion

This chapter has chronicled the steps in the nomination and confirmation process for lower court nominees and how confirmation hearings fit into the Judiciary Committee's role as a primary vetting body for nominees. We find that most nominees for both district and circuit court positions receive hearings, but that there is a notable drop-off in the probability of a nominee having a hearing if she or he is nominated in the final Congress of a presidential administration. These results suggest that when nominees fail to make the hearing stage it is typically a result of bad timing as opposed to concerns about the nominee. Finally, we examined the composition of the Judiciary Committee, which is disproportionately composed of lawyers and ideologues who represent more partisan constituencies. The composition of the committee suggests that senators are drawn to the committee due to both policy and electoral considerations. In the next chapter, we begin our analysis of levels of senator participation in confirmation hearings and give an overview of the content of the hearings to better understand how senators may use these hearings to advance both their policy and electoral goals.

APPENDIX

TABLE A2.1. Whether Nominee Received a Hearing

Logistic Regression

	Hearing in First Congress				**Hearing within Presidential Admin.**			
	District		Circuit		District		Circuit	
	Coef.	(S.E.)	Coef.	(S.E.)	Coef.	(S.E.)	Coef.	(S.E.)
Nominee Variables								
ABA Rating	0.32**	(0.08)	0.13	(0.13)	0.35**	(0.11)	0.23	(0.17)
Female Nominee	-0.18	(0.26)	0.05	(0.43)	-0.05	(0.35)	0.45	(0.57)
Minority Nominee	0.34	(0.27)	0.65	(0.46)	0.34	(0.38)	1.07+	(0.62)
Opposition Party Senator	-0.45+	(0.24)	-0.41	(0.39)	-0.80*	(0.34)	-0.26	(0.50)
Contextual Variables								
Divided Government	-0.47	(0.33)	-2.21**	(0.64)	-0.39	(0.47)	-1.28	(0.89)
Last Congress in Presidential Administration	-1.10**	(0.33)	-1.69**	(0.51)	-1.88**	(0.37)	-3.04**	(0.61)
Days Left in Congress	0.01**	(0.001)	0.01**	(0.001)	0.002**	(0.001)	0.01**	(0.002)
Clinton Nominee	0.81**	(0.28)	1.37**	(0.46)	-0.26	(0.34)	-0.07	(0.54)
Obama Nominee	-0.60+	(0.35)	-0.72	(0.69)	-0.10	(0.62)	-0.89	(1.09)
Constant	-1.35*	(0.55)	-0.63	(0.89)	1.71*	(0.73)	0.62	(1.19)
N	801		215		801		215	
LR χ^2	164.52**		67.14**		74.60**		70.10**	

$+p < 0.10$; $*p < 0.05$; $**p < 0.01$, two-tailed

THREE

An Overview of Confirmation Hearings, 1993–2012

> "Everybody knew right out of the box that [Goodwin] Liu was going to be someone who was going to be controversial."
>
> —Sen. Ted Kaufman (D-DE)

We began the book with a description of the differences between Obama circuit court nominee Goodwin Liu's two contentious appearances before the Senate Judiciary Committee and future Supreme Court justice Samuel Alito's relatively light questioning at his circuit court confirmation hearing. The quote from Senator Kaufman that leads off this chapter suggests that there was something unique about Liu that raised his profile as a nominee and prompted extra scrutiny from the committee. Although Liu's experience before the Judiciary Committee—two hearings and 150 questions—was unusual for a lower court nominee, it was not unprecedented. For example, as George W. Bush's nominee for the D.C. Circuit, Brett Kavanaugh faced roughly 400 questions during his two confirmation hearings, while Clinton nominee Rosemary Barkett fielded 130 in her 1994 hearing.

As we discussed in chapter 1, committee members pursue different goals in their participation in hearings for controversial versus typical nominees. Typical hearings provide committee members and home-state senators the opportunity to pursue their policy and electoral goals through various forms of participation. Hearings for controversial nominees present similar opportunities, though the increased attention puts additional emphasis on electoral goals. Additionally, we find that committee members also use hearings for controversial nominees to individually vet the nominee (a goal that is *not* pursued in the typical hearings, as we discuss further in chapter 4). This chapter begins, then, with an explanation of the role of controversy in lower court confirmation hearings, as well as an accounting of the disparate treatment controversial nominees receive in their confirmation hearings.

After establishing that hearings for controversial nominees are qualitatively different from the typical lower court confirmation hearing, we more fully introduce the nominee and hearing data that will be used throughout the book and provide a first look at these hearings in the aggregate from 1993 to 2012. In doing so, we have two primary objectives. First, we provide an overview of the content of lower court confirmation hearings to lay a foundation for understanding how senators use these proceedings to pursue different mixes of goals and to set up the analyses that follow in the subsequent chapters. Second, we assess whether there are any trends over time in the content of confirmation hearings during the 20 years under study. Despite the general increase in contentiousness and delay in the lower court confirmation process (see, e.g., Binder and Maltzman 2009), we find that the number and types of questions nominees face do not exhibit a clear trend over time. We do, however, identify Congress-to-Congress variation in the content of confirmation hearings, which is linked to changes in the political context. This finding sets the stage for the empirical analyses in the chapters to follow, where we consistently find that the political context is a bigger predictor of committee member behavior than individual characteristics of the nominees.

The Role of Controversy in Lower Court Confirmation Hearings

While confirmation hearings offer an important opportunity to interact with new judges who will ultimately set federal policy, senators face many demands on their time. Senators must weigh competing opportunities and make decisions about whether and how to participate in each hearing. We argue that given the competing demands on senators' time, members of the Judiciary Committee—for the bulk of nominees—see little value in using these proceedings to closely scrutinize nominees on their individual merits since most nominees are deemed noncontroversial by the time the hearings occur. Indeed, the nominees that receive a hearing have gone through extensive vetting from the White House, the Department of Justice, and committee staff; surviving this process without controversy tends to make committee members assume that the nominee is "acceptable" (Scherer, Bartels, and Steigerwalt 2008). In our interviews, one staffer referred to hearings for these nominees as "pro forma," suggesting that they have lower levels of senator participation and are not being used to vet individual nominees. This does not mean, however, that these proceedings are without value to senators; the endurance of confirmation hearings for lower court nominees suggests otherwise. Rather, we argue in subsequent chapters that larger battles over the direction of policy and a home-state connection to nominees drive engagement in hearings for noncontroversial nominees.

In some notable cases, concern over a nominee's qualifications or views, like that which accompanied Goodwin Liu's nomination, may lead to more in-depth scrutiny. As Sen. Jon Kyl noted in our interview with him, "Sometimes, especially where there was some doubt about the qualifications of the candidate or the candidate's views, the hearing would be better attended and there would be quite a bit of fairly intense questioning about qualifications or the candidate's views. In those cases, sometimes it would get pretty intense." Put simply, we argue that senators approach hearings for controversial nominees differently. We suspect that the attention of interest groups and party activists surrounding controversial nominees incentivizes increased senator attendance and rigorous individual vetting at such hearings.

Identifying Controversial Nominees

To test our argument that there are two types of hearings, we require a method of distinguishing typical nominees from controversial nominees. The bulk of lower court nominees begin and end their journey through the Senate with noncontroversial status. As Steigerwalt explains, "[s]enators' default position is to confirm lower court nominees" (2010, 30). Echoing this sentiment, Senator Kyl described the "vast majority of nominations" as lacking in controversy. How, then, can we identify the minority of controversial nominees? We are interested in a way to identify individual nominees whose fitness for the bench has been seriously questioned as opposed to the extent to which tension exists over the confirmation process itself (e.g., a belief that nominations in general are proceeding too slowly).

Scherer, Bartels, and Steigerwalt (2008) argue that senators view interest group opposition as a time-saving warning about a nominee's potential lack of fitness for the bench. In particular, they assert that interest group opposition can be a powerful signal for senators since these groups are often in a position to help or hinder senators' re-election efforts via methods such as voter mobilization. When a "fire alarm" (McCubbins and Schwartz 1984) is sounded by an interest group's formal opposition to a nominee, Scherer, Bartels, and Steigerwalt assert that the salience of a nomination increases and senators who are sympathetic to the interest group's perspective change their default presumption regarding the nominee from "acceptable" to requiring "thorough consideration" (2008, 1030). They find that such opposition results in longer times to confirmation and reduced likelihood of confirmation for opposed nominees, while unopposed nominees have similar odds of being confirmed and similar lengths of time to confirmation regardless of ideology.

Though they do not examine confirmation hearings, Scherer, Bartels, and Steigerwalt's (2008) prediction that nominees with interest group opposition will receive "thorough consideration" could apply to the way senators scrutinize nominees during hearings. While it is not tested directly, this sentiment is echoed by Steigerwalt's (2010) categorization of paths to confirmation, which also suggests that those who are opposed by interest groups will face more contentious hearings, while those without opposition will proceed smoothly to confirmation. Further, since a record of taking positions on controversial issues increases the odds of interest group opposition (Steigerwalt 2010),[1] we expect that interest group opposition generally serves as a signal of controversy surrounding a given nomination and therefore would place a nominee in the second category of hearings, which includes increased individual scrutiny. We employ this concept of interest group opposition throughout the book to distinguish controversial from noncontroversial circuit nominees.

While interest group opposition is only one manifestation of controversy, we argue that it is the most viable option for systematically capturing this concept. Its primary drawback is that public, documented interest group opposition sometimes occurs after confirmation hearings rather than before (this happens 28 percent of the time in our time period), which means we cannot conclude that interest group opposition has a direct effect on the hearing content. Our goal, however, is not to establish that interest group opposition before a hearing leads to a more contentious hearing (although we suspect it does). Instead, our goal is to establish that hearings for controversial nominees (measured through interest group opposition) look quite different than hearings for noncontroversial nominees.

Our interviews with those involved in the confirmation process suggest that interest group opposition serves as a suitable proxy for controversy surrounding a nominee and speaks to the issue of when and how controversy emerges. While it is possible that formal interest group opposition occurs as a result of what takes place during a hearing, our interviews and the interest group opposition literature suggest that this is not the typical manner in which opposition emerges (Scherer 2005; Steigerwalt 2010). For example, Senator Kyl told us that "if a nominee were going to be controversial it was manifested pretty quickly," and that he "absolutely" knew whether a nominee was controversial before his or her hearing occurred.

Second, Senator Kaufman noted that a nominee's status as controversial was widely agreed upon, saying that "there's a consensus that builds." Kaufman's comments indicate that the exact timing of formal opposition by interest groups is less critical for purposes of using it as an indicator of controversy given this broad level of agreement regarding whether a nominee is controversial. The suggestion that controversy surrounding a nominee emerges early on in the process and is widely agreed upon, combined with the empirical evidence of a clear distinction between hearings for opposed and unopposed circuit court nominees that we present below, gives us confidence that interest group opposition works well as a proxy for identifying controversial nominees.

Given their lower salience and status in the judicial hierarchy, district court nominees rarely provoke significant controversy. While interest groups routinely take formal positions on circuit court nominations, this is not the case for district nominees (Scherer 2005; Steigerwalt 2010). The lower profile and lack of ability to set precedent reduces the incentives for interest group involvement. From a theoretical perspective, we would prefer to analyze any controversial district nominees with their circuit court counterparts, but the vast majority of interest group opposition is limited to circuit nominees. Therefore, though there are some notable exceptions (e.g., Frederica Massiah-Jackson's nomination in 1997), we consider all district court nominees noncontroversial for the purposes of our analysis. Potentially including some controversial nominees in our sample of typical district court nominees would blur any distinctions between the two groups we analyze and would only work against our ability to support our contention that there are two types of hearings.

Senator Engagement in Hearings for Typical vs. Controversial Nominees

In order to compare senator engagement in hearings for typical versus controversial lower court nominees, as well as to assess the core questions of the book, we compiled transcripts for all district and circuit court confirmation hearings during the 103rd through the 112th Congresses (1993–2012), which covers the Clinton and George W. Bush presidencies and Obama's first term. This yields 929 nominee-hearings, the largest collection of lower court confirmation hearings analyzed to date. In coding the hearing transcripts, we focused on senators' questions. We recorded the senator who asked each question and placed each query into a category, which we discuss below.

To establish that hearings for controversial nominees are qualitatively different than hearings for typical nominees in the pursuit of members' different mix of goals, we examined senator engagement in these proceedings. In general, we do not expect senator attendance during the question-and-answer portion of lower court confirmation hearings to be high given the large quantity of nominees, that the vast majority of nominees are considered noncontroversial, the competing demands on senators' time, and the relatively low public salience of these proceedings. Further, since the full committee is not required for a hearing to take place, the above considerations lead us to anticipate that some committee members will participate in hearings for typical nominees at higher rates than other members. Importantly, we argue that these differences are driven by differences in Judiciary Committee members that relate to their policy and electoral goals, as opposed to differences in the nominees. In particular, we expect that junior members, committee leadership, majority party members, and senators not up for re-election will be most involved in the hearings themselves due to their institutional roles and responsibilities (or relative lack thereof). We anticipate that for controversial nominees, however, the incentive to participate across all motivations (policy, electoral, and individual vetting) increases, changing senators' calculations regarding how best to use their time. We investigate senator participation in confirmation hearings more thoroughly and test these expectations in chapters 4 and 6.

Figure 3.1 displays the distribution of the number of senators asking at least one question at three types of hearings: district court hearings, hearings for circuit court nominees without interest group opposition, and hearings for circuit court nominees with interest group opposition. To identify opposed nominees, we use Steigerwalt (2010) and Scherer, Bartels, and Steigerwalt's (2008) list for the 103rd through 109th Congresses and extend the data using Lexis and Westlaw (supplemented with Google in two instances) to determine if two or more groups, or one umbrella group, took a position in opposition to a nomination during the 110th–112th Congresses. This yields 49 controversial nominees out of the 178 circuit nominees who received a hearing during the time frame examined.

One notable takeaway from figure 3.1 is that the distribution of the

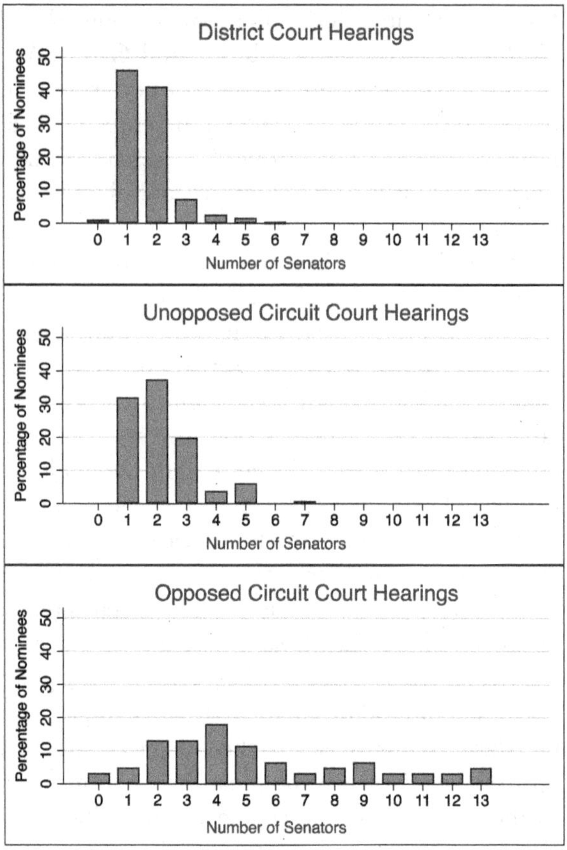

Fig. 3.1. Number of Senators Questioning Nominee

number of senators attending hearings for unopposed circuit court nominees looks similar to that of district court nominees. At both types of hearings, the median number of senators attending is two. The mean number of senators attending unopposed circuit court hearings (2.2) is slightly higher than the mean number of senators attending district court hearings (1.7), but most district and unopposed circuit court nominees face questions from two or fewer senators on average (88 percent and 70 percent, respectively).

In contrast, the median number of senators attending hearings for opposed circuit court nominees is 4, with a mean of 5.3, and only 21 percent of such nominees face questions from two or fewer senators. Figure 3.1 also shows that opposed nominees often draw more than five senators to their hearings, with 22 out of the 61 hearings for opposed nominees (36 percent) facing questions from more than five senators. For district

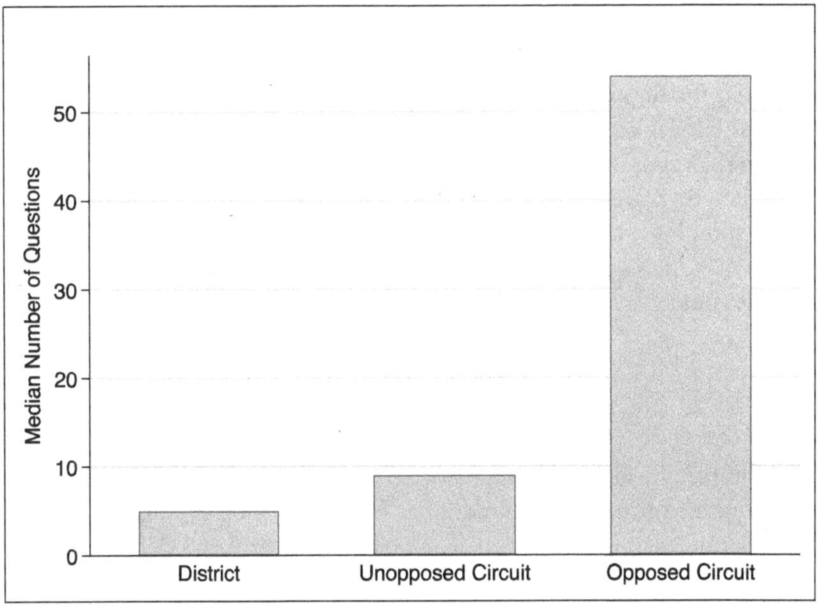

Fig. 3.2. Median Number of Questions by Nominee Type

and unopposed circuit court nominees, only 2 out of 870 nominees (0.2 percent) faced questions from more than five senators. In sum, although there are some small differences in senator attendance as we move from district to unopposed circuit court nominees, these differences are dwarfed by the change in senator attendance when we move from an unopposed to an opposed circuit court nominee.

A second way of measuring senator engagement in the hearings is the total number of questions asked. Figure 3.2 presents the median number of questions posed to each of the three types of nominees. Here again we see sizeable differences between opposed circuit court nominees and the other two types of nominees. District court nominees face a median of 5 questions, unopposed circuit court nominees face a median of 9, and opposed circuit court nominees face a median of 54 questions. The hearings for opposed nominees are therefore strikingly different from those for district and unopposed circuit court nominees. Senator engagement is greater across both measures for opposed circuit court nominees. At least in terms of the way senators treat nominees during the hearings, then, the greatest distinction is not between district and circuit court nominees but between controversial circuit court nominees and all other nominees. This suggests that the increased attention given to controversial nominees substantively changes committee members' calculations about the utility of hearing participation.

Given the important distinctions between hearings for opposed circuit court nominees compared to unopposed circuit and district court nominees, in the rest of this chapter and chapters 4 and 5, we focus our attention on explaining patterns in typical confirmation hearings, or, in keeping with our terminology, hearings for district and noncontroversial circuit court nominees. Unless otherwise noted, then, we reserve our analysis of hearings for controversial nominees for chapters 6 and 7.[2]

Senatorial Participation Over Time

The Clinton, Bush, and Obama years cover a time in which the confirmation process for judicial nominees has been described as "chaos" (Dewar 2003, A05), "vicious" (Toronto Star 2005), and "broken" (Walker 2012). That the process has changed over the past several decades is evident in declining confirmation rates and increasing delays in confirming judges (Binder and Maltzman 2009; Wheeler 2012). Has the extent to and manner in which senators engage in confirmation hearings for district and noncontroversial circuit court nominees changed over time alongside these trends in the broader confirmation process? At least as measured by senator participation in typical hearings, the answer, surprisingly, appears to be no.

Figure 3.3 graphs the median number of senators who asked at least one question at hearings for district and noncontroversial circuit court nominees in the 10 Congresses under study.[3] In all 10 Congresses, the median number of senators attending district court hearings is either one or two, while the median number of senators attending noncontroversial circuit court hearings never exceeds three. Notably, the two Obama Congresses in our time span are the only two Congresses that saw a median of three senators attending noncontroversial circuit court hearings. The data suggest a potentially small increase in senator participation at circuit court hearings, although the increase is minor and the time series ends in 2012.

Figure 3.4 shows the trend in the median number of questions asked at district and noncontroversial circuit court hearings. We again see no clear upward trend. In fact, for district court nominees, there appears to be a slight downward trend, with the median nominee facing 7 questions in the 103rd Congress (1993–94) and 8 in the 104th (1995–96), compared to 5 questions in both the 111th (2009–10) and 112th (2011–12) Congresses. No clear pattern is evident in the number of questions posed to noncontroversial circuit court nominees.

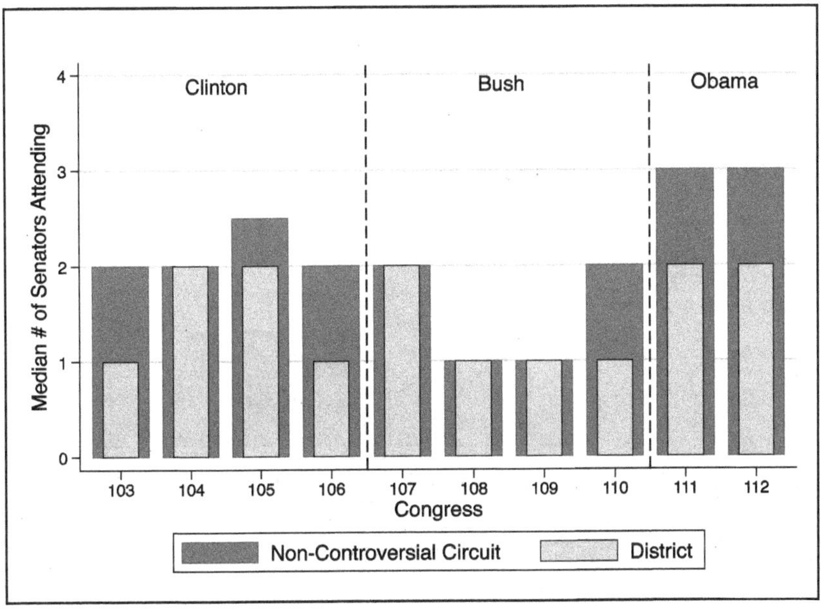

Fig. 3.3. Median Number of Senators Questioning Nominees

In sum, during a time of heightened contentiousness and delay in the lower court confirmation process, the number of senators questioning nominees and the number of questions asked of nominees do not exhibit a consistent trend. Of course, that does not mean that the number of questions posed to nominees is constant across Congresses. Indeed, we see the median number of questions asked of both district and noncontroversial circuit court nominees dropping in the 108th and 109th Congresses before returning to higher levels in the 110th through 112th Congresses. As a result, we test our core argument about policy and electoral explanations for senators' engagement in confirmation hearings at both the aggregate and individual levels in the next chapter and chapter 6 respectively. For now, we turn our attention to the content of questions that senators ask nominees.

Exploring the Content of Lower Court Confirmation Hearings

In addition to coding the senator who asked each question, we also classified each question by a senator to a nominee into 1 of 25 categories (which are grouped into 5 larger categories).[4] To construct these categories, we consulted the coding scheme used by Collins and Ringhand (2013), who

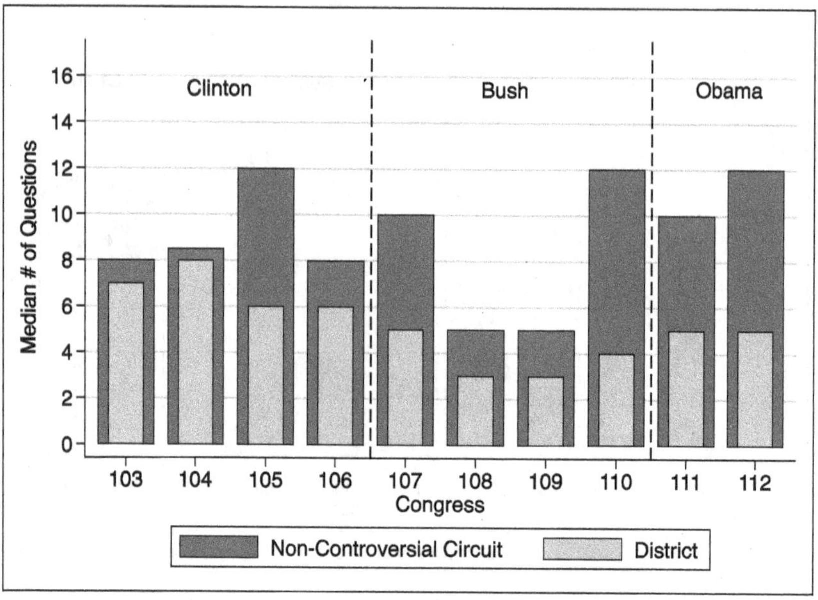

Fig. 3.4. Median Number of Questions by Congress

categorized hearings for Supreme Court nominees. These categories required some adjustment to account for the type of topics that are relevant to district and circuit court nominees. For example, since district courts do not have the same discretion over the cases that they hear that Supreme Court justices enjoy, district court nominees are sometimes questioned about managing a potentially heavy caseload.

The categories, a short description, and an example of a question from each category are included in table 3.1, which also groups the specific categories by type. There is wide variety in the rigor and frequency of these questions. Among the first type of question, *Judicial Decision Making and Philosophy*, questions about judicial philosophy are common, with 61 percent of all nominees receiving at least one question in this category.[5] Some of these questions are broad. For example, in the 112th Congress, Sen. Christopher Coons (D-DE) starts a hearing by asking, "I'd appreciate your beginning our first round of questions by just briefly describing your judicial philosophy." Sen. Charles Schumer (D-NY) asks a more specific but fairly typical judicial philosophy question when he asks circuit court nominee Charles Pickering whether the nominee considers himself to be a strict constructionist. Questions about precedent, judicial temperament, objectivity, and justiciability are also included in *Judicial Decision Making and Philosophy*.

The largest number of categories is devoted to questions that ask about specific issue areas, which make up the second type of question in table 3.1. All told, there are twelve different issues-related categories: rights for disadvantaged groups, civil rights other, criminal justice/death penalty, domestic commerce, environment, health, LGBT rights, Indian affairs, labor, right to privacy/abortion, terrorism, and other issues.[6] Questions on issues sometimes dealt with nominees' past opinions, writings, or thoughts about specific substantive issue areas or simply asked nominees to commit to following precedent in some specific issue area. For example, some Obama nominees were asked questions that we categorized as health, given that they related to comments or decisions associated with the Affordable Care Act. Sen. Chuck Grassley (R-IA) specifically questioned nominee Steve Six about comments he had made that joining a lawsuit against the individual mandate requirement in the Affordable Care Act would have been a waste of taxpayer resources.

The fact that Obama nominees were asked about the Affordable Care Act during their hearings is no coincidence. In our interview with him, Senator Kyl (R-AZ) noted that senators often had standard questions that they posed to nominees that "tended to evolve over time depending upon what kind of the hot judicial issue of the day was." Our data bear this out. Following the Supreme Court's 1995 decision on affirmative action in the *Adarand v. Pena* case, we see an increase in questions in our rights for disadvantaged groups category, with 40 percent and 42 percent of noncontroversial nominees facing questions in this category in the 105th (1997–98) and 106th (1999–2000) Congresses, respectively, compared to 16 percent and 13 percent of nominees in the 103rd (1993–94) and 104th (1995–96) Congresses. Many of the questions referenced the *Adarand* decision by name. In addition, the 107th Congress (2001–02) was the Congress where the largest percentage of nominees were asked terrorism questions, with many of the nominees' hearings coming only a few months after the September 11 terrorist attacks. Democratic senators asked many nominees in 2001 and 2002, for example, to weigh in on the proper balance between "liberty and security." As we demonstrate at different points throughout the book, the variation in questions often has more to do with changes in the political environment and senators' concerns about the direction of policy set by the courts than with the particulars of individual nominees.

The third type of question in table 3.1, *Qualifications and Judicial Administration*, includes questions that address the nominee's ABA rating, docket, experience, group affiliations, and reversal rate. These questions tend not to ask nominees to take a position on an issue or constitutional principle. Rather, this type of question deals with a nominee's credentials and fitness

TABLE 3.1. Categories, Examples, and Sample Questions

Category	Examples	Sample Question
Judicial Decision Making and Philosophy		
Judicial Philosophy	Interpretive methods, role of judges, separation of powers	"I would like your comments on the role of a judge on interpreting versus making law."
Precedent	Stare decisis, application of precedent	"Are you committed to following the precedents of higher courts faithfully?"
Judicial Temperament	Courtroom temperament, treatment of colleagues and attorneys	"What kind of judicial temperament would you say you have? And what is the proper judicial temperament?"
Justiciability	Standing, general process, jurisdiction	"What factors would you look to in deciding whether or not there is standing?"
Objectivity	Questions about bias, broad questions about being impartial	"How can you assure us that if politically sensitive cases come before you and in any case before you will be able to disregard your own personal views and allegiances and decide the case only on the law and the facts before you?"
Issues		
Rights for Disadvantaged Groups	Affirmative action, discrimination against racial minorities and women, diversity in the court	"Do you believe that racial and ethnic diversity is a compelling government interest in public education?"
Civil Rights—Other	Religion, free speech, gun rights	"And I want to bring up specifically whether you are committed to following precedent in the gun cases . . . affording the individual right to possess arms."
Criminal Justice/Death Penalty	Drugs, criminal sentencing, death penalty	"Do you believe mandatory minimum sentences are effectively deterring drug use?"
Domestic Commerce	Banking, corporate issues, product liability, intellectual property	"What would be your approach to deciding antitrust issues under the rule of reason?"
Environment	Environmental cases and policy	"Do you think that the Clean Air Act harms the environment?"
Health	Health policy and cases	"What impact would caps on damages have in our health care costs?"
LGBT Rights	Equal rights, marriage equality	"Do you support the decision of the Boy Scouts of America to use sexual orientation as a basis for determining whether an individual is qualified to be a leader?"
Indian Affairs	Cases and relevant policy	"Do you believe in tribal sovereignty?"
Labor	Worker safety, unionization rights	"Do you know whether a plaintiff has ever prevailed in your courtroom in an employment discrimination case?"

TABLE 3.1.—*Continued*

Category	Examples	Sample Question
Other Issue	Any policy or case that does not fit existing categories	"Do you believe that there is a constitutional right to sleep in the parks in America?"
Right to Privacy/Abortion	Abortion, other privacy issues (e.g., government surveillance)	"Do you believe there is a constitutional right to privacy?"
Terrorism	Security versus civil rights, detainee treatment	"What do you think the tradeoff needs to be between liberty and security?"
Qualifications and Judicial Administration		
ABA Rating	Nominee's ABA rating	"Why do you think there were some [in the bar association] who found you not qualified?"
Docket	Caseload, settlements, alternative dispute resolution	"How do you balance the need to move cases with the heavy caseload?"
Experience/Background	Professional experience, qualifications	"And how long have you been serving in judicial or judicial-like positions, how many years of experience?"
Group Affiliation	Group memberships of the nominee	"Do any of you belong to any clubs that have bylaws or have had a history of restricting membership?"
Reversal Rate	Nominee's reversal rate, nominee's cases that have been reversed	"How many times were you reversed by the Ohio Supreme Court?"
Ethics		
Conflict of Interest	Recusals, past conflicts of interest	"Do you believe that judges should disclose their financial assets so litigants can assess whether there would be an actual or apparent conflict of interest?"
Ethics	General ethics, nominee's questionable ethical behavior	"Did you report the value of these trips?"
Other		
Other	Topics not covered by the above categories	"Why do you want this job?"

for office, as well as his or her experience with or ideas about docket management. As an example of the type of question in this category, Senator Grassley asked nominee Alison Nathan the following: "Given the dates of your graduation from law school and the dates of your Bar memberships, do you believe that you meet the ABA's standard?"

The next type of question includes ethics and conflicts of interest, which addresses both questions specific to the nominee (i.e., questions about potentially unethical behavior in the past) and general questions as to the nominee's thoughts on what is and is not ethical or when judges should recuse themselves. For example, Sen. Dennis DeConcini (D-AZ) asked nominee Henry Adams Jr., "Will you please express your views as to whether or not you think there should be a judicial process for disciplining judges in the course of their action, whereby citizens, members of the bars, or clients can file a complaint or have some process?"

Finally, we created an "other" category to capture topics not covered by the aforementioned categories. Questions coded as other are sometimes less directly connected to the judiciary (e.g., a question posed to nominee Christina Armijo by Sen. Ted Kennedy: "I was interested in whether you had anything you could say about the nature of the make-up of a university in terms of one of the principal vehicles in terms of education and the future of our society.") and sometimes related to the judicial system but not overtly tied to an issue or a nominee's judicial philosophy or decision making. For example, Sen. Patrick Leahy questioned nominee Harry Barnes: "What is your feeling about lawyers and their involvement in pro bono [work]?"

Trends in Questioning

Although our analysis of senator participation revealed no clear upward trend in the number of questions nominees faced, it is possible that the content of questions has changed over time. In this section, we combine questions into the broader typology described above, focusing on three substantively important groups: *Judicial Decision Making and Philosophy* (e.g., questions related to judicial philosophy, temperament, precedent); *Issues Questions* (e.g., rights for disadvantaged groups, domestic commerce, abortion, crime); and *Qualifications and Judicial Administration Questions* (e.g., ABA rating, experience, reversal rate, docket), and we assess the extent to which senators engage with nominees on these topics over time.[7] Variation in the degree to which senators employ these broad categories could signal changes in how senators use these proceedings.

Figure 3.5 shows the proportion of questions falling into each of these three categories for both circuit and district court nominees across all 10 Congresses. With the exception of some unusual fluctuations in the 106th and 110th Congresses (1999–2000 and 2007–2008 respectively), the pattern for how senators question circuit court nominees is fairly consistent. Of our three categories, senators generally query circuit court nominees about *Issues* and *Judicial Decision Making and Philosophy* the most, while asking relatively few questions about *Qualifications*.

There is more variation in how senators engage with district court

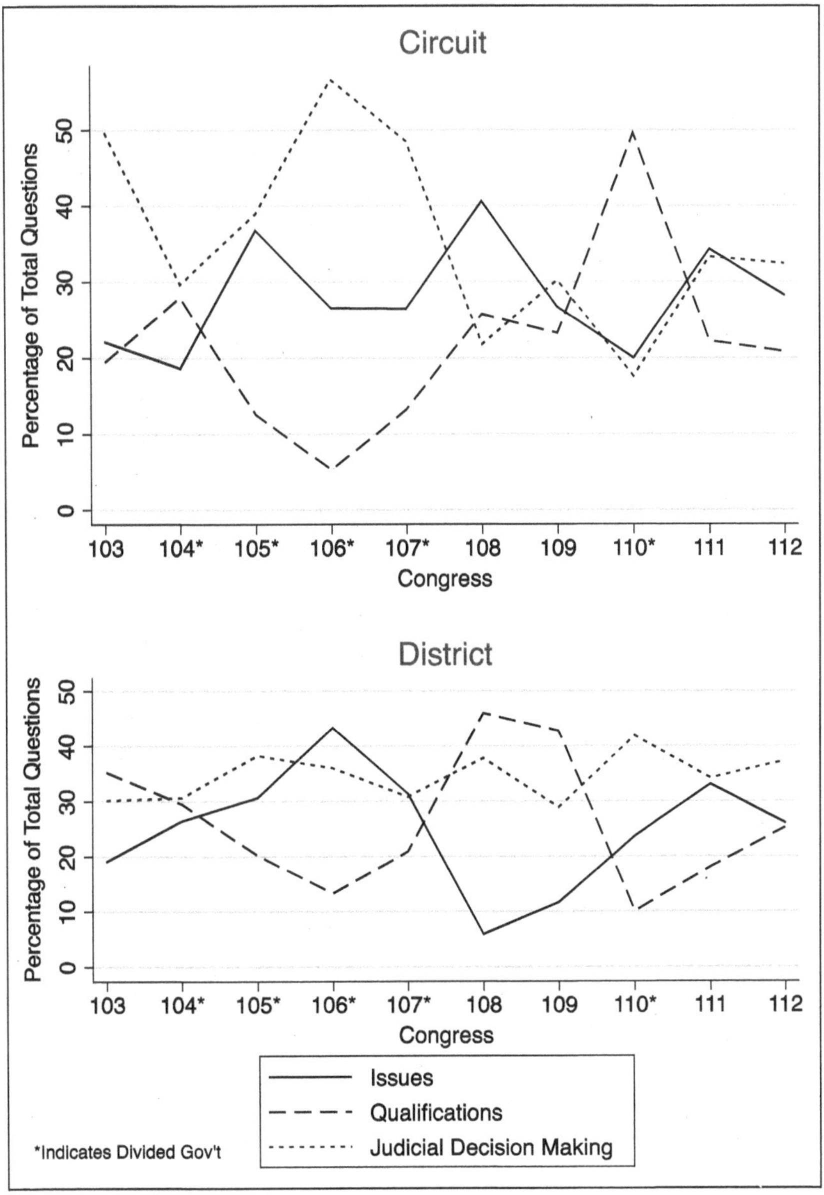

Fig. 3.5. Hearing Content Across Time

nominees, with *Qualifications* and *Issues* questions exhibiting a strong negative relationship (r = -0.85) that is weaker for circuit court nominees (r = -0.34). What explains the big changes in *Qualifications* and *Issues* questions for district court hearings? The answer appears to be divided versus unified government, with divided government defined here as when the Senate majority party and president are from different parties. The bottom half of figure 3.5 illustrates an upward trend in *Issues* questions during most divided Congresses (i.e., 104th, 105th, 106th, 107th,[8] 110th), while *Qualifications* questions generally show higher levels in unified Congresses (i.e., 103rd, 108th, 109th, 111th, 112th). This is our first piece of evidence that senators question nominees differently in response to contextual factors.

Importantly, despite escalating delays and conflict in the lower court confirmation process (see, e.g., Binder and Maltzman 2009), the data do not suggest senators are asking increasingly more of one type of question over another during the time span for either type of nominee. Variation in senators' engagement in confirmation hearings over time, however, clearly exists. Therefore, throughout the book we will examine a range of factors that may explain variation in senators' questioning during the hearings, such as nominee qualifications and contextual factors (e.g., divided government) as we test our broader argument that senators use judicial confirmation hearings as opportunities for pursing policy and electoral goals.

In Pursuit of Policy and Electoral Goals: A Preliminary Analysis

The aggregate analyses thus far have provided preliminary evidence that contextual factors matter and that one nominee-specific variable—nominee controversy—greatly shapes the rigor and substance of a confirmation hearing. Our other central argument relates to the mix of policy and electoral goals that senators satisfy with their participation in these time- and resource-intensive hearings. By examining committee members' questions about two Supreme Court cases—*United States v. Lopez* and *United States v. Morrison*—we gain preliminary insight into how these goals may be achieved. Senators' frequent invocations of these two cases—they are the second and third most mentioned Supreme Court cases in circuit court confirmation hearings (Dancey et al. 2018)—provide examples of how senators use confirmation hearings to communicate their views on policy, to explore the policy implications of specific court actions, and to pursue electoral goals. To conduct this analysis, we use the 26 and 24 unique senator mentions of *Morrison* and *Lopez*, respectively, at hearings in the 178 circuit court hearings from 1993 to 2012.[9]

United States v. Lopez is a case that arose out of the Gun-Free School Zones Act of 1990. Alfonzo Lopez was convicted on federal charges of carrying a gun on known school grounds; Congress had implemented the regulation under the auspices of the Commerce Clause. In 1995, the Supreme Court, in a 5–4 decision, ruled for the first time in 60 years that Congress had overstepped its authority to regulate interstate commerce (Greenhouse 1995; "United States v. Lopez"). Court observers at the time noted the larger policy relevance of this case and several others decided by the Supreme Court in the same session that appeared to be rebalancing congressional versus state powers (Greenhouse 1995).

Four years later, in another case that touched on the balance of congressional and state power, the Supreme Court again overturned a federal statute in *United States v. Morrison*. After her rapist's punishment was set aside by Virginia Tech for being "excessive," Christy Brzonkala sued her rapist (Antonio Morrison), a second alleged rapist (James Crawford), and Virginia Tech under a section of the Violence Against Women Act (VAWA). This section of the law provided potential civil remedies for the victims of gender-motivated violence ("United States v. Morrison"). Congress invoked the Commerce Clause (as well as the Fourteenth Amendment) as the basis for this legislation ("United States v. Morrison"). The Supreme Court, however, disagreed and, in a 5-4 decision, overturned this portion of the VAWA ("United States v. Morrison").

Observers of the Court drew a line from the earlier *Lopez* case to *Morrison*, noting they were two of several recent cases building toward a "new federalism," which the *New York Times*'s Linda Greenhouse (2000) called "a convergence between the court's focus on a Congress of limited powers and its newly found solicitude for state sovereignty." In short, journalistic discussions of these cases highlighted their substantive importance, belying a philosophical shift in the jurisprudence that underlay fundamental questions of the separation of powers (i.e., the Court's newfound bravery in overturning so many congressional acts) and federalism (i.e., striking a new state/federal government balance that leaned toward state sovereignty more than it had in previous decades of decisions).

Although these cases were not the most salient by measures of media attention (see, e.g., Clark, Lax, and Rice 2015), their frequent invocation at circuit court hearings suggests that they were particularly salient to senators. This interest should not come as a surprise given their implications both for Congress's lawmaking powers and for the larger ideological battles over federal power that the cases tap into. We find that in the course of these hearings, senators tend to invoke these cases in three general ways: first, by questioning nominees about more general implications of *Lopez* and *Morrison* in other policy areas; second, by using the cases to frame more general questions about the nominees' judicial philosophies; and third, by asking about previous statements or actions of the nominee in regard to the cases or related substance of the cases. Each of these categories vary in terms of how closely the questioning hews toward policy or electoral goals. Senators may certainly pursue electoral and policy-focused goals simultaneously within the same hearing, or even within the same line of questioning.

Broader Policy Implications. The first two categories of questioning related to *Morrison* and *Lopez* are the clearest examples of policy-related questioning. This first category of questioning includes questions where senators ask the nominee to expand on the *Lopez* and *Morrison* decisions to explore the implications for other policy areas. In this category, we observe Sen. John Edwards questioning nominee Julia Smith Gibbons in 2002 about the implications of the "new federalism"—with which *Lopez* and *Morrison* are typically associated—for the stability of civil rights, since, he notes, "the Federal laws have played a very important and significant role" in their implementation and enforcement. We also observe Sen. Dianne Feinstein in 2002 asking nominee Miguel Estrada about *Lopez*'s implications for Congress's ability to regulate firearms "when these weapons travel in interstate commerce, when they affect commerce and tourism, and when they have such a devastating impact on the children of this country[.]" Most recently, in 2011, Sen. Mike Lee uses an exchange about *Lopez* and *Morrison* with nominee Caitlin Halligan to ask whether Congress could "legislate that I need to eat four servings of green, leafy vegetables in one day?" Subsequent dialogue makes it clear that Senator Lee is exploring the constitutionality of the Affordable Care Act; nominee Halligan does not definitively answer the question, but states that a court would need to apply *Lopez* and *Morrison* to make a determination.

These examples show how one line of questioning can pursue both policy and electoral goals. These exchanges are policy-substantive and, as such, are not necessarily meant for a broader audience. It is plausible that senators are genuinely using these opportunities for dialogue to explore the implications of these cases for a wide array of policy areas. At the same time, committee members use these policy conversations to illustrate electorally useful points, such as the undesirable ends these decisions might lead to (i.e., the unaddressed "devastating impact" of firearms on "the children of this country" or the implications of the individual mandate).

Judicial Philosophy. The second category of questioning in the *Lopez* and *Morrison* cases includes situations where senators use the cases to explore the nominee's broader judicial philosophy of the appropriate balance of power between Congress and the courts and/or the federal and state governments. In these instances, the questioning senator tends to ask some manner of whether the nominee agrees with the *Morrison* and *Lopez* cases. First, Sen. Orrin Hatch questions nominee Bonnie Campbell:

> SENATOR HATCH: Are you aware of the Supreme Court's recent decision in *United States* v. *Morrison* and its 1995 decision *United States* v. *Lopez?* And if you are, please explain to the committee your understanding of these decisions and their holdings regarding congressional power.
>
> Some commentators have accused the Supreme Court of judicial activism because of their decisions in these cases. Do you agree or disagree?

Similarly, after summarizing the facts of the two cases for nominee Jeffrey Sutton, Senator Leahy asks, "Now, do you agree that Congress's power to regulate an intra-state activity should turn on whether the activity can be classified as economic or non-economic?" These types of questions are, again, policy-substantive, providing committee members with an opportunity to find out what kind of policy-relevant decisions they might expect from the nominee were he or she confirmed. At the same time, the questioning senators frame the queries in ways that would resonate with their bases (e.g., Senator Hatch's use of the phrase "judicial activism").

Previous Statements or Actions. Finally, we turn to the case-related questioning that could be characterized as the most political of the three: questioning that invokes the cases in regard to the nominee's past statements or behavior related to the case. These invocations tend to feel less policy-oriented in that they are specific to the nominee before them and, as such, can often revolve around the nominee's fitness for the bench. A good example of this comes in circuit court nominee Jeffrey Sutton's hearing, when Senator Schumer invokes Sutton's statements about VAWA and the *Morrison* case to frame questions regarding Sutton's ability to be fair and impartial:

> SENATOR SCHUMER: You discussed the *Morrison* case. [You stated,] "Unexamined deference to VAWA—Violence Against Women

Act—findings would have created another problem as well. It would give to any Congressional staffer with a laptop the ultimate Marbury power to have final say over what amounts to interstate commerce, and thus to what represents the limits on Congress's Commerce Clause powers."

Right now, I disagree with these, but that is not my point here. My point is you are not simply a lawyer who was chosen to represent cases. You have been a passionate advocate for this point of view, and you state it not only when you represent a client before a court, you state it in articles, you state it in conversation, et cetera.

And yet, even in exchanges where senators focus on the nominee's past, the senator may use this as a springboard for a policy-substantive exchange. Take, for example, Senator Leahy's exchange with nominee Sutton. After acknowledging that professors (Sutton's occupation at the time of the hearing) have a different orientation toward the law than judges, Leahy digs into Sutton's professional experience:

SENATOR LEAHY: . . . You had advocated to preclude claims for State employees with disabilities, persons that are denied Medicaid benefits. One newspaper called [you] "the leader of the States' rights revival." And then you said yourself in a *Legal Times* article, that you're quote, "on the lookout" for the types of federalism cases you have become known for. In fact you once said that while advocating for States' rights does not get you invited to cocktail parties, that nevertheless you believe in this stuff. So is this not a little bit different than a client walks in and says, "Mr. Sutton, please, take my position. Here is what I would like you to argue. If you feel I am right or not, go for it." And rather what you are doing is looking for the particular cases that you can carry out your own agenda; is that correct?

After Sutton vigorously reinforces his commitment to *stare decisis* as a judge, Leahy expands his questioning to that of the nominee's political philosophy, using a quotation from one of Sutton's law school course syllabi to buttonhole him about his feelings on the new federalism:

SENATOR LEAHY: Let me say it another way. If you were confirmed as a judge, would you be able to resist the temptation to use results oriented reasoning to implement an agenda of new federalism?

This question leads into another philosophical exchange over states' rights, where Leahy incorporates a more personal angle of the recommendations of Sutton's friends for the judicial position. Finally, this exchange, laced with potentially politically motivated questions about the nominee's past behavior, moves into exploring the broader policy implications of the decisions. Sutton brings up *Lopez* and *Morrison* in the course of discussing new federalism. This leads Leahy to ask Sutton about the economic versus noneconomic activity distinction, ultimately asking Sutton to apply the *Lopez* framework to the policy areas of human cloning and education. Leahy wraps up by returning to his nominee-specific concerns:

> SENATOR LEAHY: Is that a way of saying that people should have no fear, depending upon who they are, whether they have taken the position via the State or opposed to the State, whether they are liberal, conservative, whatever, coming before a Judge Sutton as compared to Professor Sutton?

In sum, then, we observe that even in the most political of the three categories, senators use the exchanges as an opportunity to discuss the policy implications of court decisions to further their goal of implementing good public policy. This exchange also provides qualitative evidence of committee members using the hearings of controversial nominees to individually vet the nominee, a point we will return to more fully in chapter 7.

Conclusion

In our initial examination of the data, we find substantive differences in the nature of lower court confirmation hearings depending on whether or not the nominee is controversial. These differences are consistent over time. It is also notable that while there is much around lower court confirmation hearings that is changing—in particular how contentious the process is—in the aggregate, the hearings have not significantly changed. At the same time, differences in the nature of hearings appear to be explained by senators' responses to contextual variables, a theme we return to in the next chapter. We end with a more in-depth look at the nature of questioning that highlights the ways that policy and political goals shape senators' participation in the hearings. In chapters 5 and 6, we consider these questions more fully. Finally, our focus on *Lopez* and *Morrison* highlights the individualized questioning that controversial nominees face in a way that typical nominees do not. This is a point to which we return in chapter 7.

APPENDIX

TABLE A3.1. Whether a Nomination Is Opposed

All Circuit Court Nominees; Logistic Regression Model

	Coef.	(S.E.)
Nominee Variables		
ABA Rating (Lowest)	0.54	(0.62)
ABA Rating (Middle)	0.64	(0.41)
Judicial Experience	0.28	(0.39)
Opposition Party Senator	−0.65+	(0.39)
Contextual Variables		
Divided Government	−0.27	(0.44)
Presidential Election Year	0.41	(0.47)
Party Balance of Circuit	−3.66	(2.25)
D.C. Circuit	1.03	(0.75)
Clinton Nominee	−0.98*	(0.46)
Obama Nominee	−0.85	(0.52)
Constant	−0.20	(0.58)
N	178	
LR χ^2	24.91**	

+$p < 0.10$; *$p < 0.05$; **$p < 0.01$, two-tailed test

FOUR

Why Do Senators Hold Confirmation Hearings?

An Initial Investigation

Near the beginning of the Judiciary Committee's questioning of district court nominee Frederica Massiah-Jackson, Sen. Jon Kyl (R-AZ) noted that "we have some general questions and then some specific questions that may in some respect represent criticism [of] writings or the like in your record." Kyl's comment foreshadowed what would be a challenging hearing for Massiah-Jackson. Ultimately, four senators grilled the state trial court judge extensively on her judicial record and temperament, collectively posing more than 80 questions.

Senators' questioning of Judge Massiah-Jackson focused on specific examples from her background and record rather than posing general questions that could have been asked of any nominee. For example, Senator Kyl queried Massiah-Jackson about her involvement in the Pennsylvania case *Commonwealth v. Donald Powell,* explicitly questioning her actions in the case. Kyl asked, "the Commonwealth's brief on appeal indicates that you wrote letters to both the district attorney's office and to the appellate court in an effort to discourage or dismiss the government's appeal. Do you think it is appropriate for a judge to express such strong opinions that he or she is view[ed] as acting as an advocate?" Sen. Jeff Sessions (R-AL) raised similar individualized questions about Judge Massiah-Jackson's temperament. For example, Senator Sessions stated that "I would like to follow up a little bit . . . [o]n the comments you made that you have apologized for.

I think that is a fact that I will consider, and I know there was some disciplinary action taken for misbehavior by you in that regard." Sessions then proceeded to note and question the nominee about specific comments she made while on the bench.

When contemplating why senators hold hearings for lower court nominees, one obvious answer, supported by Senator Kyl's comment and the nature of the committee's subsequent questioning of Massiah-Jackson, is that they do so to vet individual nominees. Such an explanation is intuitive and normatively pleasing. As chapter 2 explained, nominees must receive a hearing before the full Senate can vote on their confirmation. These proceedings are one mechanism through which the Senate could exercise a check on the president by rigorously vetting those he nominates to lifetime appointments. These hearings are public and contribute to the transparency of the process for a position that is otherwise characterized as undemocratic (i.e., unelected lifetime appointments). Additionally, that there is not a formal uniform set of questions asked of all nominees during their hearings allows for the possibility that senators develop nominee-specific questions and use the hearings to scrutinize nominees on their individual merits, ensuring that only the highest quality nominees make it through the process.

While individually assessing the fitness of nominees for the bench is one potential explanation for why senators hold confirmation hearings, other possibilities exist. We suggest that confirmation hearings offer senators a venue to advance their electoral and policy goals. Of course, senators could use hearings for multiple purposes. In this chapter, we look at the variation in aggregate levels of senator participation in hearings as a way of understanding what motivates senators to attend these hearings. If senators use these proceedings, at least in part, to vet individual nominees, their participation in confirmation hearings should be shaped by nominee-specific characteristics (e.g., qualifications). If senators see the hearings as an opportunity to partake in larger policy battles or attend to their electoral goals, political and contextual forces should, at least in part, shape senators' engagement in confirmation hearings. In other words, if these hearings are about more than just vetting individual nominees, we would expect the political context to serve as a key predictor of patterns of senator participation.

We focus our examination on typical nominees (i.e., district and noncontroversial circuit) who received a hearing between 1993 and 2012. These typical nominees represent the vast majority of those nominated to the lower courts. Our theoretical account of why senators hold judicial confirmation hearings and the value of these proceedings in the larger advice and consent process is in part contingent on the level of controversy associated with a nominee. As we explained in chapter 3, we use the presence of interest group opposition to identify controversial circuit court nominees (Scherer, Bartels, and Steigerwalt 2008; Steigerwalt 2010). This notion receives preliminary support in chapter 3, where hearings for nominees identified as controversial by this measure are shown to be distinct from their noncontroversial counterparts, and as a result we examine controversial nominees separately in chapter 7. The models in this chapter of hearings for noncontroversial nominees include both nominee-specific and contextual variables. Our analysis thus far provides little support for the idea that senators hold confirmation hearings in order to vet individual nominees. Instead, the results suggest that senator participation in the hearings varies as a function of changes in political context. This dynamic, we argue, reflects the fact that at the typical hearing senators are more concerned with broader trends in the policy direction of the federal courts and pursuing electoral goals than in the specific individual nominee(s) in front of them.

Do Senators Hold Confirmation Hearings to Vet Individual Nominees?

As part of the advice and consent process, all Article III nominees appear in front of the Senate Judiciary Committee to answer questions before the committee votes on whether to report the nomination to the full Senate. In the aggregate, confirmation hearings thus require nontrivial portions of committee members' time. One potential explanation for this personal interaction between a nominee and members of the Judiciary Committee is that senators believe it is important to scrutinize each nominee. Hearings can thus be viewed as an opportunity for such individual assessments. Increased contentiousness in the broader confirmation process further suggests that senators might use the hearings as an opportunity to vet individual nominees (Bell 2002a; Scherer 2005; Binder and Maltzman 2009; Steigerwalt 2010).

If senators hold hearings for the purpose of scrutinizing individual nominees, we would expect senators' engagement in the hearings to vary as a function of nominee-specific factors. In other words, we would anticipate that the number of committee members who attend the hearings and the degree of scrutiny imposed would at least in part be connected to nominees' individual characteristics, such as their qualifications and perceived ideology. Therefore, to test this possibility, we identify three key nominee-specific attributes that might influence senators' engagement in confirmation hearings.

First, an obvious marker of a nominee's potential fitness to serve on the federal bench is the rating the nominee receives from the American Bar Association (ABA). The ratings come from the ABA's Standing Committee on the Federal Judiciary, which is composed of 15 members. The committee rates every nominee to the federal bench on their "professional qualifications."[1] The rating includes both the majority and minority views if there is disagreement, so a nominee can receive one of six ratings: "unanimously not qualified," "not qualified/qualified," "qualified/not qualified," "qualified/well qualified," "well qualified/qualified," and "unanimously well qualified," with the first rating indicating the majority's rating and the second rating indicating the minority's rating. The ABA ratings have been the source of both scholarly and political controversy for their potential bias against conservative nominees (Lott 2006; Smelcer, Steigerwalt, and Vining 2012) and women and minority nominees (Sen 2014). Despite these criticisms, the ratings provide arguably the clearest signal of how a nominee's peers view his or her fitness for the bench. If senators use these hearings as an opportunity to scrutinize nominees with questionable professional qualifications, we would expect increased senatorial participation—both the number of senators asking questions at the hearing and the total number of questions asked of a nominee—when a nominee has a lower ABA rating.

> **ABA Hypothesis.** Senatorial participation in a nominee's hearing will increase as the nominee's ABA rating decreases.

Given the controversy surrounding ABA ratings, they may not be the only, or even best, indicator of nominee qualifications. We therefore consider one other measure of nominee qualifications: previous judicial experience. Nominees need not have judicial experience to be nominated to the federal bench, and in fact around half of the nominees who received a hearing between 1993 and 2012 did not previously serve as a judge. Nominees with previous judicial experience do receive higher ABA ratings on average, but the difference in ABA ratings between nominees with and without previous judicial experience is not especially large (4.9 compared to 4.6, difference = 0.3, $p < 0.01$). In addition to or instead of ABA ratings, then, senators may look at whether a nominee has previous judicial experience to decide whether the nominee warrants additional scrutiny at the hearing.

Alternatively, it is possible that judicial experience could work against a nominee by creating a record of written opinions and reversals that could open the door to more scrutiny. For the judicial experience hypothesis, then, we simply state that senator participation will vary based on whether the nominee has judicial experience without specifying whether judicial experience increases or decreases senator engagement.

> **Judicial Experience Hypothesis.** Senator participation in confirmation hearings will vary based on whether the nominee has judicial experience.

Along with nominee qualifications, senators are likely to be concerned with the ideological lean of any given nominee. One key potential signal of a nominee's ideological tendencies is the home-state Senate delegation. At the district court level, the Senate typically respects the blue slips from senators of either party (see, e.g., Binder 2007; Binder and Maltzman 2009; Sollenberger 2010). In addition, senators typically suggest a nominee or nominees to the White House based on their own assessments or a commission within the state. Senator Kyl said that he had a working relationship with the White House counsel during all three administrations (Clinton, Bush, and Obama) during his time on the committee. Speaking in reference to Arizona nominees, Kyl noted:

> It was [the White House's] selection at the end of the day, but I would give them good choices, I thought, and they thought they were good choices because they frequently continued to take my suggestions. Senator McCain and I were able to, I think, create the best district court bench in the country during the time that I was on the Committee. And that probably had as many Democratic as Republican judges and some independents.

Senator Kyl's quote illustrates the role that home-state senators play in shaping district court nominees from their state, even when the president is from the opposition party. The president therefore does not have the same latitude to select an ideologically extreme judge to fill a seat in a state with at least one opposition partisan in the Senate delegation. Research on the blue slip suggests that ideology is indeed a key factor that senators consider when evaluating a nominee (Black, Madonna, and Owens 2014). In states with two senators from the president's party, on the other hand, it is possible for the senators and president to settle on a nominee who is considered more ideologically extreme. If senators are using hearings to vet the ideological leanings of specific nominees, then, we would expect nominees from states with no opposition party senator to receive more scrutiny. While the geographic jurisdiction of circuit courts typically spans multiple states, seats within a circuit are generally considered to be reserved for each of the states within the circuit. As a result, home-state senators are generally consulted by the White House regarding nominee selection, and these senators' positions on the nominee then also carry weight during the confirmation process, though senators' influence is likely weaker on circuit court nominations (Binder and Maltzman 2009).

> **Opposition Party Senator Hypothesis.** Senatorial participation in confirmation hearings will be lower for nominees with an opposition party senator from their state.

Hearings as a Venue for Policy and Electoral Goals

Because most nominees are deemed noncontroversial by the time the hearings occur, we argue that senators may foresee only minimal returns if they were to invest time into individually scrutinizing the bulk of lower court nominees during these proceedings. As Scherer, Bartels, and Steigerwalt (2008, 1030) have argued, senators' default presumption regarding a judicial nominee is that he or she is "acceptable" and therefore it is only the relatively rare controversial nominees who require "thorough consideration." Indeed, as one Senate staffer told us, "Generally speaking, nominees are pretty good and they're pretty interchangeable." That said, senators are likely concerned about the aggregate effects of a president's nominees on the future of the court. As one former staffer told us, "The role of filling vacancies on the judiciary is really an aggregate role." At a typical hearing, then, senators may care more about promoting their vision for the future direction of the federal courts than about scrutinizing the qualifications of an individual nominee.

As chapter 2 highlighted, the Judiciary Committee is disproportionately filled by senators with legal backgrounds and from traditionally liberal or conservative states (see also Lewis 2014). Due to a mix of electoral and policy goals, then, senators on the committee are those who are inclined to care the most about policy set by the courts and the future of the federal courts more generally. Although typically low-salience affairs, these hearings offer a unique opportunity for committee members to engage directly with future, and sometimes current, members of the federal bench. As a result, we argue, hearings operate as a venue for elected officials to convey their perspectives to those about to be charged with interpreting and applying our Constitution, laws, and precedents.

With a mix of policy and electoral goals guiding committee members, the types of questions senators pose can range from one senator's narrow policy interests to queries about salient or long-standing philosophical disagreements over the role of the federal courts. As one staffer told us, senators may use the questioning to "sensitize nominees" to the senator's point of view on an issue. One senator who fit this bill, and was mentioned specifically by the staffer in question, was Herb Kohl (D-WI). One of the few nonlawyers on the committee during our time span, Kohl, a former businessman, often raised questions about corporate liability (coded in the domestic commerce category). The staffer also noted Sen. Ted Kennedy (D-MA) using the hearings to raise civil rights issues, while our reading of the transcripts uncovered several instances of Sen. Charles Grassley (R-IA) probing nominees for their views on whistleblower protections. These questions emphasized issues the senators appeared to care about in terms of their views of good policy. We document examples of these types of questions in chapter 5.

Although senators do use these hearings to engage in dialogue over their specific policy interests, many of the questions seem focused on broader partisan and ideological battles over the scope and nature of the judicial branch. As Senator Kyl told us, there were standard questions asked at hearings that "tended to evolve over time depending upon what kind of the hot judicial issue of the day was." In hearings during the Obama presidency, for example, Republicans often tried to get nominees to disagree with Obama's stated position that it was important for judges to have "empathy." Senator Grassley and Michigan District Court nominee Gershwin Drain had the following exchange in 2012:

SENATOR GRASSLEY: We have people that argue that a judge should have empathy for those who appear before them. My concern is that when someone suggests that a judge should have empathy they're really suggesting that the judge should place their thumb on the scales of justice to tilt in favor of the proverbial little guy, or some other noun you might want to use there. In your personal opinion, is it ever the role of a judge to favor, for instance, the little guy over the big guy?

JUDGE DRAIN: No, Senator Grassley. I think the little guy shouldn't be given any more fairness than the big guy. They need to be treated equally and impartially. I am committed to doing that.

Similarly, the following exchanges at Ninth Circuit nominee Morgan Christen's 2011 confirmation hearing highlight how broader disputes over judicial philosophy play out in the hearings. It begins with Sen. Orrin Hatch pushing the nominee on the empathy question.

SENATOR HATCH: Now, President Obama has said that judges should base their rulings on "one's deepest values, one's core concerns, one's broader perspectives on how the world works, and the depth and breadth of one's empathy." Do you agree with that?

JUSTICE CHRISTEN: I believe that judges have an obligation to rule based on the rule of law, and that is what I have done for nine and a half years. I think I have that track record, Senator.

I do not think that empathy plays any role in determining what the rule of law is or in how we apply the rule of law. We are not allowed to tilt the scales depending on how we feel about a case. But I believe that there are life lessons that we have all learned that are very important that judges retain and take with them to the bench. By that I mean that I think it is very important that we are always mindful that there are real people on the receiving end of our orders, and very often there are people's lives on hold or their businesses are on hold waiting for our decisions. That is why it matters very much that our work is timely, for example.

Later in the hearing, Sen. Al Franken (D-MN) offers a defense of the notion of judicial empathy by building on Christen's answer.

SENATOR FRANKEN: I have empathy so I will vote for you. Speaking of which, I noticed that—because this is interesting, because on this empathy question, which we hear over and over and over again, and I agree that you have to decide on the law and that—certainly the way you feel, but I noticed that you said that you have to apply certain life lessons, and so you answered—to me, you answered with a little nuance, which actually I find a little refreshing because I think empathy sometimes is confused with sympathy.

JUSTICE CHRISTEN: Yes.

SENATOR FRANKEN: And empathy simply means understanding human beings. And I think that the experience of a judge is whether—no

> matter how the judge factors, tries to factor that out, the experience of a judge has something to do with how they are a judge. Do you agree or not?

As the two examples above suggest, it is senators from the party opposite the president who may be most inclined to use these hearings to engage in larger philosophical discussions as they present their vision of the ideal judge and types of decisions such an individual would make. Much as Senator Franken did in the Christen hearing, however, senators from the president's party have incentives to use their time to combat the narrative that the other party is advancing.

If the hearings are in part a venue for engaging in larger battles over the direction of the courts, we expect that certain contextual factors will make conditions particularly ripe for such disputes and therefore be associated with increased senator participation. As one staffer told us, the political climate "undoubtedly" affects the content of the hearing. More specifically, we expect that senators' incentives for participation will be shaped by divided government, proximity to a presidential election, and the political or ideological importance of a given vacancy. We address each in turn.

First, during periods of divided government—which we define here as when the Senate and president are of opposite parties—the chair for all hearings and the majority of the committee's membership come from the party opposite the president. This means the opposition party is in an institutionally advantaged position from which it can publicly push back against the president's agenda by presenting its perspective regarding policy set by the courts and the broader role of the judiciary. We would therefore expect the hearings to become more of a forum for confrontation over the direction of the federal courts than when the committee and chamber are controlled by the president's party. The result, we expect, is increased senator attendance at the hearings during times of divided government.

> **Divided Government Hypothesis.** Senator participation in confirmation hearings will increase during periods of divided government.

Second, presidential election years may also increase the incentives for senator participation. With the potential for a switch in partisan control of the presidency, senators should be particularly attentive to whether a nominee, who is about to assume a lifetime position, will prove to be an ideological foe on the court for years to come. Indeed, studies show presidential election years slow down the time to confirmation and lower the probability of confirmation (see, e.g., Martinek, Kemper, and Van Winkle 2002; Binder and Maltzman 2009), while also increasing the number of votes against a nominee in committee (Steigerwalt 2010, 176). This leads to the following hypothesis:

> **Presidential Election Hypothesis.** Senator participation in confirmation hearings will increase during presidential election years.

Next, with respect to circuit court nominees whose decisions set precedent, senators' incentives to participate in hearings may depend on the overall ideological tenor of the circuit a nominee would join. The composition of the federal circuit courts fluctuates over time when vacancies arise and new judges are nominated by the current president and confirmed. Senator Kyl explicitly mentioned that the "balance of the circuit did matter" when considering circuit court nominations. Circuits that are relatively evenly split between judges appointed by Democratic and Republican presidents may be particularly salient to members of the committee as circuits in which there is an opportunity to make policy inroads. This notion of differential treatment toward nominees from closely balanced circuits has manifested itself empirically as a decreased likelihood of confirmation (Binder and Maltzman 2009). We expect that a concern over the direction of circuits approaching an even split between judges appointed by Democratic and Republican presidents will draw greater attention and scrutiny to these circuits' nominees. Importantly, this argument is distinct from a general concern about a nominee's ideology. Here, if our theoretical contention is correct, senators only engage more deeply with the same individual if she or he is nominated to a relatively balanced circuit while failing to garner any special attention and proceeding smoothly if she or he is nominated to a more lopsided circuit. Thus, we propose the following hypothesis:

> **Party Balance of Circuit Hypothesis.** Senatorial participation in confirmation hearings will increase as the proportion of judges on a circuit nominated by presidents of both parties approaches parity.

Finally, the U.S. Court of Appeals for the District of Columbia Circuit is commonly considered to be the nation's second highest court and a steppingstone to the U.S. Supreme Court. Four current Supreme Court justices—Roberts, Thomas, Ginsburg, and Kavanaugh—have prior experience serving on the D.C. Circuit court. Both Justice Scalia and the first person nominated to replace him, Judge Merrick Garland, also served on the D.C. Circuit court. Further, this court has exclusive jurisdiction over many administrative law cases and cases likely to have a national effect (Fraser et al. 2013). Given the prestige and salience associated with this court, we expect that senators would perceive greater potential policy benefits from participating in confirmation hearings for nominees to the D.C. Circuit court.

> **DC Circuit Hypothesis.** Senatorial participation in confirmation hearings will increase for hearings for those nominated to the D.C. Circuit.

The above hypotheses are designed to test whether senators hold confirmation hearings to scrutinize individual nominees, provide a forum for pursuing policy and electoral goals, or a combination of the two. If hearings for typical nominees are at least in part held out of a desire to scrutinize nominees as individuals, we should find that ABA rating, judicial experience, and the presence of an opposition party home-state senator predict senators' participation in these proceedings. If hearings are held at least in part for senators to pursue their policy and electoral goals, we expect the results will show that the presence of divided government, presidential election years, party balance on a circuit, and a nomination to the D.C. Circuit will be tied to senators' engagement in the hearings and ultimately the type of hearing a nominee experiences.

Modeling Senator Engagement at Hearings for Typical Lower Court Nominees

To understand variation in senator engagement at these hearings, we begin with a model of our first measure of senatorial participation: the number of senators attending. Members of the Judiciary Committee choose which hearings they attend. Thus we believe senators' decisions about whether to attend a given hearing can help test whether senator engagement in confirmation hearings is driven by a desire to vet individual nominees, a desire to engage in a broader dialogue to further senators' policy and electoral goals, or both. Since we have outlined different theoretical expectations for hearings for controversial circuit court nominees versus hearings for district and noncontroversial circuit court nominees, the observations for the models in this chapter come from the latter unless otherwise indicated.

The dependent variable in the regression models below is a count of the number of senators who ask at least one question during a nominee's hearing. The unit of analysis is the nominee-hearing.

To test the possible influence of nominee-specific factors, we use a modified version of the ABA's six-category rating scale. Around 44 percent of nominees in our time span received a unanimously supported "well-qualified" rating. We put all these in one category and create two additional categories: nominees who received at least a minority "not qualified" rating (8 percent of nominees) and nominees who received a rating of "qualified" or a mix of "qualified" and "well-qualified" ratings (48 percent of nominees).[2] In the models that follow, the nominees unanimously rated as "well-qualified" are treated as the base category, with dummy variables included for the lowest rated nominees (at least a minority saying "not qualified") and nominees in the middle categories ("qualified" through "well-qualified/qualified"). We also include dummy variables capturing whether a nominee had prior judicial experience and whether at least one of the nominee's home-state senators was affiliated with the president's opposition party.

With respect to contextual factors, we include measures of whether the hearing took place during divided government or during a presidential election year.[3] To these we add two measures designed to address the unique dynamics of circuit court nominations. First, we capture the current party balance of the circuit to which an individual is nominated. We employ Kastellec's (2011a, 2011b) data on the annual proportion of active judges on each circuit nominated by a Democratic president and extend it through 2012. To assess the potential influence of a closely split circuit, we then use the absolute value of 0.5 minus the proportion of the circuit appointed by a Democrat as our final measure; the closer this measure is to zero, the more evenly divided the circuit is. Second, we include a dichotomous measure of whether an individual was nominated to a position on the U.S. Court of Appeals for the District of Columbia Circuit.

Along with the variables used to test our hypotheses, we include dummy variables for Clinton and Obama nominees, with Bush nominees serving as the excluded category. In addition, for district court nominees, we include a dummy variable for D.C. and Puerto Rico judgeships. Although these nominees are considered Article III nominees, the lack of Senate representation for these jurisdictions may decrease the salience of such nominees for the committee and the Senate at large. Finally, a very small minority of the sample received two confirmation hearings. We therefore include a control variable capturing whether a hearing is the second hearing the nominee received for the same position.[4]

Number of Senators Attending

The black squares and accompanying whiskers in figure 4.1 display the coefficients and 95 percent confidence intervals from a Poisson regression model predicting the total number of senators who ask at least one question of a given district court nominee at her or his hearing, while the gray circles and corresponding whiskers report the results of the noncontroversial circuit court model.[5] In terms of nominee-specific variables, the two measures of nominees' qualifications and background—ABA rating and previous judicial experience—are not statistically significant at conventional levels. Whether an opposition party senator represents the nominee's home state is, however, negative and statistically significant in the district court model. Holding all other variables at their median or modal values, a district court nominee without an opposition party senator from his or her state faces 1.2 senators on average compared to 1.1 for nominees with an opposition party senator from his or her state ($p < 0.01$). The results provide support for the opposition party senator hypothesis, suggesting that senators may more heavily scrutinize nominees from a state without an opposition party senator, perhaps out of concern that the nominee is more ideologically extreme. Importantly, the substantive difference is minimal, with district court nominees from a state without an opposition party senator still facing questions from fewer than two senators on average, suggesting that nominee-specific factors play a minor role in explaining senator participation in hearings for typical nominees.

In terms of contextual variables, divided government is a positive and statistically significant predictor of senator participation in both types of hearings. District court nominees during divided government face questions from an average of 1.5 senators compared to 1.1 senators during unified government ($p < 0.01$). Similarly, during unified government, 1.6 senators attend and pose at least one question on average for noncontroversial circuit nominees while this number increases to 2.1 senators, on average, during times when the president's opposition party controls the Senate ($p < 0.1$). Although it is not a massive shift in the number of senators participating, divided government is associated with a larger shift in the number of senators participating (roughly 0.5 senators) than any of the nominee-level variables. Presidential election years and the circuit-specific characteristics, on the other hand, are not statistically significant predictors of senator attendance in either model.

Although we did not hypothesize differences in senator participation based on presidential administration, we do see differences across the three

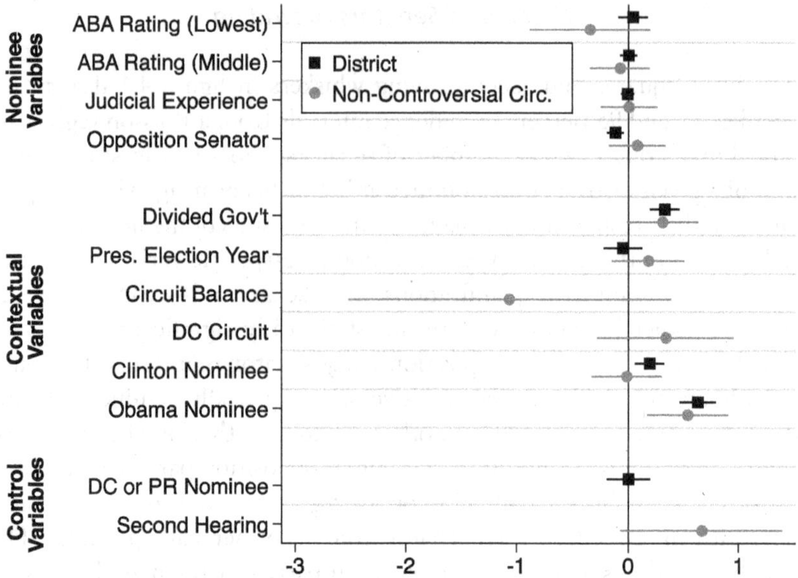

Fig. 4.1. Number of Senators Attending; Poisson Regression Models

Note: For district nominees, n = 739. For noncontroversial circuit nominees, n = 131. Independent variables for the two models are primarily the same, except that the circuit model includes variables for party balance of the circuit, whether the nominee was nominated to the D.C. Circuit, and a dichotomous measure that equals 1 if it is a second hearing for the nominee. The district model includes a variable that equals 1 if the nominee is from D.C. or Puerto Rico and is also clustered on the hearing date, to account for multiple nominees being questioned at once. The figure displays 95 percent confidence intervals. Full tables for these models are available in the on-line appendix.

administrations. Notably, Bush's district nominees faced fewer senators on average (1.1) than both Clinton nominees (1.3) and Obama nominees (2.1). Also noteworthy is the increase in senator participation at district court hearings during the Obama administration. Nominees during the two Obama Congresses in our dataset faced an average of 2.1 senators per hearing, even though these hearings occurred during unified government. This is an increase of almost one senator per hearing on average compared to district court hearings for Bush nominees during unified government. Similarly, we note that Obama's noncontroversial circuit nominees were questioned by more senators (2.7 vs. 1.6), on average, compared to Bush's nominees.

Total Number of Questions Asked

We now turn to the analysis of our second measure of senator participation: the total number of questions asked of a nominee. In these models, we again focus on district and noncontroversial circuit court nominees and test whether variation in senatorial participation is a function of nominee characteristics, political context, or a combination of the two. The dependent variable is a count of the total number of questions senators put to a nominee during his or her hearing, while the independent variables remain unchanged from the number of senators attending models presented above. The number of questions posed to each nominee is within senators' control and indicates how they approach confirmation hearings. Again, if senators hold these proceedings in order to scrutinize individual nominees, nominee-specific factors should predict the number of questions asked. If, however, senators use confirmation hearings as a venue for airing larger policy disputes or pursuing electoral goals, we expect that political context and institutional factors will shape the degree of senatorial participation in a typical nominee's hearing.

Figure 4.2 reports the results of these negative binomial regression models.[6] The black squares depict the coefficients from the model of district court nominees, while the gray circles display the coefficients from the noncontroversial circuit court model, along with 95 percent confidence intervals. Again, we see little in the way of systematic relationships between our nominee-level variables and senator participation. We do find some variation in total questions asked as a function of a nominee's ABA rating for district court nominees. More specifically, nominees who receive at least a minority "not qualified" rating from the ABA face two more questions on average (5.5) than nominees who receive a "well-qualified" rating (3.6, $p < 0.05$), although there is no significant difference between nominees who receive a rating in the middle categories and the nominees who receive a rating in the highest category. The other nominee-specific variables, however, are not statistically significant across either district or noncontroversial circuit nominees.

In contrast, many of the contextual variables are related to the number of questions asked, which lends support for the idea that senator participation varies more as a function of political context than nominee characteristics. As we have argued, we view this as evidence that hearings are about advancing senators' electoral and policy goals, as opposed to simply a venue for vetting nominee qualifications. For both types of nominees, divided government is again associated with an increase in senator engagement. District court nominees during divided government face an additional 1.0 questions on average (5.0 compared to 4.0 during unified government, $p < 0.05$). Similarly, noncontroversial circuit court nominees are asked 8.5 questions, on average, during unified government and 12.6 questions during times of divided government ($p < 0.05$).

Second, presidential election years also correspond to an increase in the

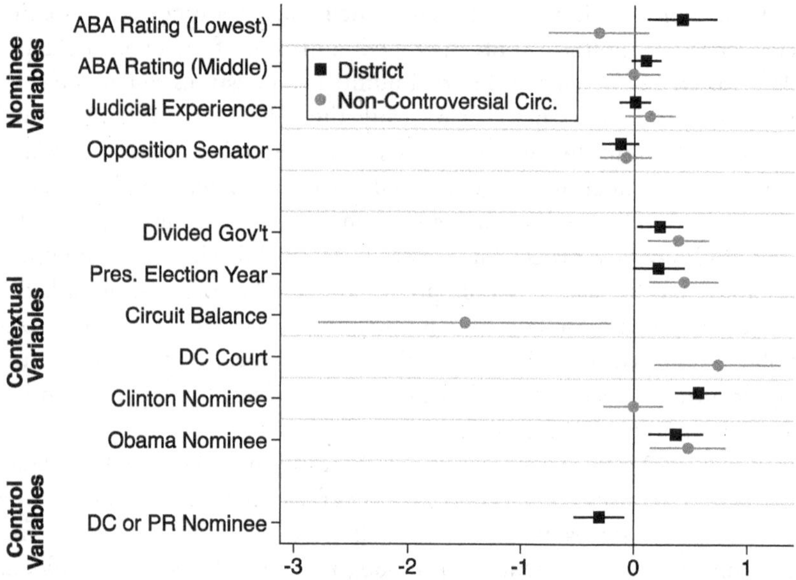

Fig. 4.2. Total Number of Questions Asked; Negative Binomial Regression Models
Note: For district nominees, $n = 732$. For noncontroversial circuit nominees, $n = 129$. Independent variables for the two models are primarily the same, except that the circuit model includes variables for party balance of the circuit and whether the nominee was nominated to the D.C. Circuit. The district model includes a variable that equals 1 if the nominee is from D.C. or Puerto Rico and is also clustered on the hearing date to account for multiple nominees being questioned at once. The figure displays 95 percent confidence intervals. Full tables for these models are available in the on-line appendix.

number of questions asked during confirmation hearings for typical nominees. For district court nominees, the predicted number of questions goes from 4.0 to 5.0 ($p < 0.10$) when comparing nonelection years to presidential election years, while noncontroversial circuit court nominees similarly increase from 8.5 to 13.2 questions on average ($p < 0.05$). This suggests that the partisan conflicts and electoral competition that accompany presidential election years alter senators' cost-benefit calculations regarding participation in confirmation hearings.

Third, the party balance of the circuit also shapes the extent to which senators engage in hearings for noncontroversial circuit court nominees. As a circuit becomes more closely split between those nominated by Democratic versus Republican presidents, the average number of questions posed to a nominee increases. Alternatively, as the circuit to which an individual is nominated becomes increasingly composed of judges nominated by presidents of one party over another, the predicted number of questions asked of a nominee decreases. For example, individuals nominated to a circuit with a 36 percent/64 percent split between judges nominated by Democratic presidents versus Republican presidents (the median value) received 8.5 questions on average, while those nominated to a circuit with a closer split—45 percent/55 percent—faced 9.7 questions (a one standard deviation change, $p < 0.05$). This indicates that senators' behavior during confirmation hearings is tied to the partisan distribution of the relevant federal circuit court, regardless of the nominee's personal ideological leanings or qualifications. We argue that senators' concerns over the implications of any given nominee for the direction of future policy outputs is heightened when a circuit is more evenly split, thereby raising the potential policy payoff for senators' participation in these proceedings.

Next, nominees to the D.C. Circuit experience disparate treatment, controlling for individual-level characteristics. Noncontroversial D.C. Circuit nominees receive 17.9 questions, on average, compared to 8.5 questions for those nominated to other circuits ($p < 0.10$). Senators' attentiveness to nominations to the U.S. Court of Appeals for the District of Columbia Circuit specifically again suggests that senators view the confirmation hearings for certain vacancies as particularly consequential.

We also see additional questions asked of Clinton's and Obama's district court nominees, which is consistent with the results from the number of senators questioning nominees. And we note that Obama's noncontroversial circuit court nominees received more questions (13.7 vs. 8.5), on average, compared to Bush nominees ($p < 0.01$).

In sum, our models for both measures of senator involvement indicate that contextual factors best explain whether and the extent to which members of the Judiciary Committee participate in lower court confirmation hearings. We submit that the influence of the political and ideological context surrounding the confirmation process on senators' engagement in these proceedings suggests that senators view the hearings as opportunities to pursue policy and electoral goals. Further, these findings suggest that senators are more attuned to the general direction of the federal courts than to individual nominees. There is some evidence that senators use the hearings as an opportunity to vet individual nominees, although no one nominee-specific variable is a robust predictor of senator engagement across the two types of models. Nominees from a state without an opposition party senator may receive slightly more scrutiny (at least in terms of number of senators who attend), as may nominees who receive one of the two lowest ratings from the ABA (at least in terms of total number of questions). In the end, however, these differences are inconsistent and small, especially compared to the differences we observe across unified and divided government and presidential administrations.

Across all models, divided government is a consistent and robust predictor of senator engagement in these hearings. When the president's opposition controls the Senate and therefore the Judiciary Committee, nominees face more senators and more questions on average. We argue that the natural tensions between the Senate and the White House during divided government over policy and the future of the federal courts incentivizes greater participation on the part of senators. In addition, district court nominees during the two Democratic administrations in our time period faced more senators and questions on average than did Bush nominees, and the same is true for Obama's noncontroversial circuit court nominees compared to Bush's. This suggests that the public proceedings for typical nominees are not used for individually vetting lifetime appointments to the federal bench. Instead, committee members use these hearings to pursue policy and electoral goals.

An Additional Look at Noncontroversial vs. Controversial Circuit Nominees

We have argued that hearings for typical district and noncontroversial circuit court nominees are not used to vet nominees individually. Alternatively, we have proposed that some circuit court nominees are considered more controversial—for reasons that are unique to the nominee and independent of these larger political considerations—and therefore receive more rigorous, nominee-specific scrutiny. As an additional investigation of the notion that senators approach hearings for controversial circuit nominees differently, we reran both models of senator engagement on all circuit court nominees, adding interest group opposition as an independent variable. If our argument is correct that interest group opposition is a proxy for controversy surrounding a given nomination, senatorial participation should be higher for opposed nominees than for their unopposed counterparts. While we explore this in much greater depth in chapter 7, we expect that the higher salience associated with controversial nominees' hearings should ramp up the potential for senators to advance their policy and electoral goals through participation in these proceedings.

The analysis reported in figure 4.3 includes all federal circuit court nominees (1993–2012) who received a hearing before the Senate Judiciary Committee.[7] Nominee controversy is a strong and statistically significant predictor of both measures of senator engagement. The model of the num-

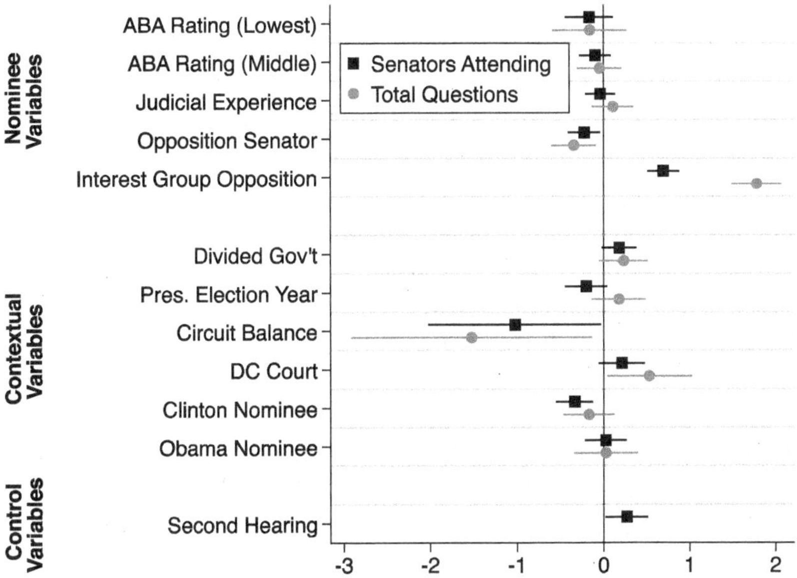

Fig. 4.3. Senator Engagement at Hearings; All Circuit Court Nominees; Event Count Models

Note: For senators attending, this is a Poisson regression model, $n = 192$. For total questions, this is a negative binomial regression, $n = 178$. Independent variables for the two models are primarily the same, except that the senators attending model includes an indicator that equals 1 when it is a nominee's second hearing. The figure displays 95 percent confidence intervals. Full tables for these models are available in the on-line appendix.

ber of senators attending (displayed in black with squares marking coefficients) predicts that approximately 2.7 senators question noncontroversial circuit court nominees, while this number almost doubles to 5.4 senators for controversial nominees ($p < 0.01$). The magnitude of this difference is especially notable given that the baseline number of senators attending a circuit court hearing is relatively low.

When we look at the model of total questions (displayed in gray with circles marking coefficients), we see that the controversy surrounding a nominee has a massive influence. Noncontroversial circuit nominees are predicted to receive 13.5 questions during their hearing, whereas controversial nominees are predicted to be asked a whopping 79.7 questions ($p < 0.01$).[8]

Combined, these findings support the use of interest group opposition as a good, albeit imperfect, indicator of controversial nominees. Additionally, these results are consistent with previous scholarship documenting the powerful influence of interest group opposition on how senators exercise their advice and consent privilege over circuit court nominees (Scherer 2005; Scherer, Bartels, and Steigerwalt 2008; Steigerwalt 2010). Further, the results reinforce our argument that senators approach and use confirmation hearings differently for controversial versus noncontroversial nominees.

Finally, figure 4.3 suggests that when considering all circuit court nominees, another nominee-specific factor—the presence of an opposition party senator—predicts senator engagement across both models. Having at least one opposition party senator reduces the number of senators posing questions and the total number of questions asked during a hearing. Upon further exploration, however, we find that this influence is limited to controversial nominees. We reran the models with an interaction term between the controversial nominee and the opposition party senator variables. The difference in the number of senators asking questions between nominees with and without an opposition party senator from her home state is only significant among controversial nominees. Among these controversial nominees, the predicted number of senators decreases from 5.9 for those without an opposition party senator to 3.0 for those with at least one opposition party senator.

Similarly, the difference in the number of questions asked between nominees who have an opposition party senator versus those who do not have an opposition party home-state senator is not statistically significant for those without interest group opposition. Alternatively, among controversial nominees, having at least one opposition party senator reduces the predicted number of questions from 101.1 for those without an opposition party senator to 31.0 ($p < 0.01$).[9] In sum, the evidence suggests that the influence of an opposition party home-state senator applies only to controversial nominees and indicates that both senators' decisions to question and the extent to which they scrutinize nominees is influenced by a concern over a nominee-specific factor: potential ideological extremity. In contrast, senator engagement in typical (unopposed) circuit court nominees' hearings is driven by contextual factors, as expected.

Conclusion

Combined, our analyses indicate that the Judiciary Committee's intense scrutiny of district court nominee Frederica Massiah-Jackson, highlighted at the beginning of this chapter, was an anomaly. The findings suggest that the value of the hearings both to senators and the larger confirmation process is most frequently not rooted in facilitating individual scrutiny of nominees. Instead, the analyses of typical hearings—i.e., hearings for district and noncontroversial circuit court nominees—indicate that contextual factors, such as the presence of divided government and the nature of the circuit for appellate nominees, are better predictors of senator engagement than nominee-specific variables such as ABA rating or previous judicial experience. The results thus serve as initial support for our argument that hearings for the vast majority of nominees are not about judging nominees on their merits. Instead, we find that senators are drawn to hearings when tensions over policy and politics are heightened, such as when the Senate and White House are controlled by different parties or when a seat is seen as particularly important given the ideological balance of sitting judges. We argue that it is in these circumstances of divided government and hearings for particularly significant circuits that senators have the greatest incentive to participate in these public proceedings to advocate on behalf of what they see as good public policy, to promote their vision for the federal judiciary generally, and to leverage their positions for electoral gain. Finally, the results suggest that with respect to hearings for typical nominees, senators are more attentive to the general direction of the federal courts and future policy rather than to individual nominees.

Our analysis of senator participation ultimately serves as a first, although not final, test of the argument that most hearings are not about vetting the qualifications of individual nominees. To further assess this argument and our broader contention that senators hold confirmation hearings in order to promote their views on policy and garner electoral benefits, we turn in the next chapter to an analysis of the content of confirmation hearings to assess the policy side of this argument. Members of the Judiciary Committee can direct the content of confirmation hearings toward whatever topic(s) they choose. Senators may focus on certain topics based on attributes associated with specific nominees, or senators can craft their questions to engage in larger political and policy discussions. We thus examine whether variation in the types of questions senators ask is best explained by nominee-specific factors, contextual factors, or both. We also delve more deeply into variation in the content of individual senators' questions and the potential motivations behind them.

FIVE

In Pursuit of Policy Goals

Explaining the Content of Lower Court Confirmation Hearings

In September of 2005, Bush nominee Brian Sandoval, who would later become the Republican governor of Nevada, appeared before the Judiciary Committee for his hearing to be a district court judge in Nevada. Sandoval received two questions from Sen. Orrin Hatch (R-UT). No other senators questioned Sandoval during his hearing. The entirety of Hatch and Sandoval's exchange is reproduced below.

SENATOR HATCH: Mr. Sandoval, you have had a lot of experience in State government as a public servant there, having served as a Nevada State Assemblyman, a Commissioner of the Nevada Gaming Commission, which in and of itself is a big-time job out there, and currently as the State's Attorney General. You have gained a lot of insight in your professional life. How has this all prepared you for being a Federal district court judge?

MR. SANDOVAL: Thank you, Mr. Chairman. I have been very blessed in my life to serve as a legislator, to serve as a regulator, and now to serve as our State's Attorney General. And through my experiences as a private practitioner and as—

SENATOR HATCH: You have been Attorney General for 7 years, right?

MR. SANDOVAL: Mr. Chairman, no; for approximately 3 years.

SENATOR HATCH: Three, OK.

MR. SANDOVAL: But my experiences in Federal and State courts as well as before our State Supreme Court and the amount of litigation that I have been confronted with and have had an opportunity to participate in, with all that experience I feel that—I believe that the Committee will feel that my qualifications satisfy the necessary requirements to be an effective Federal district court judge. If I'm fortunate to be confirmed, I will treat all litigants with dignity and respect.

Senator Hatch's questioning of Sandoval focused exclusively on straightforward queries that highlighted the nominee's experience and qualifications. The questions did not ask Sandoval to take a position or wade into partisan waters.

In contrast, Bush nominee Claire Eagan, who received a hearing for a district court judgeship in Oklahoma when Democrats controlled the Senate in 2001, was asked a similar number of questions—three total—but the nature of the questions were notably different than those asked of Sandoval. Eagan received the following three questions from Sen. Herb Kohl (D-WI) over the course of the hearing:

SENATOR KOHL: What advice would you give Senators who are drafting legislation to comply with the new federalism?

Should you be confirmed, what would be your opinion on a litigant's right to privacy when the information sought to be sealed could keep secret a public health and safety hazard?

I am sure that you have followed the debate here on Capitol Hill and, in fact, across the country, about the need to address the risk of more terrorist attacks. Without getting into any specific proposals, what do you think the tradeoff needs to be between liberty and security?

The two examples show that the number of questions asked of nominees can mask differences in the content and tone of senators' questions. Sandoval merely had to restate his resume and highlight how it qualified him for a job on the federal bench. Eagan, on the other hand, was asked to weigh in on debates over federalism, public health and safety, and the tradeoff between security and civil liberties. Such questions require nominees to state their views and opinions on more ideologically charged policy areas as opposed to simply relaying factual information (Farganis and Wedeking

2014). What explains this variation in the manner in which senators engage with nominees during confirmation hearings? Do nominee characteristics determine the types of questions senators ask, or is hearing content driven more by other motivations, as we found in chapter 4?

The previous chapter explored variations in senators' participation at lower court confirmation hearings in order to assess whether committee members use lower court confirmation hearings to individually vet nominees. We provided evidence that individual vetting is not a central purpose of hearings for typical nominees. Building on this finding, in this chapter the focus shifts to variation in the type of questioning. In so doing, we argue that senators will choose what kinds of questions to ask based on their policy goals, regardless of the specific nominees named by the president. To test this, we investigate the number of questions posed in each of three broad categories: *Judicial Decision Making and Philosophy* (e.g., questions related to judicial philosophy, temperament, precedent); *Issues* (e.g., rights for disadvantaged groups, domestic commerce, abortion, crime); and *Qualifications* (e.g., ABA rating, experience, reversal rate).[1] Members of the Judiciary Committee are empowered with broad discretion over the nature and types of questions they put to nominees. We argue, therefore, that these choices provide another indication of the value of confirmation hearings to senators and their importance within the larger confirmation process. If senators employ these proceedings, at least in part, to vet individual nominees, we expect that their questioning will be driven by nominee-specific characteristics, such as qualifications. If senators view the hearings as a place to engage in larger policy battles independent of individual nominees, political and contextual factors should, at least partially, influence the types of questions senators ask.

The advice and consent process places senators in a position to influence the composition of the federal bench, which ultimately shapes the policies set by the federal courts. As a result, confirmation hearings offer senators a venue in which to engage in larger policy battles. Additionally, senators' roles in these proceedings present an opportunity for them to claim credit for their involvement in staffing the federal bench, which can help enhance their electoral prospects (Mayhew 1974). Chapter 6 addresses and tests the possibility that the hearings can further senators' electoral goals. In short, senators may ask policy-related questions for purposes of pursuing good policy as well as for purposes of pursuing their electoral goals. Here we focus on the potential for hearings to serve as a place for waging larger policy battles, regardless of the specific motivations for engaging in those battles, though we return at the end of the chapter to a consideration of policy invocations that are plausibly primarily focused on good public policy.

In what follows, we investigate content differences in the less contentious but far more numerous cases of hearings for district court nominees and noncontroversial circuit court nominees (~90 percent of nominees from 1993–2012). Since our theoretical account of why senators convene confirmation hearings and the value of these proceedings within the larger advice and consent process is in part contingent on the level of controversy associated with a nominee, we examine typical and controversial nominees separately. As we discussed in chapter 3, we use the presence of interest group opposition to identify controversial circuit court nominees (Scherer, Bartels, and Steigerwalt 2008; Steigerwalt 2010). Given that hearings for nominees identified as controversial by this measure are shown in chapter 3 to be distinct from their noncontroversial counterparts, we examine them separately in chapter 7. Here we model the types of questions asked in hearings for noncontroversial nominees and include both nominee-specific and contextual variables.

To preview the results, there is predictable variation in the types of questions senators pose, and, as we found in chapter 4, this variation is better explained by contextual factors than nominee-specific factors. This chapter thus provides another key piece of evidence supporting our main argument that the vast majority of lower court confirmation hearings—in particular, those that involve noncontroversial nominees—are not used to vet individual nominees' fitness for the bench. Rather, these proceedings reflect senators' responses to larger political and institutional forces and their desire to influence the direction of policy.

Is Hearing Content Driven by Nominee-Specific Factors?

There is no set of required questions asked at all confirmation hearings. Instead, members of the Judiciary Committee choose the nature and types of questions they want to pose to nominees. Therefore, one intuitive possibility is that senators would, based on factors tied to individual nominees, tailor the types of questions they ask in substantively meaningful ways as they fulfill their advice and consent role. If senators hold confirmation hearings to vet nominees individually, we expect senators' behavior to be shaped by factors tied to specific nominees. In this context, that would mean that the types of questions senators ask would be driven by nominee-specific characteristics, such as their qualifications or perceived ideology.

To test this possibility, we use the three key nominee-specific attributes identified in chapter 4 as potentially influencing senator engagement in confirmation hearings: ABA rating, judicial experience, and the presence of an opposition party senator. Our argument in this chapter is similar, so we briefly reintroduce each nominee-specific factor and explain our expectations about how it might influence the types of questions senators pose.

First, senators may rely on the ratings generated by the American Bar Association's (ABA) Standing Committee on the Federal Judiciary. Given the Standing Committee's focus on a nominee's "professional qualifications," we expect that if senators adjust their questioning to a nominee based on her or his ABA rating it will most likely manifest itself in differences in the number of *Qualifications* questions. Asking more *Qualifications* questions would allow senators to probe a nominee's background and fitness for the bench. This leads to the ABA hypothesis:

> **ABA Hypothesis.** Senators will ask fewer *Qualifications* questions of nominees with higher ABA ratings.

Second, a lack of judicial experience may also raise questions in senators' minds about whether a nominee is qualified for a seat on the federal bench. Many nominees do not have judicial experience, and the absence of such experience may raise interest in discussing the nominee's judicial decision making and philosophy since the nominee does not have a previous record for senators to scrutinize. Alternatively, it is possible that judicial experience could work against a nominee by creating a record of written opinions and reversals that could open the door to more scrutiny. For the judicial experience hypothesis, then, we simply state that we expect the content of senators' questions will vary based on whether the nominee has judicial experience without specifying whether judicial experience increases or decreases questions in specific categories.

> **Judicial Experience Hypothesis.** The content of senators' questions will vary based on whether the nominee has previous judicial experience.

Finally, senators may take a cue about a nominee's ideological leanings from the composition of a nominee's home-state senators. When a president and a nominee's home-state Senate delegation are members of the same party, the lack of involvement from the opposition party could increase the likelihood, or at least the perceived likelihood, that the president—

along with the like-minded home-state senators—selected a nominee that is more ideologically extreme (see, e.g., Binder and Maltzman 2009; Black, Madonna, and Owens 2014). As a result, we expect that if senators hold hearings in order to vet individual nominees, members of the committee should respond to a lack of an opposition party senator by increasing the number of *Issues* questions they pose at a hearing to explore the nominees' stances on these issues and ensure that an ideologically extreme nominee is not appointed to a lifelong position on the bench.[2]

> **Opposition Party Senator Hypothesis.** Senators will pose fewer *Issues* questions to nominees from states with an opposition party senator.

The Influence of Senators' Policy Goals on Hearing Content

In chapter 4, we argued that the presumption of acceptability of lower court nominees (Scherer, Bartels, and Steigerwalt 2008) and senatorial control over confirmation hearings combine to reduce the incentive to use these proceedings to vet individual nominees. We suggest that senators instead use these proceedings as a venue for engaging in larger battles over the direction of policy and to pursue electoral goals. In this chapter, we consider the question of committee members' policy goals. Based on interviews with key actors in the confirmation process, Steigerwalt (2010, 108) notes that "Judiciary Committee staff all agreed that senators join the Committee out of a concern for the creation of public policy through the courts. Consequently, the policies (expected) to be created by those serving on the federal courts take center stage in these senators' deliberations." Confirmation hearings serve as a key venue for these policy-motivated senators to publicly engage with future judges over the direction of the federal courts. Senators may respond to beliefs about the likely policy preferences of *individual* nominees, which we consider with the opposition party senator hypothesis above. But given the default assumption of acceptability of lower court nominees (Scherer, Bartels, and Steigerwalt 2008), senators' behavior may also or instead be shaped by their predictions about the policy outputs of a *set* of nominees selected by a given president. Such a focus—on the general policy direction of the courts, as opposed to the impact of any individual nominee—suggests the importance of contextual and political variables for predicting types of questions.

How might confirmation hearings help senators promote their policy goals? We expect that members of the Judiciary Committee leverage their authority to choose which questions they ask during these proceedings to aid in their pursuit of what they see as good public policy. Because these proceedings are a relatively rare opportunity for interbranch dialogue, senators may view them as a venue for engaging in policy discussions with nominees who, if confirmed, will interpret and apply our Constitution, laws, and precedents with the ultimate goal of guiding future policy (Collins and Ringhand 2013). More broadly, confirmation hearings provide senators with a public forum for highlighting specific policy areas and what they see as the ideal direction of the federal courts. This notion is supported by previous work on Supreme Court confirmation hearings. Collins and Ringhand argue that "senators repeatedly frame their questions about currently contested constitutional issues in ways that flatter their preferred position" (2013, 232). This strategy then allows senators to "both signal their constitutional priorities to future justices and present their best case for what should and should not be considered part of our constitutional consensus" (Collins and Ringhand 2013, 232). Senators may find value in this public dialogue even without the expectation of changing nominees' minds on a specific policy.

In what follows, we argue that the specific topics raised by senators in a hearing are driven by whether the Senate is controlled by the president's party or the opposition, as well as other contextual factors which constrain or enhance senators' ability to use the hearings to further what they see as good policy. Scholars have demonstrated the important influence of these types of contextual factors on other aspects of the confirmation process, including the duration of the process itself and the likelihood of confirmation, which suggests they likely also influence senators' decisions about the way they engage in confirmation hearings (see, e.g., Bell 2002a; Martinek, Kemper, and Van Winkle 2002; Binder and Maltzman 2009).

The Role of Contextual Factors

Presidents' authority to appoint federal judges presents an opportunity to transform the judiciary and its policy outputs (see e.g., Goldman 1997; Nemacheck 2007). Thus, a president's policy goals play a central role in the judicial nominees selected (Goldman 1997; Nemacheck 2007). This important power is often discussed by presidents and even presidential candidates. For example, while running for president, Donald Trump promised to "appoint judges very much in the mold of Justice Scalia" (Barrett and Ingold 2017). Statements like this signal a candidate's or president's vision for the judiciary and his or her desired policy outputs from the federal bench.

Senators who belong to the president's party likely generally support the president's views on the ideal direction of the federal courts and, therefore, approve of the slate of nominees on the whole. As ideological allies, promoting the president's nominees and their confirmation aids these senators' own policy goals as well. We argue that senators from the president's party can facilitate the confirmation of these policy allies by highlighting nominees' qualifications. While *Qualifications* questions occasionally critique a nominee's preparedness to serve on the bench, these questions more typically allow nominees to showcase their resumes and credentials and focus on objective, fact-based matters that do not require the nominee to take a position on a potentially controversial issue (Farganis and Wedeking 2014), much as the Sandoval dialogue at the beginning of the chapter illustrates.

By concentrating on *Qualifications* questions, which allow nominees to tout their experience and fitness for the bench, senators can create an impression over time of the president's selections in the aggregate as well-qualified nominees with strong credentials. In a hearing for Gershwin Drain and Robin Rosenbaum, two Obama nominees to district court seats, Sen. Al Franken (D-MN) led off the hearing with a question that highlighted the nominees' extensive judicial experience: "Each of you are a judge and have experience. Judge Rosenbaum, you've been a magistrate judge since 2007. Judge Drain, you have been a State court judge for more than 25 years. How will each of your previous experiences help you in the transition to the Federal Bench, and what challenges do you anticipate in making that transition?"

By highlighting nominees' (typically) strong qualifications, senators from the president's party use the hearings to support like-minded individuals nominated to lifelong seats on the federal bench, where these future judges will make decisions on critical and divisive policy questions such as abortion and the death penalty. Given this, we anticipate an increase in *Qualifications* questions during times of unified government when a majority of senators support the president's vision for the judiciary.

Alternatively, during divided government, a majority of the Senate is likely to have different views than the president on policy and, by extension, what constitutes an ideal judicial nominee. For example, it is not difficult to imagine Democratic senators having a negative reaction to Trump's goal of filling vacancies with those "in the mold of Scalia." Further, given their status as the party in power, these opposition party senators have an institutional mechanism through which they can draw attention to those differences, since the chair for all hearings and the majority of the committee's membership come from the president's opposition party during periods of divided government. We argue that this desire of opposition party senators to publicly counter the president's policy agenda should result in a focus on *Issues* questions during confirmation hearings that occur during divided government. While unlikely to derail a nomination, *Issues* questions allow the majority of senators who disagree with the president to highlight specific policy areas and to contrast their perspective with that of the president and, presumably, his nominees. Further, the ideological nature of *Issues* questions means that nominees are being asked to take a position or express a preference on a subjective matter (Farganis and Wedeking 2014).

Returning to the hearing for Rosenbaum and Drain that Senator Franken began by highlighting the nominees' qualifications, we see how opposition party senators use hearings to raise potential objections to both the nominee under consideration and the president's vision for the courts more generally. Sen. Mike Lee (R-UT) uses his time to question Drain on Second Amendment and death penalty issues. In one question, Lee references a column the nominee authored in *The Michigan Chronicle*, noting: "You wrote that you 'look forward to the time when a person with a gun will be viewed as a coward or a chicken with an unfair advantage, a cheater in a fight.' Does that, and if so how does that, reflect in any way of your view of the Second Amendment?" Sen. Chuck Grassley (R-IA), meanwhile, uses part of his time to criticize the Obama administration's policies more broadly. Grassley argues, "Recently this administration—I should say President Obama's administration, in my view, has shown a disregard for the rights of religious liberties and exercise of conscience protected by the First Amendment." He then poses a question to Rosenbaum: "What is your understanding of the current state of law with regard to the interplay between establishment and free exercise clause of the First Amendment, and how would you approach a case where the First Amendment religious rights were an issue?"

The examples from Senators Lee and Grassley demonstrate how opposition party senators can use the hearings to emphasize the potential ideological changes that the president's nominees will bring to the bench. Unlike senators from the president's party, who have an incentive to create an impression that the president is nominating qualified candidates to the federal bench, the opposition party has incentives to paint the president's nominees as ideologues. These opportunities are present at all hearings, and hearings frequently include a mix of *Qualifications* questions and *Issues* questions. At hearings during divided government, however, opposition party senators are empowered with majority party status, control of the Judiciary Committee, and a majority of members. As a result, we expect to see more *Issues* questions in hearings that occur during divided government.

In sum, we anticipate that senators from both parties see their ability to direct the conversation during confirmation hearings as an opportunity for making headway toward policy goals. We anticipate that during periods of divided government, the incentives are strongest for senators belonging to the president's opposition party—given their different perspective and institutional advantages—to highlight their alternative perspective. During unified government we expect to see more *Qualifications* questions given that senators from the president's party are institutionally advantaged and want to use that advantage to focus on building up the qualifications of their party's president's nominees.

> **Divided Government Hypothesis.** Senators will ask more *Issues* questions and fewer *Qualifications* questions in hearings that take place during divided government compared to hearings during unified government, when we expect more *Qualifications* questions and fewer *Issues* questions.

Second, we expect that presidential election years also influence the types of questions senators ask during the hearings. During a presidential election year, senators' assessments of nominees is likely altered knowing that control of the White House could change hands. A new president may select a different sort of nominee who may, as a group of lifetime appointees, alter the future direction of policy. Previous work has demonstrated that presidential election years indeed influence the broader confirmation process by slowing down the time to confirmation, lowering the probability of confirmation (see, e.g., Martinek, Kemper, and Van Winkle 2002; Binder and Maltzman 2009), and increasing the number of dissenting votes a nominee receives in committee (Steigerwalt 2010, 176). Thus, presidential election years may incentivize a general slowdown of the confirmation process and raise the salience of policy concerns regarding the future of the judiciary, leading senators to adjust their questioning to focus more on issues and less on nominee qualifications.

> **Presidential Election Hypothesis.** Senators will ask more *Issues* questions and fewer *Qualifications* questions in hearings that take place during presidential election years.

For circuit court nominees, the ideological makeup of the circuit to which they are nominated may also influence senators' assessments. Since the composition of each circuit varies over time as vacancies arise and are filled, senators may view ideologically split circuits as more valuable opportunities to influence the direction of policy and therefore may treat these nominees differently. Previous work supports the notion that nominees from closely balanced circuits are handled differently. Binder and Maltzman (2009) find that it is more difficult for nominees to be confirmed to these circuits, and the analysis in chapter 4 finds that nominees to evenly balanced circuits elicit more questions. We anticipate that circuits approaching an even split will increase interest among senators in their ideological future and resulting policy outputs. More specifically, we expect that senators will especially want to relay their vision for the judiciary and its policy outputs to those nominated to closely balanced circuits and that they do so by posing more *Issues* questions as opposed to *Qualifications* questions.

> **Party Balance of Circuit Hypothesis.** Senators will ask more *Issues* questions and fewer *Qualifications* questions as the party balance of the nominee's circuit approaches parity.

Additionally, we expect that hearings that occur for vacancies on closely split circuits during times of divided government combine the potential for a large impact on policy with a political climate known to produce fierce competition over the direction of public policy. This combination, we argue, increases the incentive for senators to direct the content of a hearing toward policy-focused *Issues* questions. In other words, the potential policy payoff for focusing more on *Issues* questions in hearings that occur during divided government, when a majority of senators oppose the president's perspective, are even greater when the hearing is for a vacancy on a closely divided circuit where a newly confirmed judge could have a significant influence on policy outputs. Again, this expectation is based on senators having a shared presumption about the policy preferences of the president's judicial nominees as a whole—i.e., that they are generally liberal or conservative—not an assessment of an individual nominee's policy predilections. Thus, adapting language from Berry, Golder, and Milton (2012), we hypothesize:

> **Balanced Circuit and Divided Government Hypotheses.** The marginal effect of a balanced circuit on the number of *Issues* questions will be stronger for nominees whose hearings occur during periods of divided government, and, similarly, the marginal effect of divided government on the number of *Issues* questions will be strongest for those nominated to more balanced circuits.

Finally, we expect that the high-profile nature of the D.C. Circuit increases senators' perceived potential for furthering their policy goals during hearings for positions on this court. The D.C. Circuit is considered important in part due to its exclusive jurisdiction over many administrative law cases and cases likely to have a national effect (Fraser et al. 2013). Further, several current and former U.S. Supreme Court justices ascended to the High Court by way of the D.C. Circuit, bolstering the circuit's reputation as powerful and influential. We expect that the prestige and salience associated with this court increase the incentive to discuss policy topics most important to members of the Judiciary Committee. By focusing on *Issues* questions in hearings for nominees to this critical circuit, senators may see the greatest return on their efforts compared to similar opportunities to question those nominated to other courts.

> **D.C. Circuit Hypothesis.** Senators will ask more *Issues* questions and fewer *Qualifications* questions of nominees for positions on the D.C. Circuit.

The above hypotheses allow us to further test whether senators hold confirmation hearings to scrutinize individual nominees, engage in larger policy battles, or for both reasons. If senators use these proceedings at least in part to vet individual nominees, we expect that ABA rating, judicial experience, and an opposition party senator will all shape the types of questions senators ask of nominees. If senators hold confirmation hearings in part to further their policy goals, we should find that divided government, presidential election years, party balance of a circuit, and a nomination to the D.C. Circuit influence the distribution of *Issues*, *Qualifications*, and *Judicial Decision Making and Philosophy* questions senators pose. We submit that contextual factors shape senators' calculations about their ability to advance good public policy through the questioning of nominees during confirmation hearings. If the theoretical argument we have offered is correct, we generally expect that contextual variables should best explain the number of questions in the three categories rather than factors tied to specific nominees.

Modeling Hearing Content

To test the above hypotheses, we separately model the total number of questions in each of three categories using a negative binomial regression. Our models are similar to those in chapter 4, but the dependent variable in these new models is the total number of questions asked in each of three categories: *Judicial Decision Making and Philosophy* (e.g., questions related to judicial philosophy, temperament, precedent); *Issues* (e.g., rights for disadvantaged groups, domestic commerce, abortion, crime); and *Qualifications* (e.g., ABA rating, experience, reversal rate). A full list of the categories and their groupings can be found in table 3.1 (see chapter 3).

Our theoretical expectations about why senators hold judicial confirmation hearings are in part contingent on the level of controversy associated with the nominee. Given this, we focus here on the types of questions asked during hearings for district and noncontroversial circuit court nominees. We address hearings for controversial circuit court nominees in chapter 7.

As we did in chapter 4, we include three nominee-specific independent variables (ABA rating, judicial experience, and opposition party senator). We also incorporate four variables to test whether contextual factors influence the types of questions senators ask during confirmation hearings (divided government, presidential election year, party balance of the circuit, and D.C. Circuit). Variables capturing circuit-level characteristics are excluded from the district court models. See chapter 4 for additional details on how these variables are coded. Along with the variables needed to test our contextual and nominee-specific hypotheses, the models include controls for presidential administration and the total number of questions asked. The district court models also include a dummy variable for D.C. and Puerto Rico nominees, while the circuit court models include an interaction between divided government and the party balance of a circuit. While we hypothesize that senators will ask more *Issues* questions specifically for those nominated to relatively balanced circuits during divided government, we include this interaction term in all four models to explore whether a similar dynamic may influence the frequency with which senators pose the other types of questions too. The unit of analysis is the nominee.[3]

Results

District Court Hearings

Coefficients from the district court models, along with 95 percent confidence intervals, are presented in figure 5.1. Black squares, gray circles, and black triangles correspond to the *Qualifications*, *Issues*, and *Judicial Decision Making and Philosophy* models, respectively. Turning first to the nominee-specific variables, we see that they are associated with at most minor differences in the content of hearings. Nominees in our lowest ABA rating category face more *Qualifications* questions on average than nominees in our highest rating category ($p = 0.11$). Although this result is consistent with what we might expect if senators are scrutinizing individual nominees, the increase in *Qualifications* questions is reserved for the 9 percent of nominees who received a rating in the bottom two categories. There is no statistically significant difference between the number of *Qualifications* questions nominees in the middle range of ABA ratings receive compared to the nominees rated unanimously "well-qualified."

Turning to judicial experience, if senators use confirmation hearings to assess nominees based on their individual merits, we would expect this experience to affect questions about their qualifications or their judicial decision making. The transcripts reveal that senators consistently use the hearings to press nominees about their willingness to adhere to precedent or question them on how they will decide "cases of first impression." In addition, nominees during the Obama years have often been asked whether they agree with Obama's 2009 statement that he wanted judicial nominees to possess "empathy," which drew criticism from conservatives as a signal of judicial activism (e.g., Christophersen 2013). For nominees who have no record as a judge, getting a sense of how the nominee will decide cases may prove especially important to senators. The results displayed in figure 5.1 offer no support for this expectation, however. Nominees with judicial experience do not face greater or less thorough questioning about their judicial decision making. In addition, these nominees do not face more questions about their qualifications or positions on specific issues. Given that we have competing reasons for expecting more or fewer questions in these categories for nominees with judicial experience, however, it is possible that both of these mechanisms are at play, which may be canceling out any effect.

Finally, we see no change in the number of questions senators ask in our three categories as a function of nominees' home-state Senate delegation.

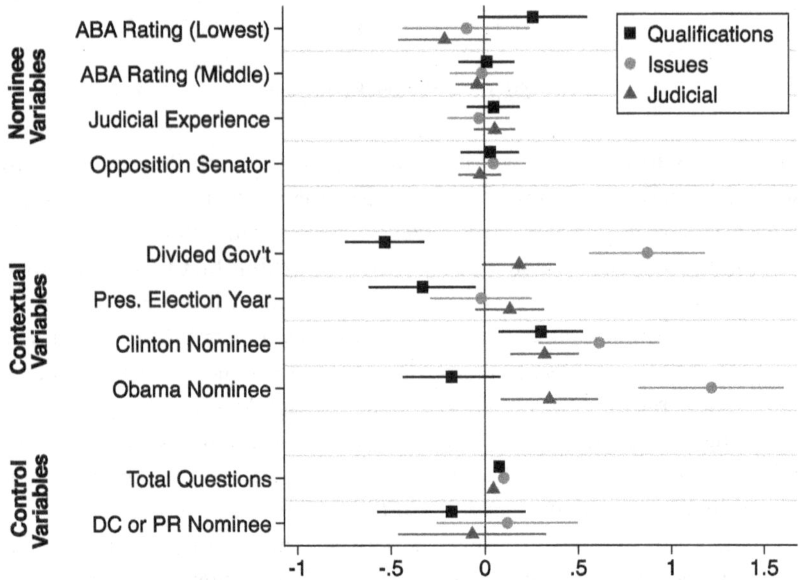

Fig. 5.1. Number of Questions by Category; District Court Nominees; Negative Binomial Regression

Note: For all models, $n = 732$. All models are clustered on the hearing date to account for multiple nominees being questioned at once. The figure indicates 95 percent confidence intervals. Full tables for these models are available in the on-line appendix.

This is perhaps especially surprising when it comes to *Issues* questions. If senators are more concerned about the ideological leanings of a nominee from a state with no opposition party senator, they do not show it by asking such nominees more ideologically charged *Issues* questions.

Turning to the contextual variables, we see support for the Divided Government Hypothesis. During periods of divided government, senators ask fewer questions about nominees' qualifications and more questions about issues. There is also partial support for the Presidential Election Hypothesis, with hearings during presidential election years focusing less on questions about nominees' qualifications.

The results indicate that divided government is a consistent predictor of content differences in hearings. Figure 5.2 shows the predicted number of questions in each of the three categories as we move from unified to divided government, with all other variables held at their median or mode, along with 95 percent confidence intervals. In general, senators do not ask district court nominees many questions at their hearings, so the absolute change in the number of questions asked in any one category is not large. The tenor of the hearings does change, however, as we move from unified

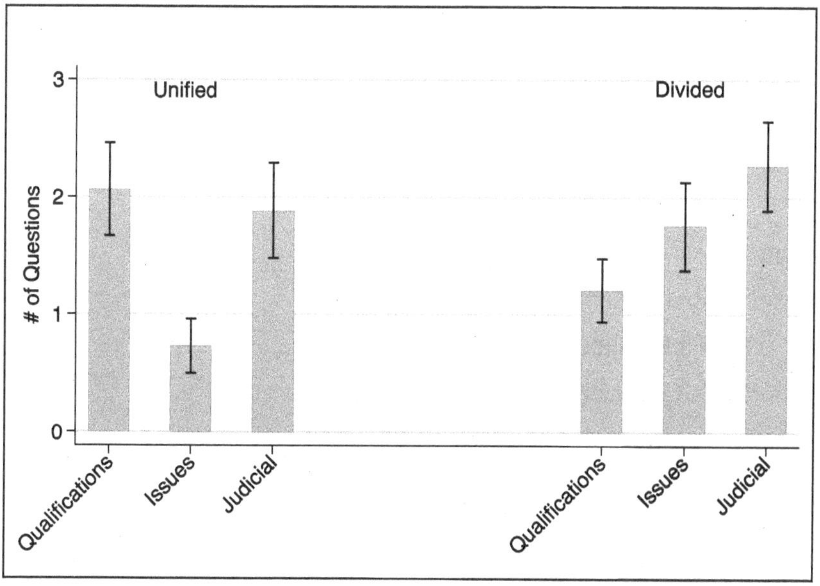

Fig. 5.2. Predicted Questions by Category (District Nominees); Unified vs. Divided Government
Figure displays 95 percent confidence intervals.

to divided government. The changes are most pronounced in the *Qualifications* and *Issues* categories. At hearings during unified government, senators pose 2.8 times as many *Qualifications* questions as *Issues* questions. During divided government, however, senators ask more *Issues* questions (1.8) than questions about the qualifications of nominees (1.2).[4]

In sum, the analysis of district court hearings indicates that the types of questions senators raise during confirmation hearings are best explained by contextual factors outside of nominees' control, such as divided government. The evidence suggests that nominee-specific factors at most only minimally influence the extent to which senators query nominees about their qualifications, issues, and judicial decision making. Instead, the predictive role of contextual factors like divided government suggests that senators use their control over the content of confirmation hearings as an opportunity to play out larger battles over policy.

Circuit Court Hearings

Are senators' choices about the types of questions to pose to noncontroversial circuit court nominees similarly influenced by contextual factors rather than nominee-specific factors? Since circuit courts are a step up in the

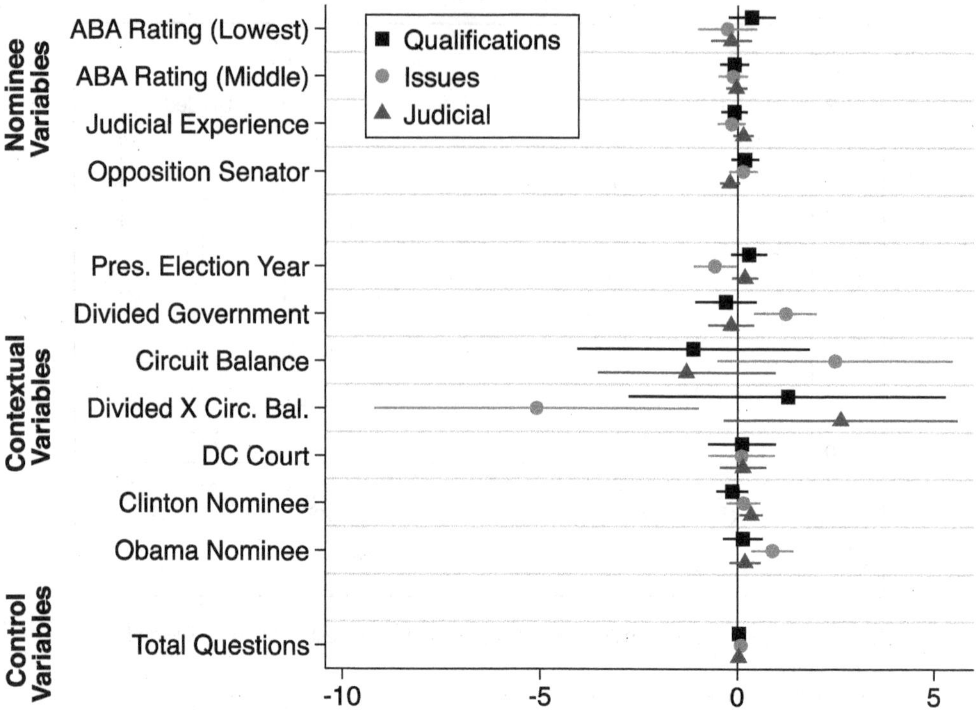

Fig. 5.3. Number of Questions by Category; Noncontroversial Circuit Nominees; Negative Binomial Regression

Note: For all models, $n = 129$. The figure displays 95 percent confidence intervals. Full tables for these models are available in the on-line appendix.

judicial hierarchy, might senators treat these nominees differently? Figure 5.3 displays the coefficients and 95 percent confidence intervals from the circuit court models. The results reported do not provide support for any of the nominee-specific hypotheses. There is little indication that senators direct the content of confirmation hearings on the basis of nominee-specific characteristics. This does not preclude the possibility that senators tailor the exact wording of questions to nominees. For example, a nominee's specific type of service may be referenced (e.g., Sen. Jon Kyl says to circuit court nominee William Pryor, "What I was curious about . . . was her reference to your work on behalf of children. And I would like to ask you to expand on that, if you could a bit." Or when Senator Franken notes circuit court nominee Scott Matheson's past experience as a professor and prosecutor, then asks, "What impact do those experiences have on your understanding of the criminal justice system and how will that impact or influence you, if you are confirmed, at the appellate court?") The models suggest, however, that any such variation occurs within categories and not between categories. In other words, a question may be worded slightly differently but still focuses on the same basic concept (e.g., qualifications, issues, etc.).

The lack of a connection between ABA ratings and qualifications may seem counterintuitive, but we believe it stems from the fact that most circuit court nominees are seen as highly qualified by their peers and likely by members of the Judiciary Committee as well. Indeed, only 8 percent of noncontroversial circuit court nominees (and 11 percent of all circuit court nominees) had at least a minority of the ABA Standing Committee rank them as "not qualified," while more than half were unanimously rated "well qualified." Furthermore, circuit court nominees are rarely asked directly about their ABA rating. Only 3 out of 129 noncontroversial circuit court nominees received at least one question specifically about their ABA rating. Given that the ABA only rarely rates a nominee as "not qualified," we believe senators on the Judiciary Committee have come to expect nominees to be reasonably qualified, and as a result there is little to no incentive to routinely ask *Qualifications* questions on the basis of nuances in otherwise relatively positive ABA ratings.

Turning to the contextual variables, we find that divided government increases the number of issue questions from approximately 1.1 to 1.9 when the circuit's party balance is at its median level, which corresponds to a circuit with 64 percent of judges appointed by presidents of one party ($p < 0.1$). In line with our interactive hypothesis, this difference increases when a circuit is more closely divided. Figure 5.4 displays the difference in the number of *Issues* questions between divided and unified government as the circuit's balance approaches an even split. The figure indicates a heightened influence of divided government only for those nominated to more evenly split circuits. This suggests that the larger tensions that occur over policy during periods of divided government spill over into confirmation hearings. Members of the Judiciary Committee use their control over the content of confirmation hearings to make headway toward their policy goals by directing the conversation toward *Issues* questions when the direction of policy is contested and the potential impact of the nomination is greatest.

In terms of the predicted number of questions, a nominee to a circuit split evenly between Republican and Democratic appointees during unified government can expect about 0.8 *Issues* questions. The predicted number of *Issues* questions increases to 2.7, a difference of almost two questions,

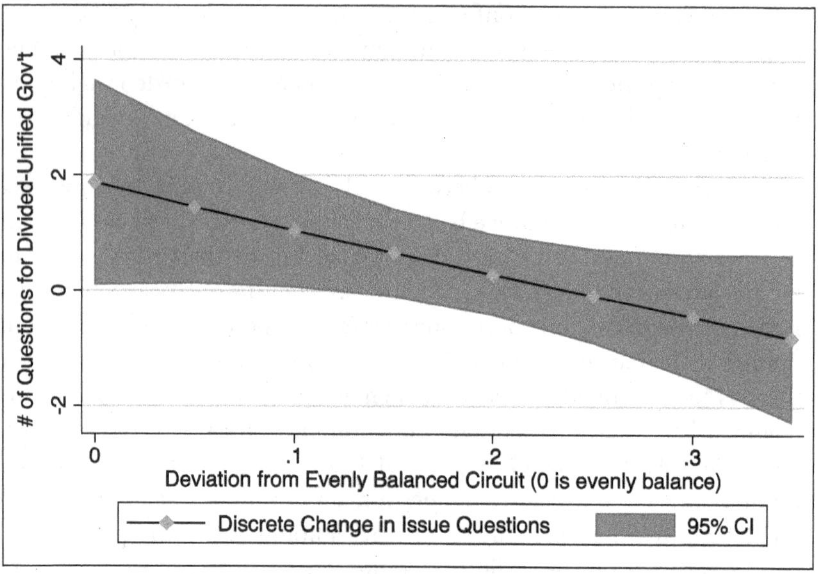

Fig. 5.4. Difference in Number of *Issues* Questions; Comparing Unified vs. Divided Government

when the same nomination occurs when the president and the Senate are controlled by opposing parties ($p < 0.05$). Given that the median number of total questions asked of noncontroversial circuit nominees is approximately nine, an increase of two questions is substantively meaningful. This behavior suggests that under divided government—when competition over policy is at a maximum—senators perceive the greatest benefit to asking *Issues* questions since these nominees, if confirmed, will be in a position to alter the direction of the circuit's policy outputs.

Though we did not have any prior expectations, we find the opposite relationship regarding the interaction between divided government and the party balance of the circuit for *Judicial Decision Making and Philosophy* questions. While figure 5.5 shows that the difference in the predicted number of *Judicial Decision Making and Philosophy* questions from unified to divided government is not statistically significant when the party balance of the circuit is at its median (a 64 percent/36 percent party split), a statistically significant difference between times of unified versus divided government is present for more lopsided circuits. More specifically, this difference between times of unified versus divided government becomes statistically significant when the partisan breakdown of Republican versus Democratic

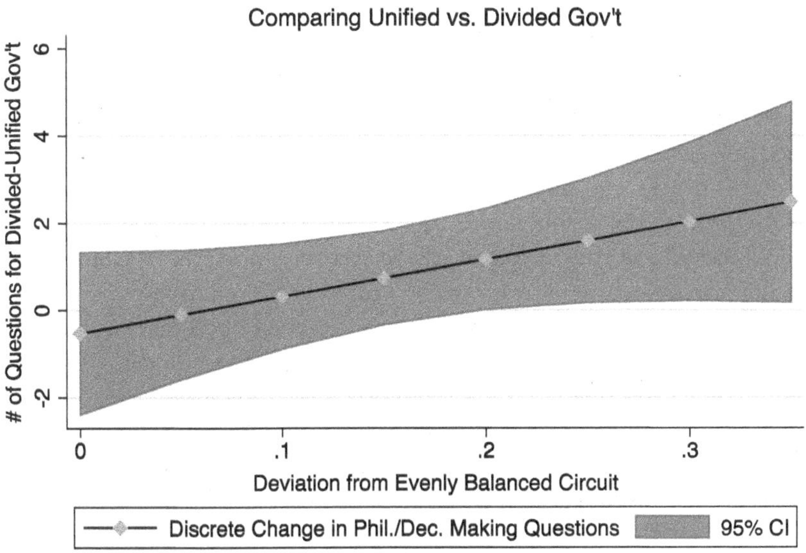

Fig. 5.5. Difference in Number of *Judicial Decision Making and Philosophy* Questions; Comparing Unified vs. Divided Government

appointees is at least 70 percent/30 percent (or vice versa). Senators are predicted to ask 2.7 *Judicial Decision Making and Philosophy* questions of an individual nominated to a circuit with a 70 percent/30 percent party split whose hearing takes place when the Senate and White House are controlled by the same party. This number increases to 3.9 if the hearing occurs during a time when the Senate majority party is the opposite of the nominating president's party affiliation ($p < 0.05$). The effect of divided government is most pronounced for those nominated to the maximum observed level of circuit party balance, an 85 percent/15 percent party split. At this level of circuit balance (or lack thereof), senators are predicted to pose 2.2 *Judicial Decision Making and Philosophy* questions of a nominee whose hearing occurs during unified government compared to 4.8 questions if the hearing takes place during divided government ($p < 0.05$).

These results again suggest that macro-level disputes over policy shape what senators seek to gain from confirmation hearings and therefore the types of questions they pose during these proceedings. This senatorial behavior fits with the notion of senators being attuned to hearings as an opportunity to promote their definition of good public policy. Given this, an increase in *Judicial Decision Making and Philosophy* questions during divided government is unsurprising since we expect greater incentives for scrutinizing nominees during times when the Senate is likely less approving of the president's selections as a group. That this increase only occurs for nominees whose confirmation would not significantly alter the partisan balance of their circuit, however, suggests that these questions are used differently by senators than are *Issues* questions, which increase during divided government only for those nominated to closely split circuits.

In terms of the other contextual variables, we also find that *Issues* questions decrease during presidential election years. More specifically, the model predicts that senators pose 1.1 *Issues* questions during years without a presidential election and 0.6 *Issues* questions for those having hearings during the year of a presidential election ($p < 0.05$). In some ways, this finding is counterintuitive in that we anticipated senators would want to voice policy arguments by focusing on *Issues* questions more during presidential election years. We suspect, however, that this finding may be due to the conventional wisdom that only the most uncontroversial of nominees proceed through the confirmation process, including having a hearing, during presidential election years.[5] If this is a shared assumption by members of the Judiciary Committee, they may view their efforts toward policy goals as being better directed elsewhere during critical presidential election campaigns. Finally, we note that the results show that senators posed more *Judicial Decision Making and Philosophy* questions to Clinton nominees compared to Bush nominees.

On the whole, contextual factors are stronger predictors of the number of questions received in these broad categories for both district and noncontroversial circuit court nominees than are nominee-specific factors. The evidence therefore indicates that senators do not hold confirmation hearings with the primary goal of vetting individual nominees. Instead, by strategically directing the content of hearings toward policy-focused *Issues* questions in some circumstances, senators use these proceedings as a place to play out broader disputes over the direction of policy.

Despite the mounting evidence that senators do not hold confirmation hearings for the purpose of vetting individual nominees, it is possible that our analysis of these broad categories has masked more subtle senatorial responses to nominee-specific characteristics. Before concluding that nominee-specific factors play only a minimal role at best in determining the types of questions senators ask, we explore whether three additional nominee-specific characteristics—race, gender, and experience as an attorney general or prosecutor—might be connected to the types of questions senators pose during hearings. In the analysis that follows, we focus on more narrow question categories selected on the basis of research on race, gender, and judicial behavior.

Differential Questioning by Race and Gender?

Along with professional qualifications, it is possible that senators and their staff make inferences about a nominee's future behavior based on the race or gender of the nominee. Such assumptions about the types of decisions a future judge might make could lead to differential questioning during confirmation hearings. Research on whether men and women judges rule differently has not produced consistent evidence on the subject, but it suggests that some differences—though perhaps limited in scope—exist (see, e.g., Westergren 2004; Martin and Pyle 2005; Peresie 2005; Segal, Spaeth, and Benesh 2005; Ostberg and Wetstein 2007). The most recent comprehensive studies on the matter suggest that systematic differences in how men and women judges rule are reserved only for sex discrimination cases (Boyd, Espstein, and Martin 2010; Haire and Moyer 2015).

Research also shows differences in the ways white and minority judges rule in certain types of cases. Haire and Moyer (2015) find that black judges are more likely to side with the plaintiff in discrimination cases. Kastellec (2013) similarly finds that black judges are more likely to vote in support of affirmative action plans and that white judges are more likely to favor affirmative action plans when a black judge is on their panel. Kastellec's finding is consistent with other work that suggests the presence of women and racial minorities may change the voting behavior of men and white judges on a panel (see, e.g., Boyd, Epstein, and Martin 2010; Haire and Moyer 2015). Finally, Scherer (2004) and Haire and Moyer (2015) find evidence that black judges are more likely to side with defendants in certain criminal cases.

Although the evidence suggests that racial and gender differences in judges' rulings are reserved for a narrow set of cases (see, e.g., Boyd, Epstein, and Martin 2010; Haire and Moyer 2015), senators and their staff members may still make inferences about judges' proclivities based on stereotypes of how women and minority judges may differ from white men judges. Research on voter stereotypes finds that women candidates are perceived to be more pro-choice and liberal than men candidates (see, e.g., Koch 2000), while research on stereotypes about black politicians suggests they are perceived to be more liberal (Schneider and Bos 2011; Jacobsmeier 2015) and particularly focused on civil rights issues (Schneider and Bos 2011). Voters also presume that women are more competent in issue areas that get tagged as "feminine," such as education, health care, and social services (Huddy and Terkildsen 1993; Sanbonmatsu 2002), while black politicians are perceived to be more competent on issues such as civil rights, unemployment, and poverty (Schneider and Bos 2011).

Voters tend to rely on gender and race as heuristics in low-information races (McDermott 1998). Although senators and their staffs may take a more sophisticated approach to evaluating nominees than voters do with candidates and politicians, political elites are not necessarily immune to biased perceptions. While there is ample information available for lower court nominees, given the number of nominees and the magnitude of senators' and their staff members' other responsibilities, unless there is an obvious reason to focus on a given nominee, senators are not likely to be effortfully processing and incorporating a lot of information about the nominee. If so, we would consider Judiciary Committee members to be operating as if they were in a low-information setting, and we might expect women and racial minority nominees to face more stereotype-related questions. What is more, there is evidence from a high-information setting—Supreme Court confirmation hearings—that the nominee's gender and race are related to the kinds of questions senators ask (Boyd, Collins, and Ringhand 2018).

To test this possibility, we examine whether senators ask a given nominee at least one question in each of four specific categories: rights for disadvantaged groups, criminal justice/death penalty, right to privacy/abortion, and judicial philosophy. The first three categories were selected because they most closely match the areas identified in the literature as where women or minority judges behave differently than men or white judges and areas in which issue-based stereotypes operate. If senators anticipate the possibility that racial and ethnic minority or women nominees would make different decisions in or pay more attention to these issue areas, they may be more inclined to scrutinize minority and women nominees on these issues. Additionally, we analyze judicial philosophy questions based on the theory that senators may expect women and minority judges to be, on balance, less competent than their white male counterparts, and judicial philosophy questions present an opportunity to more fully explore a nominee's judicial competence (Boyd, Collins, and Ringhand 2018).[6]

We explore potential differences first in senators' questioning of district court nominees. The coefficients from the regression models are presented in figure 5.6, along with 95 percent confidence intervals. Since we now focus on more specific question categories, the models are binary logistic regression models with the independent variables from the previous models included, along with the nominee's race (white = 0, racial minority = 1) and sex (male = 0, female = 1). In addition, given our focus on crime questions in the second model, we control for one other nominee qualification variable in these models: service as an attorney general or prosecutor.

The results in figure 5.6 show no consistent evidence of differential

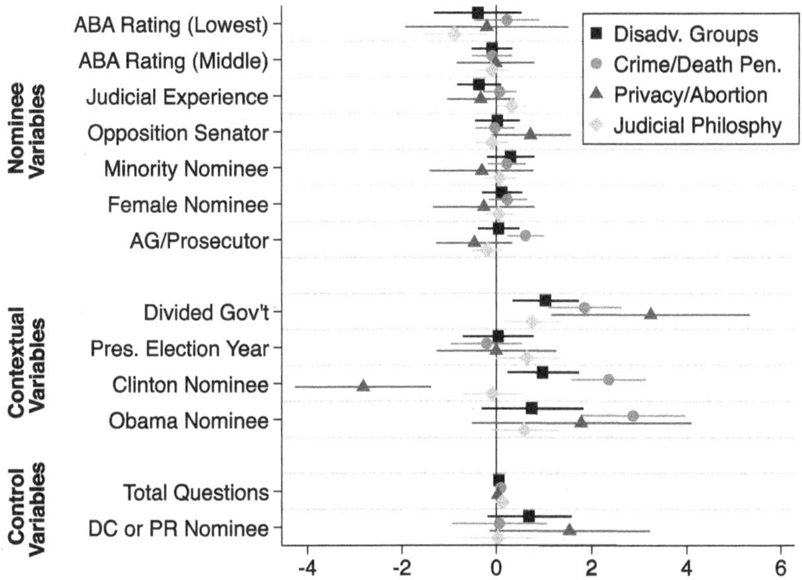

Fig. 5.6: Whether Nominee Received a Question in Category; District Court Nominees; Logistic Regression

Note: For all models, *n* = 732. All models are clustered on the hearing date to account for multiple nominees being questioned at once. The figure displays 95 percent confidence intervals. Full tables for these models are available in the on-line appendix.

questioning based on the race or gender of the nominees, at least as it pertains to the likelihood of receiving a question in the four categories we examine here. Despite evidence that black and women judges are more prone to side with plaintiffs in discrimination cases (Boyd, Epstein, and Martin 2010; Kastellec 2013; Haire and Moyer 2015), we see no evidence that women and racial minority nominees are more likely to be asked about the rights of disadvantaged groups than their white male peers. The same is true for racial minority judges in criminal justice cases, in spite of empirical evidence that black judges are more prone to side with defendants in certain criminal cases (Scherer 2004; Haire and Moyer 2015) and in spite of general stereotypes about black judges' ideology and policy competence (Schneider and Bos 2011; Jacobsmeier 2015). On the issue of abortion, where stereotypes suggest that women are viewed as more liberal (Koch 2000), we see no evidence of differential questioning. Finally, despite evidence that women Supreme Court nominees face more judicial philosophy questions, this difference does not emerge for district court nominees. In sum, on the questions where previous literature would suggest we should be most inclined to find differences, none emerge. These findings are consistent with an earlier analysis of a smaller sample of district court nominees, which showed little indication of differential questioning based on nominee gender or race (Dancey, Nelson, and Ringsmuth 2014).

Once again, we find evidence that divided government changes the tenor of district court hearings. Senators are more likely to raise questions in these policy-focused categories during divided government than during unified government. With all other variables held at the median or mode, moving from unified to divided government increases the probability of a nominee facing a question about disadvantaged groups from 0.1 to 0.3, crime/death penalty from 0.2 to 0.6, privacy/abortion from 0 to 0.01, and judicial philosophy from 0.4 to 0.6 (though the difference is not statistically significant for privacy/abortion).

For circuit court nominees, the models include most but not all of the variables from earlier models. Because we now focus on a much narrower set of questions in each model and have fewer than 130 observations, variation in each category is sometimes limited. Further, some of the independent variables also occur rarely, such as presidential election year. This combination leads us to rely on a pared down set of core independent variables.[7]

The coefficients and 95 percent confidence intervals from the logistic regression models for circuit court nominees are presented in figure 5.7. The results again show no consistent evidence of differential questioning on the basis of a nominee's race or gender. We do find modest evidence that minority nominees are less likely to receive at least one question about privacy/abortion than are white nominees. But this is not consistent with the documented stereotypes about black politicians being more liberal (Schneider and Bos 2011; Jacobsmeier 2015), and the difference in the predicted probabilities for white and minority nominees is not itself statistically significant. Similarly, minority nominees appear less likely to face a question in the judicial philosophy category, though again the difference in predicted probabilities between white and minority nominees is not statistically significant. As in the case of district court nominees, on the questions where previous literature would suggest we should be most likely to find differences in how senators question nominees, none emerge.

The strongest evidence that senators tailor questions to specific nominees on the basis of nominee-level factors comes in the criminal justice models. For both district and circuit court nominees, we find that senators are more likely to ask at least one criminal justice question of nominees with a background as an attorney general or a prosecutor (a 0.3 probability

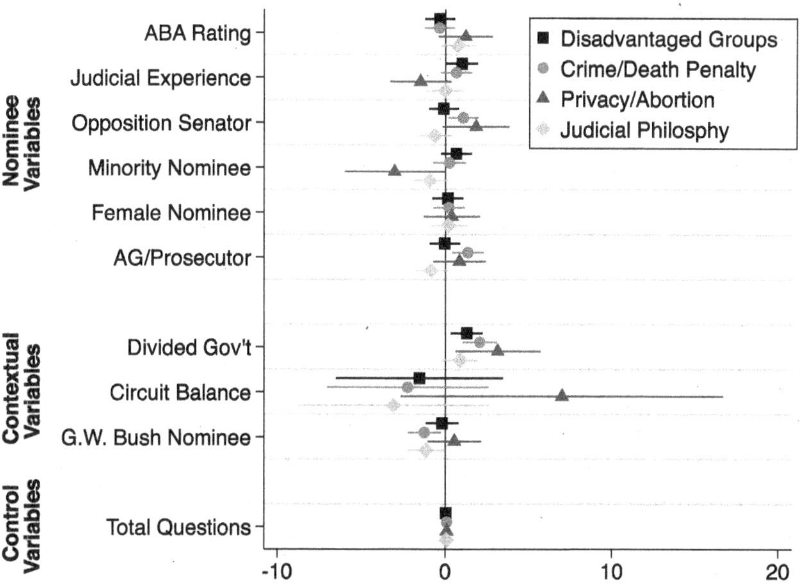

Fig. 5.7. Whether Nominee Is Asked a Question in Key Categories; Noncontroversial Circuit Nominees; Logistic Regression

Note: For all models, $n = 129$. The figure displays 95 percent confidence intervals. Full tables for these models are available in the on-line appendix.

versus 0.1 in the circuit court model and a 0.4 probability versus 0.2 in the district court model). This result suggests that senators respond to this type of professional experience and are inclined to discuss the criminal justice system with nominees who have experience as an attorney general or prosecutor. Often these questions include subjects like the death penalty and mandatory minimum sentencing. For example, Second Circuit nominee Pierre Leval, who had previous experience as an assistant U.S. attorney, was asked by Sen. Larry Pressler, "Do you feel the federal sentencing guidelines have been effective in the equitable administration of justice at the federal level?"

While we find some evidence that nominee-specific variables play a role in determining the likelihood of senators questioning a circuit court nominee in specific issue areas, most of these findings are in the opposite direction than theory and previous evidence would lead us to expect. For example, the coefficient for opposition party senator is statistically significant for the criminal justice and privacy categories. If senators see a lack of an opposition party senator as increasing the likelihood that the president would name a more ideologically extreme nominee, we would expect a negative relationship here. Instead, the presence of an opposition party senator *increases* the likelihood that the Judiciary Committee will ask at least one question in each of these categories.[8]

Combined with our earlier findings, the results suggest that while there is some evidence that nominee-specific factors influence how senators question nominees during confirmation hearings, the models do not present a widespread pattern or indicate a systematic influence of nominee-specific factors on senators' behavior. Consistent with our earlier results, however, we see evidence that divided government changes the tenor of circuit court hearings. Senators are more likely to question nominees in these more policy-focused *Issues* categories when tensions over policy are highest, that is, during divided government. With all other variables held at the median or mode, moving from unified to divided government increases the probability of a nominee facing a question about disadvantaged groups from 0.2 to 0.3 and crime/death penalty from 0.1 to 0.5.[9] Thus divided government has a substantial impact on the types of questions senators ask and the overall tone of a nominee's hearing. This evidence, combined with the district court results, reinforces our argument that contextual factors have a strong influence on the incentives for senators to direct the substantive focus of hearings during these public proceedings.[10]

Pursuing Policy Goals: An Examination of Four Committee Members

As we have noted throughout, senators' decisions to engage with certain policy areas can be a function of electoral goals, policy goals, or a mix of the two. One claim we seek to advance in this book is that senators use confirmation hearings in part as a forum for policy discussion that is about more than simply electorally motivated position taking. In that sense, we view senators as having policy motivations (Fenno 1973) that are frequently tied to electoral motivations but may also arise due to a senator's personal background (Burden 2007); race, gender, or class identity (see, e.g., Minta 2009; Carnes 2013; Swers 2013); committee assignments and jurisdictions (see, e.g., Adler and Wilkerson 2013, chap. 4); or other factors.

To help demonstrate this claim, we tracked the questioning of four long-serving senators to document the types of questions they ask and identify the potential motivations behind those questions. The four senators—Herb Kohl (D-WI), Dick Durbin (D-IL), Jeff Sessions (R-AL), and Chuck

Grassley (R-IA)—served on the Judiciary Committee during all three presidential administrations from 1993 to 2012. Kohl and Grassley served on the committee during our entire 20-year time span, while Durbin and Sessions joined the committee in 1997 and served beyond the 2012 ending point of our data, although Durbin was not on the committee in the 106th Congress (1999–2000). For each senator, we randomly selected one district and one noncontroversial circuit court hearing date for each year they participated in a hearing. We then randomly selected one nominee's questions from that date. The goal was to create a sample of questions that the senator poses over time while minimizing the number of repeat questions that would appear in our sample if we selected hearings from the same date.[11] In keeping with the rest of the chapter, we choose to focus on district and noncontroversial circuit court nominees.

Kohl clearly fits the pattern of a senator who uses the hearings to engage with nominees on a policy interest of his, and one that appears distinct from his electoral goals. One of the few nonlawyers on the committee during our time span, Kohl, a former businessman, was a key member of the Judiciary Committee's Subcommittee on Antitrust, Competition Policy and Consumer Rights, including time as the chair of the subcommittee (Barone 2013, 1757). In one of our interviews, a former Democratic staffer noted that "some senators have particular concerns" that they raise at hearings and noted Kohl's business background and interest in antitrust. Consistent with this observation, in the 19 randomly selected hearings that Kohl participated in, he asked at least one question that fell into the domestic commerce category in 9 hearings. The 14 total domestic commerce questions, which primarily focused on the use of protective orders in product liability cases, made up 19 percent of the 73 questions Kohl asked during the hearings in our sample. By way of comparison, Durbin, Sessions, and Grassley asked only 1 domestic commerce question out of the 243 combined questions in our sample (0.4 percent of questions).

Kohl's interest in the topic of corporate liability also seems consistent across time and presidential administrations. In 1995, for example, he asked Clinton D.C. Circuit Court nominee Merrick Garland, "Should a judge consider public health and safety when reviewing a request for a secrecy order, and should that be written into law?" In 2001, he asked Bush district court nominee Claire Eagan, "Should you be confirmed, what would be your opinion on a litigant's right to privacy when the information sought to be sealed could keep secret a public health and safety hazard?" Similarly, in 2009, he asked Obama district court nominee Abdul Kallon whether a "judge should be required to balance the public's right to know against a litigant's right to privacy when the information sought to be sealed could keep in secret a public health and safety hazard?"

Kohl's repeated invocation of corporate liability issues could serve his policy goals in at least two ways. First, as one of our interviewees noted, senators may use the questioning to "sensitize nominees" to the senator's point of view on an issue. Obviously any influence senators have over nominees is considerably reduced once a nominee assumes a judgeship, but the senator can use the hearing to signal the importance of an issue to elected officials and the public. In this vein, too, senators may be offering the nominee information in the event that the nominee is ambitious and may want to move up the judicial hierarchy. Sen. Ted Kaufman indicated that "every circuit court judge thinks he or she is going to be a Supreme Court justice, so people start early in planning for what they're saying." This may overstate some circuit court judges' ambitions, but it does raise the possibility that policy discussions at one hearing could signal to nominees which issues might be key to their judicial ascendance. It may also signal to future nominees, who may be watching current hearings, what the parameters of certain issues are in case they want to establish a noncontroversial record.

Second, the hearings offer a forum for information gathering. Although prominent theories of congressional committee formation highlight the informational role that committees play (Gilligan and Krehbiel 1990; Krehbiel 1991), there is skepticism in the literature that senators actually use hearings for meaningful information gathering rather than as a venue for waging political battles or garnering publicity (Truman 1951; Huitt 1954; Berry 1997). The hearings are a forum for senators to hear the perspectives of current members of the legal profession who may have unique insights into the policies senators care about, and we do see examples of senators and nominees engaging in dialogue that appears on its face to be more about the exchange of information than making a partisan point. For example, responses to Kohl's corporate liability questions sometimes provided insight into how the nominee sees the issue playing out in the courts. In response to a standard Kohl question about his concerns regarding the use of protective orders, Bush district court nominee Stephen Limbaugh gave the following response that highlighted his own concerns and the possible need for legislation in the area.

> MR. LIMBAUGH: I understand well your concern. I have a concern of my own, and that is, so many settlements—most settlements are entered into without any admission of liability by one party or the other. So I'm trying to figure out what kind of mechanism could be used

> to address your concern and still protect the legitimate interests of the other side. It is something that needs to be addressed. Perhaps legislation is the right way.

Of the four senators selected, Kohl provides the best example of a senator who uses the hearings to engage on a specific policy topic of interest. Other senators do frequently ask "pet" questions, whether they be about policy or the role of judges and the judiciary. Durbin, a former lawyer, asked 6 of the 19 nominees in our sample about their views on the importance of a judge's temperament (compared to 1 out of 19 nominees for Kohl). Durbin frequently grounded the question in his personal experiences, noting in a 1997 hearing for Clinton district court nominee G. Patrick Murphy that "one of the issues that I can recall from my own private practice of great interest was judicial temperament." When he asked Obama nominee Miranda Du about judicial temperament 14 years later, he began by recalling his "shadowy memories of the days when I appeared before Federal court judges in Springfield, Illinois and Chicago." Although the content of their questions differed, both Kohl's emphasis on corporate liability and Durbin's focus on judicial temperament seem better grounded in motivations based on personal and/or policy interests than electoral incentives.

On the Republican side, 22 percent of Jeff Sessions' questions in the 18 hearings we examined were about crime or the death penalty. As a former prosecutor (and future attorney general) with what the *New York Times* describes as "ultratough-on-crime views" (Hulse 2017), Sessions' focus on criminal justice issues fits with his issue priorities. The 22 percent of questions about crime and the death penalty also exceed the percentages for Grassley (17 percent), Durbin (15 percent), and Kohl (8 percent). He also spread the crime questions out across presidential administrations, asking crime or death penalty questions to 4 out of 6 Clinton nominees, 2 out of 7 Bush nominees, and 2 out of 4 Obama nominees in our sample.

Electoral motivations could of course explain senators' focus on certain policy areas. Sessions is a former prosecutor with a tough-on-crime approach, which could also be seen as an electoral advantage in deep red Alabama. Grassley, a farmer from Iowa, also asks more crime and death penalty questions than any other category, and crime is typically thought of as a Republican-owned issue (Petrocik 1996; Holian 2004). Sessions' and Grassley's focus on crime questions may therefore represent a strategy of furthering the Republican Party's image as the party most committed to law and order.

In a line of questioning that is similarly difficult to disentangle from electoral considerations, Durbin devotes more time in his questioning to issues related to race than does his co-partisan Kohl. In total, 11 percent of Durbin's questions fell into the rights for disadvantaged groups category, compared to 0 percent of Kohl's. In general, these questions frequently focus on racial disparities in the criminal justice system, such as when Durbin noted to Bush circuit court nominee Consuelo Callahan the "disproportionate number of people of color being arrested, tried, convicted, and incarcerated in America" and asked about "a judge's responsibility in light of that fact." Durbin's concern about these statistics could of course be a result of any number of factors, but his Illinois constituency was notably more racially diverse than Kohl's Wisconsin constituency. According to the 2000 census, 15.1 percent of Illinois residents were black compared to 5.7 percent of Wisconsin residents, and the number of persons of Hispanic or Latino origin was 12.3 percent in Illinois compared to 3.6 percent in Wisconsin (U.S. Census 2011–2012). Even in the event that this policy issue may be electorally advantageous, the venue in which Durbin raises the issue supports the idea that his primary motivation is good public policy; given that there is little public attention on these hearings, the pursuit of good public policy plausibly seems like the primary motivation in this setting.

In the end, lower court confirmation hearings are a venue for legislators and current and future members of the federal bench to enter an exchange on a diverse array of topics, from corporate liability to judicial temperament to racial disparities in the criminal justice system. Differences across senators with respect to background, policy interests, jurisdictions, etc. lead to multiple reasons senators may choose to engage nominees on these topics. In some circumstances, senators may probe nominees on issues in which the senator has a policy interest, whether for the purposes of "sensitizing" nominees or gathering information. At other times, senators may be using questions as a forum for position taking or electoral posturing for attentive publics and interest groups. The two motivations are of course not mutually exclusive, and both types of motivations, we would argue, can lead to substantive discussions over a diverse set of issues.

Conclusion

In this chapter, we set out to further test potential explanations regarding why senators hold confirmation hearings for typical lower federal court nominees. One intuitive possibility is that senators hold hearings so they can vet individual nominees to determine their fitness for the federal bench. As was the case in chapter 4, we find little evidence to support this explanation. Our results show the types of questions asked during hearings have only a minimal connection to key nominee-specific factors (i.e., ABA rating, prior judicial experience, and having at least one home-state senator from the president's opposition party). Such a finding is consistent with a staffer who told us that objections to lower court nominees are "very rarely on the merits."

Instead, the results suggest that senators participate in confirmation hearings in order to further their policy goals, which are independent of the specifics of the nominee appearing before them. Further, the results show that senators adjust the topics upon which they question nominees in conjunction with contextual indicators of broader tensions over policy. Thus, rather than questioning on the basis of nominee-specific factors, senators use the hearings as a venue for advocating on behalf of their policy preferences. We find that both district and noncontroversial circuit court nominees receive more issue-based questions on topics such as abortion, the death penalty, affirmative action, etc. during times of divided government, all else equal, and this influence is heightened for those nominated to closely divided circuits. Additionally, district court nominees face fewer *Qualifications* questions during periods of divided government and presidential election years. *Issues* questions are closely linked to policy topics and ask nominees to take a position on a subjective matter (Farganis and Wedeking 2014), thereby permitting senators to highlight their own positions on an issue important to them. In contrast, *Qualifications* questions often address positive aspects of a nominee's record and are commonly objective, fact-based matters, such as how long a nominee has served in a former job. Such questions leave little leeway for senators to advance their policy goals. Our findings, therefore, indicate that contextual factors such as divided government and the party balance of the circuit thus shape senators' strategies for pursuing policy gains through the hearings.

Our analysis suggests that senators engage in conversations with nominees over policy in different ways during hearings for lower court nominees than they do when holding hearings for future Supreme Court justices. Collins and Ringhand's (2013) examination of Supreme Court confirmation hearings shows that senators frequently invoke Supreme Court precedents during these proceedings as a mechanism for verifying justices' views on core, widely accepted aspects of constitutional policy. For lower court nominees, members of the Judiciary Committee instead typically focus on ongoing policy debates (i.e., *Issues* questions) as they articulate competing visions about the future of the federal courts without necessarily invoking specific case law.

We also examined whether additional nominee-level factors—the nominee's race, gender, and experience as an attorney general or prosecutor—influence senators' propensity to pose a question in an issue area theoretically linked to one of these factors. While we found that those with experience as an attorney general or prosecutor are more likely to be asked at least one criminal justice question, in the areas where we would expect the greatest likelihood of differential treatment on the basis of the nominee's race or gender, no difference emerges.

On the whole, we find support for our argument that senators view the bulk of confirmation hearings as opportunities to advocate on behalf of what they see as good public policy. While the idea that broad partisan-fueled battles over policy exist is not surprising, this book presents systematic, large-scale evidence that contextual factors beyond nominees' control best predict the scrutiny nominees receive during their public confirmation hearings. Despite the seemingly individualized nature of confirmation hearings—small sets of nominees questioned directly by senators, often with personalized questions—we find that when we examine these proceedings systematically, senators' participation in and the *types* of questions raised during confirmation hearings are driven by broad contextual factors rather than by nominee-specific factors. We submit that this reflects senators' desire to advance their policy interests through confirmation hearings. At times, individual senators may benefit from the exchanges with specific nominees, while in the aggregate the hearings serve the role of providing both the larger Judiciary Committee and the two parties with a forum for both engaging with current and future members of the judicial branch and articulating competing agendas for the future of the federal courts.

In chapter 1 we laid out our theoretical argument that confirmation hearings are held because doing so provides a platform for engaging in policy debates and for procuring electoral benefits. Thus far we have focused on the potential for policy gains. We turn our attention in chapter 6 to examining how senators may garner electoral benefits from convening and engaging in judicial confirmation hearings.

SIX

Hearings as a Venue for Pursuing Electoral Goals

The preceding two chapters offer evidence that the vast majority of judicial confirmation hearings are not about scrutinizing the qualifications of individual nominees. Instead, our analysis thus far suggests that senators use these proceedings as a venue in which to make headway toward their policy goals. These findings provide support for the first component of the explanation we offer in response to the core question of the book: *Why do senators hold confirmation hearings for lower federal court nominees, and what is the value of these hearings in the larger advice and consent process?* This chapter focuses on testing the second component of our theoretical explanation: that senators also convene and participate in confirmation hearings in order to advance their electoral prospects. In doing so, we expand the scope of our analysis to look at the potential electoral benefits for all senators, not just those who serve on the Judiciary Committee. While others also argue that Mayhew's (1974) classic electoral incentives exist for senators' engagement in hearings for Supreme Court nominees (Watson and Stookey 1988; Collins and Ringhand 2016), we submit that this framework applies to senators' participation in lower court confirmation hearings, but with the electoral benefits being procured through different mechanisms given the reduced salience of these proceedings.

The potential for a senator to realize electoral benefits from lower court confirmation hearings, we argue, depends on the type of nominee under consideration and whether the senator represents the nominee's state. As we demonstrated earlier, the hearings for most nominees bear little resemblance to the grilling Supreme Court nominees typically face. At typical district court hearings—and many circuit court hearings—senators are generally not looking to "score points" with attentive interest groups (Scherer 2005) or expose the ideological extremity of a nominee. The presumption of acceptability (Scherer, Bartels, and Steigerwalt 2008) and lower profile of such nominations render these ends superfluous. The hearings, however, can serve senators in other ways. We argue that for home-state senators, confirmation hearings for typical nominees—whether through introductory remarks or direct questioning—create opportunities for credit claiming (Mayhew 1974) that can promote senators' electoral goals.

Unlike the question-and-answer portion of these proceedings, which is limited to Judiciary Committee members and nominees, district and circuit court hearings nearly always begin with introductory remarks from the nominee's home-state senators. As we demonstrate in this chapter, home-state senators, who are typically not on the committee, frequently use these remarks to promote their own role in the judicial selection and confirmation process. The hearings thus serve the interests of all senators by offering them an opportunity to "credit claim" (Mayhew 1974) for the selection and confirmation of judicial nominees from their home state.

After showing how these hearings potentially serve a universal credit-claiming goal for senators, we consider the specific electoral benefits of hearings for members of the Judiciary Committee. For committee members, we argue that the typical hearing does not have obvious electoral payoffs, although when home-state nominees appear before the committee at a hearing it provides committee members with the same opportunities—or perhaps greater opportunities—to claim credit for their role in selecting and confirming judges from their state. Consistent with this argument, our analyses of individual committee members' participation in confirmation hearings show that the single biggest predictor of a senator asking a question at a hearing is whether or not the nominee is from the senator's state.

Aside from the home-state connection, committee member attendance at hearings is often reserved for more junior senators, those not up for reelection, or senators with some institutional responsibility, such as majority party members and committee leadership. These results, combined with qualitative accounts from our interviews with staffers and two former senators, suggest that committee members do not see great personal value in attending these hearings and instead are often tasked with attending due to institutional responsibilities. This is not to say that committee members see *no* value to the hearings for nominees, as such hearings do remain a site for policy-motivated senators concerned with the judiciary to question future federal judges (see chapters 4 and 5).

Hearings for controversial nominees, however, change the calculus for committee members. We argue that the higher salience associated with these hearings both allow committee members to "score points" with attentive interest groups (Scherer 2005) and provide opportunities to vet nominees senators may see as too ideologically extreme for the bench. Our analysis supports this contention and reveals changes in participation patterns among committee members for hearings featuring controversial nominees. Most notably, the president's opposition becomes significantly more likely to attend hearings for controversial nominees. We view this increased participation as a function of senators' re-election and policy goals (Fenno 1973). Before we explore the benefits that are specific to committee members, however, we begin with an exploration of the potential for confirmation hearings to serve more universal electoral goals that all senators share.

The Value of Hearings for Home-State Senators

Introductory Remarks

Nearly all work on congressional behavior operates under the assumption that members are driven, at least in part, by a quest for re-election (Mayhew 1974). The optimal re-election strategy for any given senator will vary depending on the nature of the state that senator represents. Grimmer (2013), for example, finds that senators who represent a greater percentage of copartisans focus more attention on national policy debates in their communications while senators from more politically diverse states are prone to advertise their role in securing federal funding for their state. In the end, most members adopt a "mix of strategies," with attention paid to both major policy debates and home-state service (Grimmer 2013, 60). Even the most ideological or partisan senators still need to fulfill their role as representatives of their state. Indeed, as one former Judiciary Committee staffer told us, "The motivations of senators are multiple. . . . Even ideological senators are not universally ideological." Given the geographic jurisdiction of federal district and circuit courts and Senate norms that empower home-state senators (Binder 2007), the judicial nomination and confirmation process is one venue for senators to fulfill their role as representatives of their state. In this section, we show how senators use both introductory remarks and press releases to highlight that role.

In his classic work on the re-election incentive, Mayhew (1974) identifies credit claiming as one way members seek to curry favor with constituents. When one thinks of members claiming credit, it is not typically the process of judicial selection and confirmation that comes to mind. The focus of empirical work on credit claiming frequently explores members' efforts to secure and/or advertise federal funding for their congressional district (see, e.g., Fiorina 1989; Grimmer 2013; Grimmer, Westwood, and Messing 2014). Of course, there are many ways that members can claim credit, or, in Mayhew's (1974, 53) words, "generate a belief in a relevant political actor (or actors) that one is personally responsible for causing the government, or some unit thereof, to do something that the actor (or actors) considers desirable." The following exchange at the confirmation hearing for a district court vacancy in Massachusetts shows how Sens. John Kerry (D-MA) and Scott Brown (R-MA) used their introductory remarks before the Judiciary Committee to claim credit for selecting the nominee.

SENATOR KERRY: Thank you for the privilege of being here today to introduce Judge Tim Hillman. And I can reaffirm in doing so what Senator Scott Brown and I said when we recommended Judge Hillman jointly to President Obama. This jurist is the best of the best, and we are convinced that he is going to do a tremendous job.

SENATOR BROWN: I, too, first of all, want to thank Senator Kerry for the process that we went through. It was clearly bipartisan and it was actually quite informative for me personally, being my first go-around in this endeavor, and the fact that we were able to come up with a nonpartisan Committee to make the recommendations to us, and which we took the time to interview each and every candidate. So, John, I want to thank you for that opportunity, and I think we have done a great job.

The exchange above between Kerry and Brown suggests that senators see value in presenting themselves as taking a bipartisan or nonpartisan approach to staffing the federal bench in their state. Fenno (1977) conceptualizes members' constituencies as a series of concentric circles, with the geographic constituency—in this case the residents of a senator's state—serving as the largest circle. When members claim credit for selecting someone to serve on the federal bench in their state, it is an opportunity to appeal to a wide swath of the member's geographic constituency. Few, if any, constituents would object to news that their senators are committed to selecting, in Senator Kerry's words, "the best of the best" to serve on the federal bench in their state. In line with such expectations, senators dedicate a significant amount of their introductory remarks to reading out the nominee's list of accomplishments and credentials.

Since each senator gets to choose whether to introduce a nominee from his or her home state—these remarks are not required—this choice can provide insight into the benefits senators believe confirmation hearings provide. To better understand how home-state senators use introductory remarks at hearings, we coded all introductory remarks at hearings in 2006 and 2007. We chose these years for two reasons. First, the two years offer variation in key contextual variables, with 2006 being an election year during unified government and 2007 being a non-election year during divided government. Second, we were able to use the Grimmer (2010) dataset of senators' press releases, which covers 2005 through 2007, to explore the extent to which senators advertise their participation in hearings and broader efforts during the confirmation process.[1]

During 2006 and 2007, the Judiciary Committee held 27 hearings for 75 nominees (18 circuit court nominees and 57 district court nominees). Occasionally these hearings would allow senators to introduce multiple nominees from their state. In these cases, the senators introduced all the nominees from their state in one set of remarks, which we treat as one observation. When we talk about a senator introducing a nominee, then, it includes instances in which a senator introduced multiple nominees on a single panel.

Across the 27 hearings, there were 116 unique opportunities for senators to attend and introduce one or more nominees from their state.[2] In total, senators took this opportunity 72 percent of the time, with both senators showing up for 55 percent of hearings. Given senators' busy schedules, the 72 percent attendance rate suggests that introducing a home-state nominee is something senators prioritize. Indeed, given the generally low attendance rate from committee members documented in previous chapters, the senators attending a hearing to introduce nominees frequently outnumber the committee members in attendance. For example, a hearing on October 24, 2007, for district court nominees from North Carolina, Texas, Kentucky, and New Hampshire drew eight senators for introductory remarks, but only one committee member—Sen. Sheldon Whitehouse (D-RI)—asked any questions of the nominees. To understand senators' rationale for holding these hearings, then, it makes sense to consider the value of hearings to all senators and not just those on the Judiciary Committee.

The 72 percent number also underestimates the extent to which senators show support for the nominees during the process. In some cases, senators who miss introductory remarks will submit their remarks for the *Congressional Record*. On rare occasions, senators on the committee do not use the opportunity to introduce the nominee but are in attendance for the question-and-answer session of the hearing. If we count submissions to the *Record* and senator participation in the question-and-answer portion of the hearing, home-state senators participate in the hearings 83 percent of the time.[3]

Senators may use these hearings in part to claim credit for helping select the nominee or move her or him through the confirmation process. Of course, although home-state senators typically have veto power over at least district court nominees (Binder and Maltzman 2009), senators' ability to claim credit may depend on whether they are from the president's party. With George W. Bush in the White House in 2006 and 2007, Republicans may have been more likely to show up to support nominees or highlight the senator's role in the process. Consistent with this expectation, figure 6.1 shows that Republican senators were more likely than Democratic senators to deliver introductory remarks (87 percent of the time compared to 56 percent of the time) or participate in any way (95 percent of the time compared to 69 percent of the time). The differences between Republicans and Democrats on both measures are statistically significant at $p < 0.01$.

Although we observe differences based on the party of the senator, it is worth noting that the default position for senators is to introduce their home-state nominee or participate in the hearing in some way. Even during the highly contentious fights over judicial selection in the Bush years, we see Democratic senators attending and introducing nominees from their home states. In none of these cases did we see senators actively opposing nominees from their home states in opening statements. Instead, opening statements are almost uniformly positive endorsements of the nominees. The frequent participation of senators from both parties is further evidence that these introductory remarks serve a universal electoral goal for senators who have incentives to present themselves as advocates for their state.

To get a better sense of how senators use these hearings to promote their role in the nomination and confirmation process, we coded the introductory remarks on several dimensions. First, to measure explicit credit claiming, we coded for any time a senator took credit for helping select a nominee, establishing a commission to vet nominees in the state, or expediting the nomination and confirmation process for the nominee in some way. Second, senators can also create an "impression of influence" (Grimmer, Westwood, and Messing 2014) by urging the Judiciary Committee to act in some way, whether it be expeditiously moving the nominee through the process or treating the nominee fairly. We coded such statements as "calls to action." Ultimately, these calls to action varied from senators "urging" the committee to act, which we coded as true calls to action, to

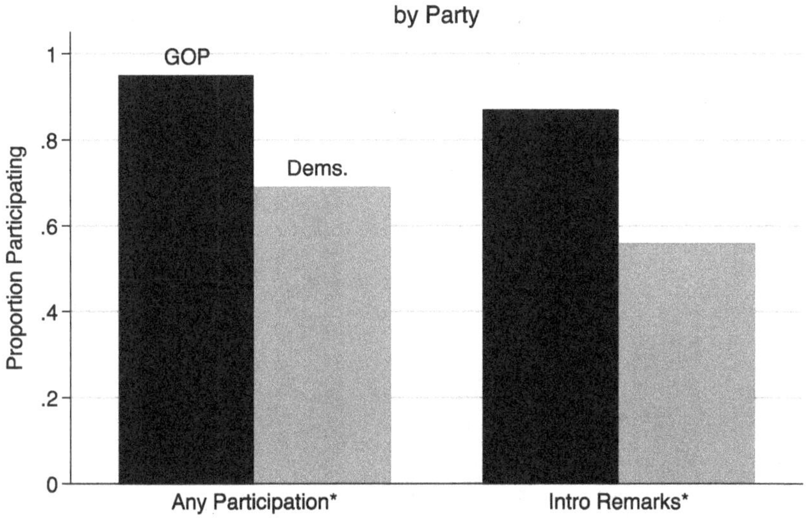

Fig. 6.1. Home-State Senator Participation in Hearings (2006–07); by Party
*Difference in proportions is significant at $p < 0.05$

simply "hoping" the committee would act in some way. We therefore distinguished between what we call true "calls to action" (e.g., urging) and "any calls to action" (e.g., urging *or* hoping). Finally, we coded for cases in which senators highlighted the bipartisan nature of the selection process in their state. As we discuss below, senators often used these statements of bipartisanship to highlight how well the judicial selection process in their state, for which the senators often take credit, operates. Figure 6.2 shows the proportion of times the different types of appeals appeared in introductory remarks by the level of court.

Across the two types of hearings, senators claimed credit 28 percent of the time. Senators are afforded more opportunities to influence the selection process when it comes to district court nominees, and, not surprisingly, senators more frequently engaged in credit claiming during their introductory remarks for district court nominees than for circuit court nominees. In the 68 introductory remarks from district court hearings, senators claimed credit 34 percent of the time compared to 12 percent of the time in the 26 introductory remarks from circuit court hearings (difference = 0.22, $p < 0.05$). The credit claiming sometimes came in the form of senators noting that they influenced the president's selection, as when Sen. Elizabeth Dole (R-NC) said of two nominees from her state that she was "proud to have recommended them to President Bush." Other times, credit claiming came

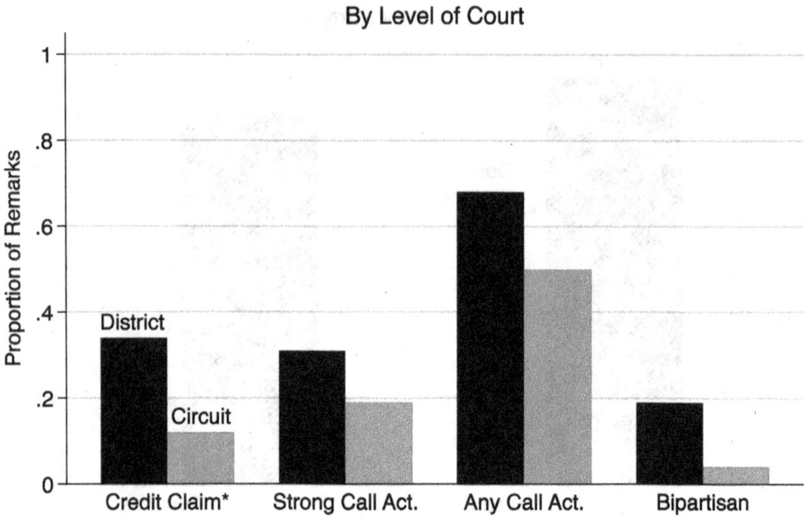

Fig. 6.2. Content Coding of Home-State Senator Remarks (2006–07); by Level of Court

*Difference in proportions is significant at $p < 0.05$

in the form of highlighting the role senators played in creating a panel to select nominees. In an example that was coded as both credit claiming and bipartisanship, Sen. Mel Martinez (R-FL) noted in his remarks at a hearing for Marcia Morales Howard, "I am very proud of the fact that Judge Howard was recommended by the Florida Judicial Nominating Commission, which Senator Nelson and I empaneled, which ensures that Florida has a nonpartisan judicial nominating process and allows us to move candidates forward in a timely manner."

Based on our coding, senators made "calls to action" 31 percent of the time in their introductory remarks for district court nominees and 19 percent of the time in their introduction of circuit court nominees. To qualify as a "call to action," senators had to make a direct request that the Judiciary Committee take some action, such as at Lisa Goodby Wood's confirmation hearing when Sen. Saxby Chambliss (R-GA) "urge[d] the Committee's swift and enthusiastic action to advance her nomination." If we include a more expansive view of "calls to action," such as senators saying they "hope" a nominee would be confirmed, then we see some sort of call to action 68 percent of the time at district court hearings and 50 percent of the time at circuit court hearings ($p = 0.11$).

Finally, it is worth noting that even when senators are not explicitly claiming credit or urging the committee to action, it is possible for senators to generate an "impression of influence" by simply attending and presenting the nominees. The following exchange at the hearing for Indiana District Court nominee Joseph Van Bokkelen between Sens. Richard Lugar (R-IN) and Charles Schumer (D-NY), who was chairing the hearing, illustrates the point:

SENATOR LUGAR: I would like to thank you again, Mr. Chairman, for this opportunity to present Joe Van Bokkelen to the Committee. I believe that he will demonstrate remarkable leadership to northern Indiana and will appropriately uphold and defend our laws under the Constitution. Thank you, sir.

SENATOR SCHUMER: Thank you, Senator Lugar, and your strong recommendation of Mr. Van Bokkelen will go a long way with this Committee, so we thank you for being here.

Although Republican senators were more likely to deliver introductory remarks during these two years, the content of introductory remarks showed minimal differences across parties. In the remarks we coded, Democrats claimed credit 26 percent of the time while Republicans did so 29 percent of the time. Democrats were more likely than Republicans to mention bipartisanship in their remarks, although this difference is likely due to the presence of a Republican in the White House, which necessitated bipartisanship on the part of Democrats. In general, the results suggest that senators from both parties use the opportunity to deliver introductory remarks at both district and circuit court hearings as a way to claim credit and create an impression of influence. In the next section, we look at how senators advertise their roles in the nomination and confirmation process, including their introductory remarks, to constituents through press releases.

Conveying Influence in Press Releases

Hearings provide an opportunity for home-state senators, through their introductory remarks, to affirm their role in the process in front of the nominee and his or her family and friends, who, by nature of the nominee's status as a nominee to the federal bench, are potentially influential leaders in the senator's state. With the exception of those who know the nominee, however, the number of constituents attending or watching a district court confirmation hearing is likely to be zero. It is reasonable, then, to question whether senators actually view participation in these hearings as something that pays off electorally.

If our argument is correct that senators see these hearings as an opportunity to claim credit or generally promote their role in the confirmation process for electoral gain, we should see evidence of senators advertising their participation externally. We therefore searched the Grimmer (2010) dataset of press releases from 2005 through 2007 for any press releases that used the name of any nominee during this time span. We find that senators do frequently issue press releases about nominees from their state. At least one home-state senator put out a press release for 53 percent of the nominees in our time span, and both senators put out a press release for 37 percent of nominees. As Grimmer (2013) shows, press releases find their way into media coverage, with some newspapers reprinting content from senators' press releases verbatim. In our time span, we see quotes from senator press releases about nominees appearing in the *Atlanta Journal-Constitution* (Ahmed 2006), *Toledo Blade* (Gilbert 2006), and *The Journal Record* (a daily business and legal publication based in Oklahoma City) (Shottenkirk 2006). More recently, we were able to find examples of home-state senators' introductory remarks during 2018 hearings being covered by local media outlets in Connecticut (Mahony 2018), Indiana (Francisco 2018), and West Virginia (LeRose 2018).

Senators frequently issue press releases after a nominee is selected or confirmed, which often include quotes from the senator lauding the nominee. In several of the press releases, senators explicitly mentioned introducing the nominee at their Judiciary Committee hearing, and typically these press releases reproduce the remarks. For example, Sen. Elizabeth Dole (R-NC) put out a press release on June 20, 2007, titled "Sen. Dole Voices Support of Two N.C. Nominees for U.S. District Judgeships," which included the remarks she delivered. In another example, Sen. Mark Pryor (D-AR) highlighted his role in supporting Bobby Shepherd's nomination and confirmation to the Eighth Circuit Court of Appeals:

> Senator Mark Pryor today announced Senate confirmation of Bobby E. Shepherd to the US Court of Appeals for the Eighth Circuit. Shepherd was confirmed unanimously by voice vote Thursday evening. Pryor said he was proud to work with President Bush to ensure an Arkansan was nominated to replace Morris Sheppard Arnold, who is taking senior status, and honored to help advance Judge Shepherd's nomination through the Senate confirmation process. Pryor testified on Shepherd's behalf during the Senate Judi-

ciary Committee's confirmation hearings on June 28th and helped expedite a vote on the nomination by the full Senate.

The credit claiming from Pryor, a Democrat, is all the more noteworthy given that the nomination and confirmation of Shepherd to the circuit court bench occurred during a Republican administration. As a Democrat from a state Bush carried in both 2000 and 2004, Pryor had electoral incentives to present himself as a Democrat who was willing to cooperate with President Bush, especially when it came to advancing the interests of Arkansas.

In the end, at least one senator expressed the view that all this credit claiming pays off. At a hearing for circuit court nominee Thomas Hardiman, Sen. Rick Santorum (R-PA) noted, "I can tell you that I get—as I know, Senator Specter, you do—compliments for the people that we have nominated to the bench." Following up, Specter used some of his time to ensure that the two Pennsylvania senators received credit for Hardiman's nomination as well, stating to Santorum, "You and I have had a voice in the submission of Judge Hardiman's name to the President, and the President has agreed, which is a great tribute to Judge Hardiman."

The Value of Confirmation Hearings for Non-Home-State Senators

The previous section highlighted the ways hearings serve the electoral interests of all senators by affording them opportunities to advocate for their state and create an impression of influence over the nomination and confirmation process. Senators on the Judiciary Committee are unlikely to receive similar electoral benefits from hearings, unless the nominee happens to be from their state. Of course, senators may have non-electoral reasons for wanting to hold these hearings. As previous work has demonstrated and chapter 2 confirmed, senators on the Judiciary Committee are disproportionately drawn from the legal community and tend to represent the ideological wings of their party (Lewis 2014). As Sen. Ted Kaufman noted in his interview with us, the issues the Judiciary Committee deals with, especially social issues, attract many of the more ideological senators to the committee. Further, as we show in the previous chapter, the ability to choose the topics discussed offers committee members the opportunity to advocate on the record for their views on the ideal direction of public policy.

The potential for these hearings to provide electoral benefits to Judiciary Committee senators are also not completely absent. Although committee members' opportunities for credit claiming at these hearings are limited, the hearings do offer an opportunity for position taking, which Mayhew (1974, 61) defines as "the public enunciation of anything likely to be of interest to political actors." Although the purpose of the question-and-answer portion of the hearing is to question nominees, even casual observers of Congress will recognize that senators' questions often look more like speeches than questions. These questions therefore often either explicitly or implicitly contain an element of position taking. Returning to the four long-serving senators we examined in the previous chapter, one sees examples of Sen. Herb Kohl position taking on the issue of protective orders when he notes in one hearing that "Critics like myself argue that these protective orders sometimes prevent the public from learning about the health and safety standards in the products that they use." Similarly, in a question about the death penalty, Sen. Jeff Sessions calls Justices Marshall, Brennan, and Douglas's position that the death penalty is cruel and unusual punishment "the high-water mark of judicial activism." In two other hearings, he argues that based on his experience as a prosecutor that sentencing guidelines "work pretty well" and that "probably 90 percent of death penalty cases are really open and shut facts."

Even if senators are not taking an explicit position on how to solve a problem, the mere fact that they raise an issue at hearings can suggest to interest groups and other attentive audiences that they are prioritizing the issue. The question from Sen. Dick Durbin is a variant on a question he frequently asks nominees that does not take an explicit position but tries to elevate the salience of a problem:

> SENATOR DURBIN: I have made it a policy of asking every Attorney General and every Assistant Attorney General with jurisdiction in this area what they thought about the fact that although we have 12 percent of our American population African American and only 11 percent whom we can say commit drug crimes, when we look at the rates of arrest and conviction they approximate 50 percent of the convictions for drug crimes are African Americans and over 58 percent of the incarcerations are African Americans. If we hope to maintain credibility in our system for all Americans so that the laws are seen as just, what is the responsibility of a judge in this context? Are you only to take the cases as they are brought to you or do you have a larger responsibility when it comes to the issue of racial profiling?

The audience for the position taking that occurs at judicial confirmation hearings is not the same audience that senators have in mind when they claim credit for advancing home-state nominees. In press releases, senators are targeting their geographic constituency, while in confirmation hearings senators are appealing primarily to party activists and interest groups. These hearings, then, are a primary opportunity for senators to engage in what Scherer (2005) refers to as "elite mobilization strategies," whereby senators seek to curry favor with the interest groups that have the ability to mobilize resources in support of or opposition to a senator.

As we have noted elsewhere in the book, the ability to differentiate policy and electoral goals is difficult, and senators likely participate in hearings and ask specific questions for a mix of reasons. There are hearings, however, where we would expect senators to perceive greater electoral payoff for their participation. As chapter 3 shows, hearings for controversial nominees attract more senators, and, as a former Judiciary Committee staffer told us, part of the rationale for this increased participation is senators' desire to be seen by interest groups. At such hearings, senators may perceive electoral benefits to position taking on or simply raising the salience of issues of concern to interest groups. Senators can also take a position on the nomination itself, arguing that some aspect of the nominee's record raises questions or compels the senator to support or oppose the nominee.

Interviews with interest group and Judiciary Committee staff confirm that interest groups do not pay the same level of attention to all hearings, although the extent to which a group chooses to selectively monitor hearings may depend on the organization. One staffer at a liberal advocacy group noted that his organization "pay[s] some level of attention to every single hearing," whether it be the question-and-answer portion, nominee questionnaire, or questions submitted for the record. In contrast, a former staffer for a different liberal advocacy group said her organization did not pay attention to hearings if the nominee was not controversial. When the group opposed a nominee, however, the hearing was key: "If it's a nominee about whom there are very serious concerns on the part of progressive groups, we would want the hearing to highlight those concerns to the public and to any undecided senators."

Senators' strategy of appealing to interest groups and party activists is not unique to judicial confirmation hearings. Sinclair (1989, 2012) documents the rise of the "individualistic Senate" in the 1960s, with senators affording themselves more opportunities to participate in committees and on the floor. The growth in the interest group community, and senators' desire to secure support from these interest groups, is a leading explanation for the institutional changes that enhanced the power of individual senators. Sinclair (2012, 3) argues, "The myriad interest groups needed champions and spokesmen, and the media needed credible sources to represent issue positions and provide commentary. Because of the prestige and small size of the Senate, senators fit the bill." Similarly, Binder and Smith (2001, 17) trace the rise of the filibuster in part to changes in the political environment that prompted senators to "champion a cause and attract support."

The electoral payoff for partisan and ideological position taking at contentious confirmation hearings may redound to senators in multiple ways. In Scherer's (2005, 23) theory, interest groups help "mobilize the mass electorate on Election Day." In an era of increasing polarization and the nationalization of congressional elections (Abramowitz 2012; Jacobson 2015), senators may also feel more pressure from constituents to support or oppose controversial presidential nominees. One need only look to the debates over staffing President Trump's cabinet for an example of both interest group and constituent mobilization around such issues (Hefling 2017).

Finally, senators' electoral considerations may not solely be focused on re-election but also ascension to higher office. Although their success rate is not particularly impressive, especially when compared to governors, senators frequently aspire to the presidency (Abramson, Aldrich, and Rohde 1987; Burden 2002; Treul 2009). As senators lay the groundwork for a presidential campaign, the backing of leading advocacy groups is undoubtedly valuable. The Judiciary Committee, like the Senate as a whole, has a list of former presidential aspirants, including Sens. Joe Biden (D-DE), John Edwards (D-NC), Ted Cruz (R-TX), Lindsey Graham (R-SC), and Ted Kennedy (D-MA). These senators can use the hearings to increase their notoriety. A *New York Times* story from 2002, for example, noted that Bush nominee Charles Pickering "seemed to wither visibly under the questioning of Senator John Edwards." Nearly 15 years after this hearing, in an interview with us, a former staffer for a liberal advocacy group recalled this line of questioning as particularly memorable and "an example of where the hearing really created public attention to the nominee."

We see similar dynamics play out in position taking in support of or opposition to one nominee from the 2006–07 time span of press releases we examined. With the exception of Sen. Patrick Leahy, who served as the ranking member of the committee in 2006 and chair in 2007, we rarely encountered press release from senators taking a position on a nominee from another state. Fifth Circuit nominee Leslie Southwick proved to be an exception. With liberal interest groups such as the NAACP raising concerns over Southwick's views on racial issues (Stout 2007), Southwick faced a difficult confirmation fight and was confirmed by a 59–38 vote. In total, 21 senators issued press releases related to Southwick's nomination and confirmation.

Six senators in 2007—Barack Obama (D-IL), Hillary Clinton (D-NY), Joe Biden (D-DE), Chris Dodd (D-CT), John McCain (R-AZ), and Sam Brownback (R-KS)—were actively seeking their party's nomination for president in 2008.[4] Four of the six senators in this group—Obama, Clinton, McCain, and Brownback—issued at least one press release on Southwick. Not surprisingly, McCain's and Brownback's press releases supported Southwick, while Obama's and Clinton's expressed their opposition. Then senator Barack Obama (D-IL), the only African American serving in the Senate at the time, issued a press release following Southwick's confirmation highlighting concerns similar to those of civil rights groups opposed to Southwick's nomination, "Southwick has shown hostility toward civil rights and a disregard for equal rights for minorities, women, gays and lesbians." In the appendix to this chapter, we show that being a presidential candidate was a statistically significant predictor of taking a position on Southwick, even after controlling for Judiciary Committee membership, ideological extremity, and other factors. The fact that Southwick's nomination prompted press releases from McCain, Obama, and Clinton—the three senators with the most plausible path to the presidency in 2007—highlights the extent to which controversial nominees become fodder for a national audience.[5]

In sum, judicial confirmation hearings can serve senators' electoral interests in multiple ways. For all senators, the opportunity to introduce nominees from their home states and highlight the senator's role in the nomination and confirmation process is an opportunity to claim credit. For Judiciary Committee members, the electoral payoffs of the typical hearing are relatively small, but hearings for controversial nominees provide senators with another opportunity to highlight their partisan and ideological credentials to activists and interest groups. These approaches need not be mutually exclusive, as senators can use one hearing to highlight the nonpartisan approach they take (or claim to take) in staffing the bench in their home state, while using another hearing to criticize the ideological nature of a presidential appointee to another circuit. In short, senators should not solely be thought of as either partisan warriors or champions of their state. As Grimmer (2013, 60) argues, "The Senate is filled with senators who adopt a mix of strategies—so any explanation of how legislators engage constituents must explain how senators mix the two strategies." Confirmation hearings are structured in such a way as to allow senators to fulfill multiple roles.

Drawing the Short Straw—Committee Member Attendance at Confirmation Hearings

As we have argued throughout this chapter, Judiciary Committee members and home-state senators likely participate in these hearings for different reasons and with different audiences and goals in mind. Earlier in the chapter we showed that home-state senators of both parties, regardless of whether they are on the committee, frequently take the opportunity to attend hearings and issue press releases highlighting their role in the nomination and confirmation process. Previous chapters, however, show that relatively few committee members—often just the minimum required to conduct a hearing—attend a typical hearing. In this section, we provide a more systematic exploration of which committee members are most likely to attend these hearings, with particular attention paid to how these senators' electoral incentives to participate vary depending on the controversy surrounding the nominee. As a result, our focus shifts from examining introductory remarks by home-state senators to participation in the question-and-answer portion of the hearing, which is reserved for members of the Judiciary Committee. For the typical hearing, we expect little electoral payoff for committee members, and the results suggest that attendance at the hearings is largely reserved for more junior members, those not up for re-election, or members with some responsibility on the Judiciary Committee. When a nominee is controversial, senators may see greater electoral payoff to position taking for attentive interest groups, and, indeed, we see fairly uniform increases in participation. Senators from the party opposite the president see larger increases in participation when a nominee is controversial, however, which we argue is likely because much interest group energy is focused on opposing nominees. Finally, we find that senators on the committee typically attend the question-and-answer portion of the hearings when there is a home-state nominee, which we attribute to the same electoral incentives that we explored in the previous section.

To examine individual Judiciary Committee members' participation in district and circuit court hearings (1993–2012), we treat each senator-nominee dyad as an observation. As a result, we have multiple observations per senator, ranging from 72 for Robert Smith (R-NH), who served on the committee only in the 106th Congress, to the more than 900 observations each for Dianne Feinstein (D-CA), Orrin Hatch (R-UT), Chuck Grassley (R-IA), Herb Kohl (D-WI), and Patrick Leahy (D-VT), who served on the committee in all 10 Congresses under study.

Since we expect that electoral benefits will vary depending on the type of nominee, we examine participation in three types of hearings: district court hearings, hearings for noncontroversial circuit court nominees, and hearings for controversial circuit court nominees.[6] One of the key questions we test, then, is whether patterns of participation vary across the different types of nominees.

The dependent variable in our model is binary and coded 1 if the senator asked at least one question of the nominee and 0 if not. This variable takes on the value of 1 in approximately 11 percent of the senator-nominee dyads. To account for repeated observations, we run an OLS regression with senator fixed effects. Even though our dependent variable is binary, we elect to run a linear probability model because it allows us to estimate marginal effects, which is not possible in the traditional conditional fixed effects logit setup.[7]

The potential electoral benefits for Judiciary Committee members are greatest in hearings for controversial nominees. As the potential for attention from other important elites increases, more committee members are incentivized to participate. To begin with a clear example, at Supreme Court confirmation hearings, all senators can be expected to utilize the opportunity to question nominees, leaving no variation to be explained. Controversial circuit court nominees do not draw the full committee but, as chapter 4 shows, senator participation does increase substantially. As a result, we expect that senator participation at hearings for controversial circuit court nominees will provide the largest opportunity to fulfill potential electoral and policy motivations.

Although senators from both parties may be motivated to attend hearings for controversial nominees, those senators who are inclined to oppose the nominee may be the most incentivized to attend. The focus of much scholarly research on the role interest groups play in the nomination and confirmation process has addressed interest group opposition (Bell 2002a; Scherer 2005; Scherer, Bartels, and Steigerwalt 2008; Steigerwalt 2010) instead of interest group support, which reflects the fact that interest groups play their most active and public role when opposing a nominee. As one staffer for a liberal interest group told us, his group rarely issued public statements in support of nominees during the Obama years. Another staffer at a different liberal interest group during the Clinton and Bush years also noted that her organization rarely publicly advocated for nominees during the Clinton years but opposed many during the Bush years. Of course, interest groups can support nominees behind the scenes by communicating their preferences directly to Senate offices, but liberal and conservative interest groups often avoid public endorsements of a nominee, perhaps out of fear of solidifying opposition on the other side. Given the more aggressive oppositional role that interest groups play, senators inclined to oppose a nominee may have the greatest opportunity to "score points" (Scherer 2005) with interest groups by attending a hearing for a controversial nominee. There is thus reason to expect that senators from the opposite party of the president will have the greatest incentive to show up at hearings for controversial nominees.

In contrast, at hearings for noncontroversial nominees (i.e., district and noncontroversial circuit court hearings), we expect that the modal Judiciary Committee member will see little electoral value in attending and questioning the nominee. Along with serving the interests of home-state senators, the value of these hearings, we have argued, is in providing a forum for exchanges over both specific policies and also broader ideological and partisan battles. The policy benefits of the hearings are therefore more aggregate in nature, benefiting the policy interests of the committee and the parties as a whole. Of course, at least one senator, and typically one from each party, is needed to ensure the hearings serve this function. Our interviews confirmed that most committee members do not prioritize low-salience hearings, with Sen. Jon Kyl jokingly noting that attendance was determined by "whoever drew the short straw." Instead of drawing straws, participation is more likely a result of the different institutional responsibilities and roles among committee members (see, e.g., Hall 1987; Evans 1991; Duffin 2003), which means participation, instead of being determined randomly, should vary as a function of senator-level factors.

Seniority was one factor consistently mentioned by staffers when asked the question, "How is it decided which senators show up at which hearings?" Staffers frequently noted that junior senators have fewer responsibilities elsewhere and thus disproportionately get tapped to serve as the chair or ranking member at hearings. As an example, one former Democratic staffer noted that when Senator Biden chaired the committee in the early 1990s, he and his staff were unlikely to ask Senator Kennedy to chair a hearing due to Kennedy's more senior status within the chamber and Kennedy's responsibility chairing the then Labor and Human Resources Committee (now the Health, Education, Labor, and Pensions Committee). We therefore include in our model a measure of seniority on the committee (Stewart and Woon 2017).

Along with more junior members, majority party members should be more likely to attend, since at least one is needed to chair the hearing. Previous chapters show that it is not uncommon to see only one senator question a nominee at a hearing, and that one senator is almost always the chair of that hearing and thus a majority party member.[8] Committee leadership may also play a unique role in the confirmation hearings, so we include a variable that is coded 1 if the senator served as the chair or ranking member of the Judiciary Committee at the time of the hearing, and 0 otherwise. These data are available from Stewart and Woon (2017). Research on committee participation typically finds that members with leadership roles on a given committee are the most active participants (Hall 1987; Evans 1991; Duffin 2003; Gamble 2007; Minta 2009), although these studies tend to focus on bill markups and oversight hearings, which differ in purpose from confirmation hearings.

Senators up for re-election are likely to have more constraints on their time and should be especially unlikely to attend hearings that have little bearing on their re-election prospects. We therefore include a variable coded 1 if the senator is up for re-election in the year of the hearing,[9] with the expectation that senators up for re-election will be less likely to attend the hearing for a noncontroversial district or circuit court nominee.

We see some initial evidence that senators' roles and responsibilities help explain their level of participation at hearings. Turning to two senators whose questioning we examined earlier in the book—Senators Grassley and Sessions—we see their participation patterns change in notable ways over the course of their careers. In his first Congress (1997–98), Sessions asked a question of roughly 36 percent of nominees who appeared before the Judiciary Committee. As he became more senior inside the institution, however, his participation decreased, with the Alabama senator asking a question of roughly 11 percent of nominees in the 109th Congress (2005–06) and less than 2 percent of nominees in the 110th Congress (2007–08). In the 111th Congress (2009–10), Sessions took over as ranking member of the committee, and his participation increased dramatically, with 70 percent of nominees in that Congress facing at least one question from Sessions. In the next Congress, Grassley assumed the position of ranking member. No longer in a party leadership position on the committee, Sessions asked a question of less than 1 percent of nominees. Grassley, meanwhile, went from asking questions of zero nominees in the 111th Congress to asking questions of 58 percent of nominees in the 112th Congress when he took over as ranking member. These two Congresses are the two in our dataset that occur during the Obama presidency, which can help explain why the leading Republican on the committee may have been particularly interested in questioning nominees at their hearings.

In sum, we expect that Judiciary Committee member participation at hearings for noncontroversial nominees will fall disproportionately on certain members—junior members, committee leadership, majority party members, and senators not up for re-election—due to their institutional roles and responsibilities (or relative lack thereof). Moreover, our expectation, then, is that individual senators' participation decisions will vary in part as a function of the controversy surrounding the nominee, which influences the electoral benefits attendance at a particular hearing offers. One key exception to this expectation is that home-state senators, whose incentives to participate are driven by the nominees' connection to their state, should be similarly incentivized to attend the hearing regardless of the controversy or lack thereof associated with a nominee. Home-state senators are usually in attendance for introductory remarks, and we therefore expect home-state senators on the committee to be more likely to ask questions of the nominee as well. The binary variable of home-state senator captures whether a senator is from a nominee's home state.

Given our expectation that patterns of senator participation will vary depending on the type of nominee, we interact each of our six senator-level variables—election year, majority party status, seniority, chair or ranking member status, presidential opposition party, and home-state senator—with separate indicator variables for whether the nominee is a district court nominee, a noncontroversial circuit court nominee, or a controversial circuit court nominee. The model includes a host of nominee and contextual controls consistent with the models in chapter 4 (coefficients and robust standard errors can be found in the appendix). Again, the coefficients are from a fixed-effects OLS regression with the dependent variable coded 0 if the senator asked no questions at the nominee's hearing and 1 if the senator asked at least one question at the hearing. Figure 6.3 graphs the probability of a senator attending across the different senator-level attributes that are interacted with the three types of nominees, with hearings for district court nominees appearing on the left, noncontroversial circuit court nominees in the center, and controversial circuit court nominees on the right side of each of the six panels.[10]

Although the 95 percent confidence intervals overlap in some of the graphs, figure 6.3 shows that junior members, home-state senators, committee leadership, and senators not up for re-election are more likely to attend all types of hearings. The results are consistent with our expectation that senators' roles and responsibilities on the Judiciary Committee and

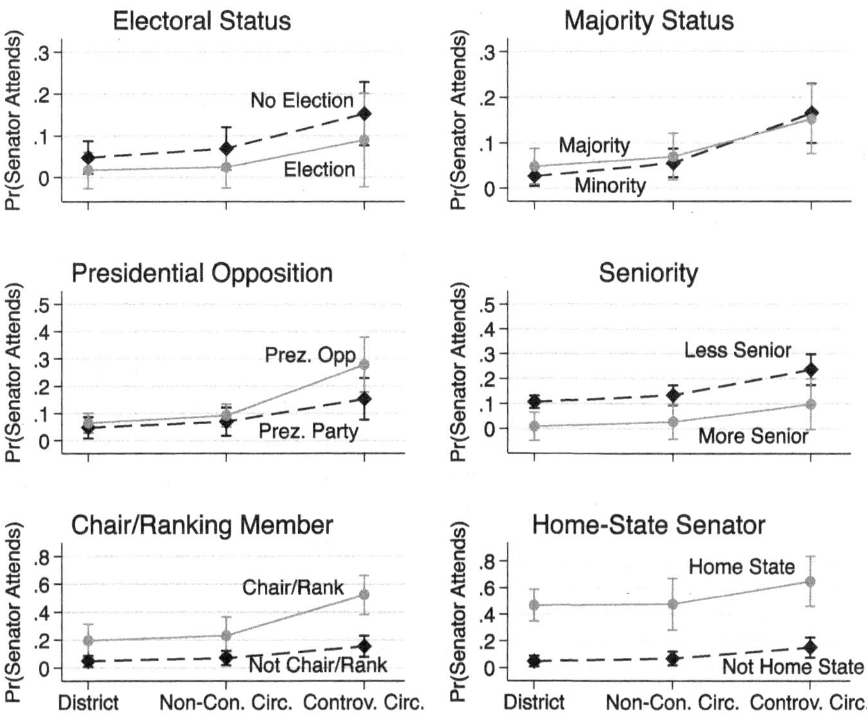

Fig. 6.3. Probability of Senator Participating; by Senator Variables and Nominee Type

inside the chamber more broadly will shape their participation patterns in these hearings. In contrast to our expectations, however, these institutional roles and responsibilities are not necessarily more predictive of attendance at lower salience hearings.

For two of our senator-level independent variables—opposition partisans and chair/ranking member—participation patterns do vary based on the level of controversy surrounding a nominee. Given the central role interest groups play in opposing nominees, we expected that senators from the opposition party would have the greater incentive to curry favor with interest groups by participating in the hearing, and we find evidence consistent with this expectation. There is a 0.07 probability that a senator from the president's party asks a question at a hearing for a noncontroversial circuit court nominee, which doubles to 0.15 for a controversial circuit court nominee. By comparison, a senator from the opposition party is roughly three times as likely to attend a hearing when a circuit court nominee is deemed controversial, with the probability of attendance increasing from

0.09 to 0.29. The interaction between opposition party senators and controversial nominees is statistically significant at $p < 0.05$.

Along with differences in attendance based on whether a senator is from the president's party, the probability that Judiciary Committee leaders will attend a hearing substantially increases for controversial nominees. Rank-and-file members' probability of attending increases from 0.07 for noncontroversial circuit court nominees to 0.15 for controversial circuit court nominees. The corresponding increase for a chair or ranking member is 0.23 to 0.53. The interaction between chair/ranking member and controversial nominees is statistically significant at $p < 0.05$. In sum, controversial nominees attract more senators but also different configurations of senators to their hearings. Committee members from the party opposite the president, as well as committee leadership, are especially likely to attend hearings for controversial nominees.

Finally, the results confirm the expectation that home-state senators will be motivated to attend hearings and that this motivation will not change across the level of the court or the amount of controversy surrounding a nominee. Across all three types of hearings, the home-state senator effect is large and consistent. Committee members are regular attendees when nominees from their home state appear before the committee, with their probabilities of participating exceeding even that of committee leadership. Combined with the exploration of introductory remarks earlier in the chapter, the results affirm the primary role that home-state interests play in drawing senators to lower court confirmation hearings.

Conclusion

This chapter started from the premise that what senators hope to get out of confirmation hearings depends on the type of nominee under consideration and whether the senator represents the nominee's state. For home-state senators, the hearings offer an opportunity to claim credit for their role in selecting qualified nominees and helping these nominees advance through the confirmation process. Participation levels suggest that home-state senators prioritize attendance at these hearings, with members of both parties using their introductory remarks as an opportunity to credit claim, promote their bipartisan approach to selecting judges, and urge the Judiciary Committee to take action on nominees from their state. Committee members also participate at substantially higher rates when a nominee from their state is before the committee. Finally, senators advertise these behaviors in their communications, issuing press releases chronicling their activities. In sum, hearings provide a venue for home-state senators to highlight the role they play in representing their home state's interests and generating an "impression of influence" (Grimmer, Westwood, and Messing 2014) over the nomination and confirmation of federal judges that will aid their re-election efforts.

Committee members, in contrast to home-state senators, do not prioritize attendance at the modal confirmation hearing. As we showed in previous chapters, many district and circuit court nominees face questions from only one or two senators. One reason for these low participation levels is that senators see little in the way of electoral benefits from attending a hearing for a noncontroversial nominee. Senators' motivation to attend, then, is likely due either to a specific interest in a set of nominees or out of an institutional responsibility to keep the hearings in place in order to serve the collective goals of the committee and parties. The participation patterns of Sessions and Grassley help demonstrate this point. In the two Congresses in our dataset that take place during the Obama administration (111th and 112th), these two Republicans served consecutively as the ranking member of the committee and frequently served as representatives of their party in the questioning of nominees.

In this chapter we find that senator participation at hearings for district and noncontroversial circuit court hearings are reserved mostly for those senators with the fewest institutional responsibilities (junior members) or less electoral pressure (senators not up for re-election) or who hold positions of leadership on the committee. These members are also more likely to attend hearings for controversial nominees, but the patterns of participation at these hearings changes in other ways. Senators from the president's opposition party are more likely to attend hearings for controversial circuit nominees, presumably due in part to the desire to be seen by interest groups who oppose the nominee (Scherer 2005; Scherer, Bartels, and Steigerwalt 2008).

Overall, this chapter offers fresh insight into what senators stand to gain from confirmation hearings and how individual senators' participation decisions vary as a function of context. The findings ultimately provide additional evidence for two core arguments of the book. First, senators perceive that these hearings provide opportunities to procure electoral benefits. These benefits are clearest for home-state senators, whose participation levels remain high regardless of the level of controversy surrounding a nominee. Potential electoral benefits are not solely reserved for home-state senators, however, with controversial nominees providing an opportunity for senators to curry favor with interest groups and partisan activists. The chapter thus provides evidence for a second argument advanced in this book, which is that there are two types of confirmation hearings. In the next chapter, we explore the second type—hearings for controversial nominees—in more depth.

APPENDIX

TABLE A6.1. Senator Position Taking on Leslie Southwick Nomination/Confirmation

Logistic Regression Model

	Coefficent	(S.E.)
Democrat	–0.56	(0.63)
Ideological Extremity	-2.58	(2.04)
Presidential Candidate	2.82**	(1.00)
Judiciary Committee Member	1.32+	(0.70)
Party Leadership	2.93*	(1.31)
Fifth Circuit State	3.64**	(1.23)
Constant	-1.12	(0.85)
N	99	
LR χ^2	29.43*	

+$p < 0.10$; *$p < 0.05$; **$p < 0.01$, two-tailed

TABLE A6.2. Predicting Individual Senator Attendance

Fixed Effects OLS Regression Model

Nominee Variables	Coef.	(Robust S.E.)
Noncontroversial Circuit	0.04*	(0.02)
Controversial Circuit	0.18**	(0.05)
ABA (Lowest)	0.002	(0.01)
ABA (Middle)	-0.002	(0.004)
Previous Judicial Experience	-0.01	(0.01)
Opposition Party Senator	-0.01**	(0.004)
Divided Hearing	0.02*	(0.01)
Presidential Election Year	0.004	(0.02)
Clinton Nominee	-0.03+	(0.01)
Obama Nominee	0.05	(0.03)
Senator-Level Variables × Nominee Type		
Election Year	-0.03*	(0.01)
× Non-Controversial Circuit	-0.02	(0.01)
× Controversial Circuit	-0.04	(0.04)
Majority Party	0.02	(0.01)
× Non-Controversial Circuit	-0.01	(0.01)
× Controversial Circuit	-0.03	(0.03)
Senator-Nominee Same State	0.44**	(0.07)
× Non-Controversial Circuit	-0.02	(0.07)
× Controversial Circuit	0.08	(0.07)
ln (Seniority)	-0.06**	(0.01)
× Non-Controversial Circuit	-0.004	(0.01)
× Controversial Circuit	-0.02	(0.02)
President Opposition Party	0.02	(0.01)
× Non-Controversial Circuit	0.01	(0.01)
× Controversial Circuit	0.12*	(0.05)
Chair/Rank	0.15*	(0.07)
× Non-Controversial Circuit	0.01	(0.02)
× Controversial Circuit	0.23**	(0.07)
Constant	0.16**	(0.03)
N	17,093	
Senators	46	
F	69.61**	

+$p < 0.01$; *$p < 0.05$, **$p < 0.01$

SEVEN

The Content and Consequences of Hearings for Controversial Nominees

Judge Priscilla Owen, who now sits on the Fifth Circuit Court of Appeals, did not have an easy path to her seat. First nominated by George W. Bush in 2001 while she was a justice on the Texas Supreme Court, she was not confirmed until 2005. In the interim, controversy raged around her as interest groups mounted campaigns both in support of and in opposition to her confirmation. A coalition of conservative groups organized a press conference in Texas to highlight their support of Owen's nomination, calling her "a highly qualified, independent mainstream justice"; they also noted their "condemnation of liberal special interest groups who oppose[d] her nomination."[1] On the other side, one liberal interest group referred to Owen as a "particularly egregious example of extremist nominees that President Bush has chosen for key courts."[2] As these examples suggest, the rhetoric from players outside the Senate was direct and aggressive.

Within the Senate, her supporters and detractors also went toe-to-toe, reiterating the interest groups' concerns. Owen appeared twice before the Senate Judiciary Committee, where she answered nearly 400 questions from committee members. Her allies and detractors pressed her on a range of topics, from employment law to abortion decisions to ethics. These questions tended to explore specific writings or decisions attributed to Owen. For example, Sen. Dianne Feinstein and Sen. Orrin Hatch, in particular, sparred over the significance of Owen's several decisions regarding minors' applications to bypass the parental notification requirement for obtaining an abortion in Texas. While Senator Feinstein focused her questions in this area around accusations that Owen added requirements for minors to bypass parental notification that the state legislature had not included, Senator Hatch used some of his questions to help Owen place these decisions in context, in particular, in the context of how often her bypass decisions agreed with the majority. This pattern played out with other issue areas. Sen. Ted Kennedy represents the strategy of committee Democrats, pressing the nominee on specific decisions as part of a larger narrative that paints Owen not only as harsh, but so harsh that other judges felt compelled to note how far she fell outside of the court's consensus:

> SENATOR KENNEDY: Numerous examples occur in other cases involving labor protections, consumer protections and environmental protections. In one case the private landowners tried to obtain an exemption from the environmental regulations, and the court majority specifically criticized your harsh dissent, saying it was nothing more than inflammatory rhetoric which merits no response.
>
> In a case involving whether an insurance company had acted in bad faith, you joined a partial dissent that would have limited the rights of jury trials for litigants, and this dissent was criticized by other judges as a judicial slight [sic] of hand to circumvent the constraints of the Texas Constitution.
>
> In another case a worker's arm had been partially amputated as he inspected a chopping machine. Your dissent would have severely limited the ability of injured individuals to obtain compensation from product manufacturers. The majority criticized your dissent for imposing a test more broad than any holding in this area so far.
>
> . . .
>
> Because of such cases—and these are just a few examples—how we can have confidence that you will fairly interpret the law and fairly consider the claims of workers, victims of discrimination or other injured individuals, and how can we have the confidence that you will review the cases with an open mind?

The Democrats threatened to filibuster the nomination, though Owen eventually received a vote as part of a compromise deal to preserve the filibuster and was confirmed by a vote of 55–43 (NBC News 2005).

Five years later, the Senate Judiciary Committee was presented with another controversial nominee, but this time with Democrats in control of the presidency and Senate. The controversy that surrounded Goodwin Liu's nomination was just as fierce as Owen's, and, like Owen, Liu was subject to two hearings before the Senate Judiciary Committee, during which he answered 152 questions. Sen. Chuck Grassley summarized the concern over Liu when he said, "If confirmed, Mr. Liu would advance his progressive philosophy for years to come" (Doyle 2011). As a prolific academic, Liu had extensive writings for the committee to parse. Senators Hatch, Coburn, and Sessions all asked Liu to clarify the philosophy of constitutional interpretation that Liu and his coauthors developed in the book *Keeping Faith with the Constitution*. Republican senators also focused on Liu's comments in opposition to Justice Samuel Alito's nomination to the Supreme Court. Senator Sessions took the time to extensively quote Liu:

> But in your testimony, in the Alito nomination, I had not recalled the intensity of your remarks. You said at that time, "Judge Alito's record envisions an America where police may shoot and kill an unarmed boy to stop him from running away with a stolen purse; where Federal agents may point guns at ordinary citizens during a raid, even after no sign of resistance; where the FBI may install a camera where you sleep on the promise that they won't turn it on unless an informant is in the room; where a black man may be sentenced to death by an all white jury for killing a white man, absent, say, multiple regression analysis showing discrimination; and where police may search what a warrant permits, and then some. Mr. Chairman, I humbly submit, this is not the America we know, nor is it the America we aspire to be."
>
> Do you think that's a fair analysis of his record? Do you think it meets the standards of civility that we would normally seek to achieve in this Senate confirmation process?

Unlike Owen, Liu was never confirmed. After a filibuster by Senate Republicans, Liu withdrew his nomination. Shortly thereafter, he was nominated and confirmed to a seat on the California Supreme Court.

These highly individualized questions stand in contrast with the argument throughout the rest of the book—that the number and type of questions senators ask during these hearings have little to do with the nominee himself or herself. While we have documented policy and electoral reasons for senators to participate in these hearings, there is a distinct lack of evidence that senators typically use these hearings as opportunities to question nominees based on the nominees' past experience, writings, or behavior. In this chapter, however, we turn our attention to the roughly 25 percent of circuit court nominees who can be considered controversial: those who are opposed by interest groups.

We have generally found a lack of evidence that senators use confirmation hearings to scrutinize nominees based on individual characteristics such as previous experience and ABA rating. By examining a subset of these nominees, however, we find that senators reserve that rigorous individual scrutiny for controversial nominees and that senators, with the help of interest groups, pepper these controversial nominees with questions that are highly tailored to the nominee's past. At the same time, the nature of this questioning reinforces the policy and electoral goals of the questioning senators, as senators focus on policies that are important to them and their constituents, while knowing that electorally helpful interest groups are watching. In fact, these three goals—individual scrutiny, policy, and electoral—come together most seamlessly in hearings for controversial nominees.

In what follows, we focus on controversial circuit court nominees in order to understand how controversy changes the nature of confirmation hearings and how senators use them. We first discuss how increased attention to controversial nominees' hearings changes the electoral and policy calculus for Judiciary Committee members. We then go on to describe the circumstances under which nominees tend to be controversial. Finally, we analyze some of the most controversial nominees' hearings and find support for the idea that controversy changes judicial confirmation hearings, particularly by providing electoral and policy incentives for committee members to scrutinize the nominees on highly individualized topics. These findings provide additional explanation for the larger purpose of these hearings, as Judiciary Committee senators can use the hearings to amplify the controversy that brews behind the scenes among committee senators, home-state senators, and relevant interest groups. Judiciary Committee senators can draw attention to aspects of specific nominees that they find particularly offensive, in a way that is harder to get lost in the shuffle of large quantities of nominees (and other business). In other words, while most of the time the hearings may not serve as a venue to individually scrutinize nominees, in a small but salient subset, senators do use this opportunity to vet nominees on specific past behaviors and opinions. For controversial nominees, then, senators employ highly individualized scrutiny in pursuit of their policy and electoral goals.

What Is Different about Hearings for Controversial Nominees?

What does it mean to be a controversial nominee? Certain nominees are clearly controversial, by any measure, such as nominees Owen and Liu. Both of these nominees answered hundreds of questions, had two hearings, were opposed by interest groups, and generally garnered significant attention from members of the Judiciary Committee, senators more broadly (who threatened or launched filibusters), and the media. Other cases are not so clear-cut. As we detail in chapter 3, we use interest group opposition as a dichotomous measure of controversy. In other words, we consider opposition by interest groups as an indicator that the nominee was experiencing increased activity around his or her nomination (Scherer, Bartels, and Steigerwalt 2008).

We used this controversy distinction previously to demonstrate that senators approach hearings for controversial nominees differently than hearings for run-of-the-mill nominees. Judiciary Committee members are more likely to attend hearings for controversial nominees, and, on average, committee members ask more questions when they do attend these controversial hearings (chapter 4 and chapter 6). We theorized that a controversial nominee will cause a change in focus for committee members. While noncontroversial nominees present easy opportunities for home-state senators to "credit claim" in their support for a typical nominee and for committee members to have substantive exchanges about public policy, the involvement of national interest groups in controversial nominees' processes changes the focus to a national, more ideological and partisan, audience. In short, interest groups' access to a politically engaged sliver of the electorate increases the potential benefits of vigorously participating in a hearing; there are, after all, potential policy and electoral benefits that are greater than those available at a hearing for a typical nominee.

How, then, might senators change the nature of their participation in controversial nominees' hearings? The increased labor of interest groups may provide an answer. When interest groups invest time and resources to flag the most worrisome aspects of a nominee's record, they reduce the member's cost of being prepared to participate vigorously.[3] As we noted in chapter 3, members of the Judiciary Committee and their staffs have the expertise to know, with minimal digging, which nominees are bound to be controversial; committee staff members circulate reports about each nominee and flag for themselves any aspects of the nominee's background that might be controversial. Above and beyond such reports, though, interest groups have the motivation and resources to link those general concerns with specific, often issue-related, details about that nominee and to share this information with allies on the Judiciary Committee (Steigerwalt 2010). Accordingly, we would expect interest groups to invest significant resources in researching and flagging aspects of the nominee's past that are most predictive of future policy proclivities. While Judiciary Committee members may legitimately share the policy concerns of their allied interest groups, their electoral goals reinforce the policy goals; asking questions aligned with interest group policy concerns—which would often fall under our *Issues* questions category—may redound to them if the interest group allies mobilize their members to support the senator's campaign. Thus, we hypothesize:

> ***Issues* Questions Hypothesis.** Senators will ask controversial nominees more *Issues* questions than they will ask of noncontroversial nominees.

Even within issues-related questions, we expect that the controversy surrounding a nominee changes the nature of senators' questions, specifically incentivizing questions that are highly individualized and grounded in the nominee's record. The basis of these questions is two-fold. First, the very fact that a nominee is controversial is presumably based on *something*; some decision or behavior from the nominee's past that falls outside the parameters of an elite consensus. Second, however, is the increased attention to controversial nominees' records—by senators, their staffs, interest groups, and the media—that means Judiciary Committee members will be knowledgeable about these controversies and equipped to grill the nominees about them. In other words, the members will not just be prepared with a question or two about *Roe v. Wade* for controversial nominee Priscilla Owen, but, with the resources of several groups scouring her record, they will be prepared to push her on specific abortion-related decisions she has authored and cases in which she has been involved.

In sum, we expect that hearings for controversial nominees will involve more nominee-specific scrutiny. Our second hypothesis, then, is as follows:

> **Individualized Questions Hypothesis.** Senators will ask controversial nominees more individualized questions than they will ask of noncontroversial nominees.

Methods and Analysis

As in previous chapters, we draw on transcripts from Judiciary Committee hearings in the 103rd through 112th Congresses (1993–2012). We use the presence of interest group opposition to identify controversial circuit court nominees (Scherer, Bartels, and Steigerwalt 2008; Steigerwalt 2010). Chapter 3 describes the transcript coding process in more detail, as well as the procedure for identifying interest group opposition.

We turn first to describing the circumstances under which we see different rates of controversial nominees. Table 7.1 displays the proportion of nominees within various subgroups who are controversial. Some key differences emerge. First, a greater proportion of Bush's nominees were controversial by our measure: 41 percent of his circuit court nominees were controversial, as compared to 16 percent of Clinton's and 24 percent of Obama's. Bush's rate of controversial nominees is statistically significantly higher than Clinton's rate but not Obama's rate. The question, then, is what these numbers mean. The jump from Clinton to Bush might reflect several different changes. For example, it may be that Bush was nominating more controversy-prone individuals; this would fit with one Democratic staffer's perspective that Bush nominated more ideological individuals, at least compared to Obama. Or it may reflect a shift in opposition strategies during that time, that Democrats and their allied interest groups saw it as important or strategically beneficial to oppose nominees at an increased rate. And, of course, it may be that both of these mechanisms were at work. That the rate of opposed nominees does not return to Clinton-era levels in the Obama administration, however, may reflect a larger trend of increasing interest group opposition.

The bivariate comparisons also reveal a statistically significant difference between nominees from states with at least one senator in partisan opposition to the president and those without any opposition party senators. Nominees from states that have at least one senator from the president's opposition party have lower rates of controversial nominees than those from states with no opposing senators (20 percent versus 35 percent respectively, $t = 2.26$, $p < 0.01$). Again, this is consistent with the idea that presidents may feel more empowered to select controversial nominees when there is no opposition party senator from the nominee's state. It may also be that interest groups pay more attention to these nominees without an ally home-state senator to object early on.

Given the increased importance of the D.C. Circuit (Steigerwalt 2010), we might also expect to see greater attention and, by extension, increased controversy around individuals nominated to the D.C. Circuit. The data verify this, with 55 percent of D.C. Circuit nominees qualifying as controversial, as compared to 26 percent of non-D.C. circuit court nominees ($t = -2.08$, $p = 0.03$). Two other central variables are related to the rate of controversy. The ABA rating of controversial nominees is lower than the

TABLE 7.1. Bivariate Comparisons by Subgroup

	Percent of Subgroup That Is Opposed (frequency)
Nominating President	
Clinton	16* (11)
Bush	41* (29)
Obama	24 (9)
Unified or Divided Government	
Unified	32 (32)
Divided	22 (17)
Election Year	
Presidential election year	38 (11)
Non-presidential election year	26 (38)
Circuit	
D.C. Circuit	55* (6)
Non-D.C. Circuit	26* (43)
Experience	
Judging experience	27 (25)
No judging experience	28 (24)
Home-State Senators	
Opposing party senator	20* (17)
No opposing party senator	35* (32)
	Mean Level of Subgroup
Average ABA Rating	
Opposed nominees ($n = 49$)	4.6+
Unopposed nominees ($n = 129$)	5.0+
Average Circuit Balance	
Opposed nominees ($n = 49$)	0.11*
Unopposed nominees ($n = 129$)	0.15*

Note: An asterisk (*) indicates that subgroups are statistically significantly different from one another at the $p < 0.05$ level. A plus-sign (+) indicates statistical significance at the $p < 0.1$ level.

ABA rating of noncontroversial nominees (4.6 versus 5.0), and controversial nominees tend to be those nominated to more closely balanced circuits than noncontroversial nominees (0.11 versus 0.15, with higher numbers indicating circuits that are more lopsided in the partisanship of their nominating president). On the other hand, there is no bivariate relationship between divided government, presidential election years, previous judicial experience, and the proportion of nominees deemed controversial by our measure.[4]

Types of Questions

Does controversy change the kinds of questions senators choose to ask of nominees? The first hypothesis posits that senators' policy and electoral goals incentivize focusing their questioning of controversial nominees on *Issues* questions. Using the same method as in previous chapters, we group our narrower question categories into three broader categories: *Judicial Decision Making and Philosophy* (e.g., questions related to judicial philosophy, temperament, precedent); *Issues* (e.g., rights for disadvantaged groups, domestic commerce, abortion, crime); and *Qualifications* (e.g., ABA rating, experience, reversal rate).[5] As stated above, our hypothesis suggests that because interest groups and Judiciary Committee members will be particularly focused on policy outcomes for controversial nominees, controversial nominees should field a higher proportion of issues-based questions. For this analysis, we use the proportion of total questions as the dependent variable (as opposed to total number of questions in each category). This controls for the total number of questions regardless of the overall length and tenor of the hearing.

Figure 7.1 shows that senators focus more on *Issues* related questions for controversial nominees than they do for noncontroversial nominees. On average, 38 percent of the questions posed to controversial nominees are *Issues* questions, compared to 24 percent of the questions posed to noncontroversial nominees ($t = -3.63, p < 0.01$), a statistically and substantively significant difference. This increase is primarily offset by the percentage of *Judicial Decision Making* questions that each type of nominee faces; senators ask noncontroversial nominees higher proportions of *Judicial Decision Making* questions (40 percent) as compared to controversial nominees (26 percent) ($t = 3.43, p < 0.01$). This trade-off means that senators ask controversial nominees more questions related to *Issues* than any other category. This could explain Walker's (2012) concern that judicial confirmation hearings make "persistent probes into [the nominees'] personal

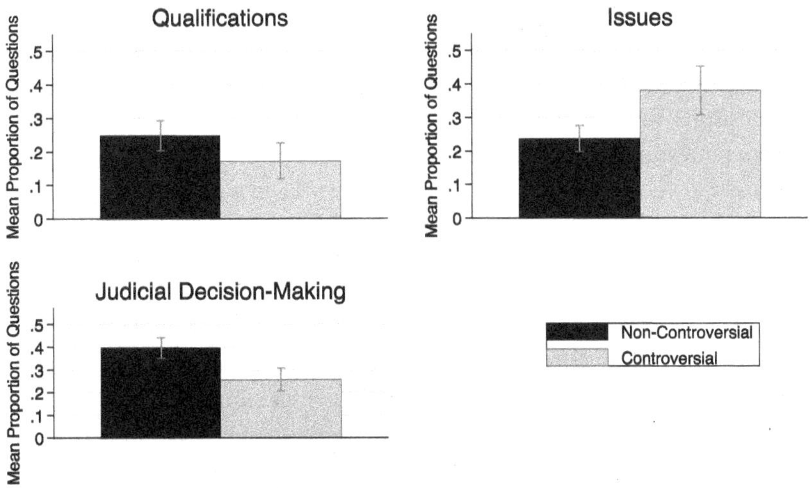

Fig. 7.1. Proportion of Questions in Major Categories; by Level of Controversy
Note: Figure displays 95 percent confidence intervals.

views on charged issues," given that it is these controversial hearings that earn the most attention. For the majority of hearings, this concern may be misplaced. Judiciary Committee members ask noncontroversial nominees the highest proportion of *Judicial Decision Making* questions, which would largely include questions Walker refers to as "appropriate questions about nominees' decision making processes." To a lesser extent, an opposed nominee can also expect a lower percentage of *Qualifications* questions (17 percent versus 25 percent), though this difference falls just above standard statistical significance levels ($t = 1.87, p = 0.06$). In sum, we find support for our first hypothesis that senators ask controversial nominees more *Issues*-related questions.

Individualized Scrutiny

Thus far, then, we have evidence that controversy changes the substance of hearings by providing senators policy and electoral incentives to focus more heavily on *Issues*-based questions. Next, we examine whether those controversial nominees senators scrutinize most intensively are, in contrast to noncontroversial nominees, questioned in highly individualized ways that are grounded in the nominee's record. We began by randomly selecting 25 controversial nominees (out of a possible 47) and 50 noncontroversial nominees (out of a possible 125). Within each nominee's hearing, we randomly selected 3 questions from the noncontroversial nominees (which represents one-third of the median number of questions for noncontroversial nominees) and randomly selected 9 questions from the controversial nominees (which represents about 15 percent of the median number of questions for controversial nominees). This results in 150 randomly selected questions posed to noncontroversial nominees and 225 randomly selected questions asked of controversial nominees.

We then coded each of these randomly selected questions on a dichotomous measure of "individualization." The question is coded 1 if the question refers to specific statements the nominee has made, previous decisions, writings, or potentially unethical, intemperate, or negative behavior. More general references to the nominee's background are coded 0, along with all questions that make no reference to the individual nominee.[6]

Sen. Herb Kohl provides an excellent example of a question that would be coded 1 on this measure when he asks controversial nominee Dennis Shedd the following:

> One more question. In 1994, you considered a lawsuit brought by several South Carolinians who asserted that flying the Confederate flag over the State house was unconstitutional. In that case, you suggested that the American flag, or even the palmetto tree, could be just as objectionable as the Confederate flag. In addition, at the end of the proceedings you expressed your frustration with the time being spent on discussing the flag when there were other, quote, "real problems which merited more attention." Judge Shedd, we don't need to tell you that the Confederate flag and the ideas that it represents offend a great number of people who live in the area covered by the Fourth Circuit. They believe the presence of the Confederate flag over the State house is a real problem, and these people turn to you and the system of justice in which you serve for a fair hearing of their complaints. It sounds like you were minimizing the importance of the issue at the time. Looking back at the comments you made at that time, would you change some of those comments if you could today?

This sample of controversial and noncontroversial nominees' questions provides evidence of the relatively individualized nature of controversial nominees' hearings. Sixty-two percent of questions asked of controversial nominees are individualized, compared to 24 percent of questions to noncontroversial nominees ($t = -7.72, p < 0.001$).

We have initial evidence for our second hypothesis: that controversial nominees receive individualized scrutiny from the Judiciary Committee. For a more in-depth analysis, we focus on controversial nominees who receive the most questions from members of the committee. Bush nominees top this list, making up 10 of the 11 highest question getters. This is unsurprising since the rate of controversy for Bush's nominees was statistically significantly higher than Clinton's rate. To get an idea of how nominee controversy varies across presidents, then, we have selected the top two question getters from each administration. This yields a sample of 6 individuals selected from the 14 nominees with the most questions, with a range of questions from 402 (for Bush nominee Kavanaugh) down to 111 (for Clinton nominee Sarokin). Table 7.2 lists the nominees with some additional characteristics.

Looking to the top question category, there is a fair amount of variation in terms of the proportion of the total hearing that is devoted to one or two categories. Obama nominee Robert Chatigny, for example, had a hearing where more than 50 percent of his questions related to criminal justice/death penalty; only 34 percent of his questions came from categories that were not the top two.[7] Clinton nominee H. Lee Sarokin and Bush nominee Priscilla Owen, on the other hand, had more evenly distributed questions; their top two categories only accounted for 41 and 37 percent of their total questions, leaving plenty of room for questions in several other categories.

Turning to the substance of the categories, criminal justice and other each are a top category for three nominees. That might speak to a pattern,

TABLE 7.2. Top Question Getters

Nominating President and Nominee		Total Questions (*N*)	Circuit	Top Question Category (%)	Second Question Category (%)
Clinton	Barkett	130	11th	Criminal Justice/ Death Penalty (41)	Judicial Philosophy (17)
	Sarokin	111	3rd	Criminal Justice/ Death Penalty (22)	Precedent (19)
Bush	Kavanaugh	402	D.C.	Objectivity (27)	Other (26)
	Owen	398	5th	Right to Privacy (27)	Other (9)
Obama	Chatigny	113	2nd	Criminal Justice/ Death Penalty (53)	Conflict of Interest (13)
	Liu	152	9th	Philosophy (43)	Other (15)

as criminal justice is a top category for three of the four Democratic nominees; this emphasis would be consistent with the expectations of issue ownership theory, where the Republican advantage on security issues like crime would incentivize senators to press Democratic nominees on these points (Petrocik 1996; Holian 2004; Egan 2013). The transcripts reveal, however, that the questioning within the criminal justice category is specifically tailored to dig in to decisions or behaviors unique to each nominee. Each of the three nominees who have criminal justice as their top or second-highest proportion category were already sitting judges, though judicial experience is not a reliable predictor of question type among nominees more broadly (see chapter 5 and Dancey, Nelson, and Ringsmuth 2014). The questions for each nominee emphasized *specific cases* in the nominees' backgrounds and, even in focusing on these specific cases, highlighted different aspects of the criminal justice category in doing so. For example, Clinton nominee Rosemary Barkett was grilled extensively on what Republican senators aimed to characterize as a pattern of dissent in death penalty hearings, dissents that argued against the application of the death penalty. Senator Thurmond uttered the phrase "6-to-1"—referencing her lone dissent in several cases—ten times to emphasize not just Barkett's apparent opposition to the death penalty, but also to highlight that she was out of step with the rest of the Supreme Court of Florida.

Barkett was also questioned specifically on dissents that cited racial disparities in the application of the death penalty as a reason to overturn it and, finally, on decisions that aimed to overturn convictions due to illegal searches and seizures. Through all three topics, these questions were specific to the nominee and, indeed, contrasted with some of the more general criminal justice questions many other nominees fielded (such as several versions of whether or not the nominee would uphold precedent related to the death penalty). It is also interesting to note that Chairman Biden, obviously aware of where the questioning would go, kicked off the hearing with friendly questions emphasizing how many times Barkett upheld the death penalty and her overall record, which boasted high rates of agreement and low rates of reversal by higher courts. Biden's pre-emptive questioning here reinforces Sen. Jon Kyl's assertion that individuals knew that nominees were controversial and why before the hearing took place, as this line of questioning was known before it started.

Sarokin represents a whole different line of questioning within the criminal justice category, although one still focused on specific behaviors and decisions in his past. While he only fielded one general question about the death penalty—Senator Thurmond asked him about his view on the "constitutionality of the death penalty"—his other questions touched on due process violations, mandatory minimum sentencing, drug testing, habeas corpus petitions, and pretrial detention, and they all pertain to decisions he rendered or statements he made on these topics. The most extensive line of questioning related to a habeas corpus petition he granted in 1989, in which Chairman Biden elicited the details of the case and concluded the questioning by placing the decision (as he did with Barkett) into the larger context of Sarokin's caseload and the number of habeas corpus petitions he actually granted (5 out of 500–1,000 petitions).

Finally, similar to Barkett, Obama nominee Chatigny faced extensive questioning related to the death penalty and his record in this area. His questions homed in on one case in which Chatigny did not support the imposition of the death penalty even when the convicted individual wanted to forgo appeals, based on questions Chatigny had about the defendant's competence. Questioning senators seemed particularly disturbed by some of Chatigny's comments he made outside of the official decision in the case. Senator Sessions noted a conversation between Chatigny and the defendant's lawyer:

> SENATOR SESSIONS: And you also said at that time, "We're not in this profession to help people get killed." A lawful execution does not meet my definition of killing. Do you think that's a bad choice of words?

Chatigny is also questioned about specific decisions and comments he made regarding mandatory minimums and sex offender laws. While much shorter lines of questioning than that related to his involvement in the death penalty case, these questions also related to specific decisions.

The category that appears second most often in the top categories of the most intensively questioned controversial nominees is the category of "other." This category fundamentally speaks to a lack of pattern, as it is the catch-all category for questions that fit in no other category. It is the second most common category for both Bush nominees, a close second for Kavanaugh with 26 percent of questions in this category and a more distant second for Owen with 9 percent. Obama nominee Liu faced 15 percent of his questioning that fit into the "other" category, which also represents his second most common category. For all but Owen, this is a notably higher proportion of "other" questions as compared to the full sample. The median circuit court nominee fields 7 percent of his or her questions from the "other" category. The median controversial nominee is slightly higher, at 9 percent, and the median noncontroversial nominee is slightly lower, at 6 percent.

As with the criminal justice category, there is a range of question topics, which is particularly diverse given the nature of this category. And, as with the criminal justice category, most of these questions relate to specific behavior or opinions of the nominees, attesting to the individualized nature of the hearings. Kavanaugh, for example, fielded a fair number of questions in the "other" category that had to do with his work for Ken Starr when Starr was investigating President Clinton, as well as Kavanaugh's work in the Bush White House with preparing other nominees for their hearings. Bush nominee Owen's "other" questions were a bit more scattered than Kavanaugh's, but the plurality of these questions assessed how fairly Owen thinks her hearings have been, as well as aimed to clarify understanding around specific incidents in her past. For example, Chairman Hatch noted, in the course of questioning, that "Justice Owen was not lectured by her colleagues in the case of *Weiner v. Wasson*. Your detractors, I think, had confused you with the defendant in that case . . . we have also clarified once again that Judge Gonzales' often-repeated comments about judicial activism were not directed at you at all." Both of these questions are good representations of the type of nominee-specific questioning taking place at Owen's and others' hearings. Similar to Owen's "other" questions, Liu's tended to be more about follow-up and clarification, though again they tended to be nominee-specific. For example, Liu was twice asked whether he still stood behind comments he had made about (then-) Judge Alito's record on the Third Circuit Court of Appeals, in addition to several questions about his understanding of the process surrounding his nomination and confirmation process.

While "other" is Liu's second-most common category of questioning, his most common category, judicial philosophy, accounts for a portion of his hearings that is three times as big as "other." As with criminal justice, that Liu, a Democratic (Obama) nominee, received so many questions in this category fits with party-based expectations, in particular, beliefs that Democratic nominees may tend toward judicial activism (Scherer 2005). Moreover, this category in particular can lend itself to general and broad questions; other noncontroversial nominees face plenty of judicial philosophy questions, though these usually manifest in terms of questions like, "What is your philosophy of interpreting the Constitution?" or "I would like your comments on the role of a judge on interpreting versus making law." Contrast these general questions, then, with the specific manifestation of this category for Liu, which is specially tailored to his individual circumstances and focuses on specific actions and espoused beliefs from his past. Senator Hatch, for example, begins with Liu's own words to grill him about his judicial philosophy:

> SENATOR HATCH: So I want to note some of the things you have written that appear to relate to this question. In your book, *Keeping Faith With the Constitution*, you wrote that the Supreme Court looks to "social practices, evolving norms, and practical consequences" to give meaning to the Constitution. In an interview about that book you said that, "the Constitution should be interpreted in ways that adapt its principles and its text to the challenges and conditions of our society in every single generation." In a *Stanford Law Review* article you wrote that courts must determine "whether our collective values on a given issue have converged to a degree that they can be persuasively crystallized and credibly absorbed into legal doctrine." Now, it seems to me that this type of an approach gives all of the power to the judges . . .
>
> Let me ask you this: do you stand by these approaches that you have written and spoken about, and do you really think that judges should have this much power over the law? What is left that can be identified as the Constitution after judges have finished adapting it generation after generation to changing conditions and challenges? What will be left of the Constitution if that is the approach? . . . Do you still stand by these approaches as though you can just about make of the law anything you want to? I know you can't mean that, but tell me what you think.

Judicial philosophy also appears as a top category for Clinton nominee Barkett which again fits with partisan expectations for this to be a popular category with Democratic nominees. While philosophy represented a much smaller proportion of the hearing than it did in Liu's, Barkett's questions were specific to her experience and were substantively rigorous. She did receive a warm-up question of sorts when Chairman Biden asked her to consider how a circuit court judgeship would differ from her role on the Florida Supreme Court. Senator Hatch, however, soon turned the questioning over to a substantive analysis of equal protection interpretations and circumstances under which the state versus federal clause would apply, as well as the application of substantive due process. As with other categories and nominees, all of these issues were broached in the context of decisions and behavior of the nominee, including Barkett's previous decisions.

If we expand our analysis to include the top five most intensively questioned controversial nominees for each president, we observe a similar pattern.[8] Judicial philosophy remains a common top category for this range of nominees; it is the first or second highest proportion of questions for 3 out of the 9 added nominees (for a total of 5 out of 15 nominees). Criminal justice (which includes questions about the death penalty) appears in another two nominees' top question categories, while rights for disadvantaged groups is a top category for three nominees. This tier of nominees is noticeably characterized by the diversity of top categories: for all 15 nominees, out of 30 first- and second-place categories, there are 9 categories that show up exactly once; 6 of these are attributable to the second tier of nominees.

Moreover, in the categories that show up repeatedly for this second tier, the questions within those categories continue to be highly tailored to the specific circumstances of the controversial nominee. For example, nominees Sutton and Fletcher faced judicial philosophy questions rooted in statements they had previously made about the role of lawyers or judges. Senator Hatch used Fletcher's past written critiques of Rehnquist's judicial philosophy as an opportunity to press him on his judicial philosophy. Sen. Chuck Schumer did likewise with Sutton's previous comments on the *Morrison* case, which struck down portions of the Violence Against Women Act on the grounds that Congress overstepped its authority to regulate interstate commerce, as did Senator Kohl, who used Sutton's previous opposition to applying the Fourteenth Amendment to the states as the basis for broader questions about Sutton's judicial philosophy. Even within the usually-mundane category of justiciability, questioning is individualized. This is Clinton nominee Fletcher's highest category. Senators questioned him extensively about his previous writings arguing for the expansion of the concept of standing. Chairman Hatch, for example, pressed Fletcher as to whether advocates working with the homeless would be able to legally challenge cuts to human services, based on Fletcher's argument that "injured in fact" should be broadly construed.

In sum, this section highlights how the questioning can be both highly individualized, substantive, *and* contingent on politics. For instance, through these examples we see that the questions may be attuned to specific facts of an individual while still being tied up with political considerations. Senators from both sides of the aisle questioned nominees on these topics, though we see friendly and sometimes protective questioning from members of the president's party, while opposition party members approach the same categories in a more antagonistic fashion. For example, before a single Republican senator could begin questioning Barkett on her dissents in death penalty cases, Chairman Biden kicked off the hearing with a litany of questions highlighting how often Barkett upheld the death penalty. Republican Senator Cohen immediately picked up a string of death-penalty-related questioning that was highly critical of specific times Barkett overruled a death penalty verdict. Second, consistent with party expectations theory, we observe Democrats, particularly the most controversial of nominees, facing extensive questioning on issues of criminal justice, an issue on which Republicans typically hold a competence advantage. This questioning, however, is driven by the specifics of the individual nominees' stories.

Do Confirmation Hearings Forecast Confirmation Outcomes?

Our theoretical argument about why senators hold and attend confirmation hearings does not create a strong expectation of a connection between what occurs at the hearings and the fate of specific nominees in the confirmation process. As we show throughout the book, senators use features of these proceedings, such as the ability to introduce nominees from their home state and their autonomy to guide the discussion toward issues they value, as opportunities for garnering electoral and policy benefits. These benefits are not, with the exception of controversial nominees, tied to specific, individual nominees. Even so, a natural question that flows from these analyses is whether the content and nature of the hearings have impact on the outcome of the confirmation process; more specifically, can we predict the likelihood of confirmation based on the hearing? Our larger argument would say no; the content of the hearings is divorced from the nominees themselves and, therefore, we would expect little predictive power.

The primary exception to this is hearings for controversial nominees. As we have argued previously, a nominee's status as controversial changes senators' calculations about engagement in the confirmation hearing. The opportunity to publicly question controversial nominees corresponds with a higher salience environment and the potential to "score points" with attentive interest groups (Scherer 2005). Therefore, senators might see a related advantage to grilling a controversial nominee during her hearing and then to voting in a specific direction on confirmation. More specifically, a senator's behavior could be driven by a desire to vet a nominee on which the senator was undecided, to curry favor with advocacy groups, or both.

We examined whether the number of questions senators pose to a nominee foreshadows the fate of that nominee in the confirmation process.

Figure 7.2 depicts the average number of questions at a hearing for circuit court nominees, comparing controversial and noncontroversial nominees and those who were ultimately confirmed and those who were not. Certain aspects of these data complicate their interpretation. First, variation in confirmation among noncontroversial circuit court nominees is quite low; approximately 98 percent were confirmed. Second, a bit more variation exists among controversial nominees (approximately 66 percent were confirmed), but there are fewer of these nominees. With these caveats in mind, the figure suggests a substantive difference in the average number of questions between confirmed and unconfirmed nominees. This difference runs in the direction we would expect, with nominees who were unconfirmed appearing to face more questions, on average, than those who were confirmed.

We do not want to overplay this potential difference. These differences, while visually large, do not quite meet conventional levels of statistical significance ($p = 0.12$ for controversial nominees; $p = 0.11$ for noncontroversial nominees). Further, when we test this relationship in a multivariate model predicting whether a nominee was ultimately confirmed, the total number of questions is not statistically significantly related to the likelihood that a nominee is confirmed, even among controversial nominees. Finally, even if this relationship exists, it is impossible to untangle the causal direction of the relationship. Did more questions increase the likelihood that a nominee was not confirmed? Or did Judiciary Committee members, already set against confirmation, use the hearing to go on record with their concerns?

Thus we have suggestive though not definitive evidence of a link between what occurs during confirmation hearings and confirmation outcomes. This may seem counterintuitive, given that we have argued that hearings are not generally used to vet individual nominees. We have provided evidence throughout the book, however, that senators' engagement in confirmation hearings is linked to a set of motivations that are, for the most part, related to the opportunities associated with the hearings themselves. Thus while we do have theoretical reason to believe senators' behavior during hearings for controversial nominees may be tied to the fate of individual nominees, for the bulk of nominees, hearings provide senators with less readily apparent yet still valuable policy and electoral benefits.

Conclusion

Though previous chapters show that Senate Judiciary Committee hearings for typical nominees are generally not driven by nominee-specific con-

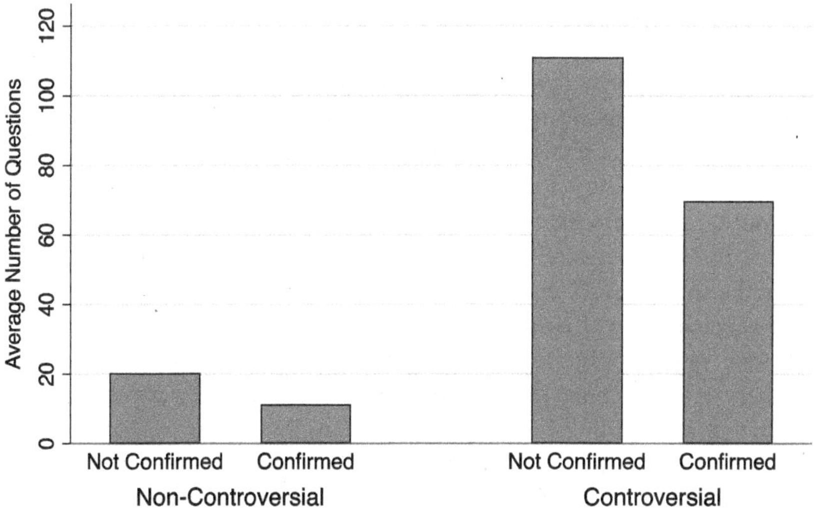

Fig. 7.2. Average Number of Questions Posed to Circuit Nominees; by Confirmation Status and Type of Nominee

siderations, this chapter demonstrates that confirmation hearings are not entirely bereft of individualized scrutiny. In fact, in the case of controversial nominees, senators pursue their policy and electoral goals by substantively grilling these nominees on their previous behaviors, writings, and decisions.

Hearings for controversial nominees present heightened potential benefits of participating paired with lower costs for committee senators of obtaining relevant, often policy-related, information. The participation of interest groups in the confirmation process for controversial nominees means that senators have an increased chance of scoring political points with interest groups who can mobilize attentive publics *and* have easy access to policy-relevant information about the nominee (Scherer 2005). This chapter presents specific evidence for this in terms of the nature of increased participation in controversial nominees' hearings by Judiciary Committee senators and an increased focus on *Issues*-related questioning during the hearing. Finally, a more in-depth examination of some of the most controversial nominees provides evidence that the questioning in controversial nominees' hearings is rigorous and individualized. Senators ask questions about specific writings, decisions, or behavior from nominees' pasts.

The hearings for controversial nominees are rare but provide another answer to the question of why Senate Judiciary Committee members devote so much time and energy to hearings in general. In the rare cases when committee members *do* use them to individually vet nominees, the exchanges are policy-substantive and provide the potential to score points with interest groups. Thus, when the need arises, the hearings provide a critical public arena in which the legislature can openly raise objections to a nominee and ultimately attempt to check the president. Accordingly, committee members may maintain the norm that each nominee gets a hearing in part to ensure that the opportunity will exist to publicly scrutinize the most controversial nominees. The result, as we have shown in previous chapters, is that the average hearing is used not for scrutinizing individual nominees but for advancing members' policy and electoral goals in other ways. We conclude the book, then, with an accounting of our core arguments and findings and ultimately what these hearings add to the advice and consent process. In so doing, we address how the role of hearings for lower court nominees compares to that of hearings for Supreme Court nominees. Next, we discuss what our results suggest about the consequences of proposals to reform the hearings themselves or the confirmation process more broadly. We end by offering our final thoughts on the value of public judicial confirmation hearings in a democratic society.

EIGHT

The Value of Lower Court Confirmation Hearings

The vision of judicial confirmation hearings that is most salient to the general public—and, specifically, most salient to those individuals who can retrieve any vision of a judicial hearing—would almost certainly be the optics of a Supreme Court confirmation hearing. Panoramas of the full senators' table, all members of the Senate Judiciary Committee in attendance and ready to engage with the nominee; the flashes of media cameras; the packed room behind the nominee, including the nominee's family, friends, and colleagues, but also the lucky staffers and interested citizens who were able to secure a seat. Even the most straight-laced, noncontroversial nominee will experience days of substantive questioning and, with more controversial nominees, perhaps dives into past behavior.

As with much of politics, the judicial confirmation hearing that happens *most of the time*—that of district and circuit court nominees—is far less dramatic and gets far less attention from a narrower audience. We set out in this book to understand why senators hold confirmation hearings for lower federal court nominees and the value of these hearings in the larger advice and consent process. It would seem that the lack of public attention to these hearings diminishes senators' usual benefits for participation. The hearings will not directly advance specific pieces of legislation, for example, that a member of the Judiciary Committee might champion, nor is it likely that footage from a nomination hearing will make the cut in a campaign commercial. Yet since the hearings persist, it stands to reason that senators benefit from them.

How Hearings Serve Senators' Interests

Instead of holding hearings for the primary purpose of vetting individual nominees, we have argued that the time-consuming practice of confirmation hearings for district and circuit court nominees continues because the hearings provide an important venue in which senators can advance their policy and electoral goals. Our analyses suggest that senators pursue these goals in different ways through confirmation hearings, depending on the level of controversy surrounding a nominee. As a result, hearings for controversial nominees look quite different from hearings for noncontroversial nominees (see chapter 3).

Since federal courts play a significant role in setting policy through the decisions they make, we argue that senators on the Judiciary Committee, who tend to have a legal background, are particularly interested in and knowledgeable about the future of the federal judiciary and its impact on policy. We submit that senators use hearings as an opportunity to engage future members of the judiciary in a dialogue regarding senators' competing visions for the direction of the federal courts. Judiciary Committee members are in a position to steer the content of these proceedings in order to discuss policy with those who, if confirmed, will have the authority to interpret and apply our Constitution, laws, and precedents.

Chapters 4 and 5 demonstrate that contextual factors related to senators' policy and electoral goals, not nominee-specific factors, drive the variation in the number and types of questions senators ask noncontroversial nominees, as well as how many senators attend these proceedings. In particular, times of divided versus unified government alter the incentives for Judiciary Committee members' engagement in confirmation hearings. Divided government inspires far more questioning related to issues, while questions around the nominee's experience decline. Moreover, for noncontroversial circuit court nominees, there is an interactive effect between divided government and the partisan composition of the circuit to which the person has been nominated. Those who stand to make the largest policy impact—those who could tip the balance of an evenly divided circuit—face more *Issues* questions, especially under times of divided government. Ultimately then, our findings suggest that Judiciary Committee members are attuned to the political landscape and the conditions under which a judicial nominee would have the most policy impact. Even though committee members may not directly influence the policy preferences of an individual nominee, senators use these hearings to attend to the aggregate policy consequences of the judiciary.

When considering controversial nominees, we argue that senators' use of hearings to pursue their policy goals expands to include individual vetting. Given senators' interest in the policy direction of the federal judiciary, the hearings are a venue for exploring the policy ramifications of confirming a particular nominee about whom red flags have been raised. In particular, these proceedings are an opportunity for Judiciary Committee members to learn about the views of nominees whom senators may be uncertain about confirming. As chapter 7 shows, senators employ individually tailored questions to both assess controversial nominees' policy positions and grill these nominees to curry favor with interest groups.

Confirmation hearings come into play in calculations of electoral benefit in other ways, too, for both Judiciary Committee members and for home-state senators from the wider chamber. As chapter 6 illustrates, the nearly universal participation in introducing nominees from a senator's state—regardless of the party of the nominating president—suggests that the hearings provide an opportunity for senators to create an "impression of influence" (Grimmer, Westwood, and Messing 2014) and present themselves as bipartisan boosters of their state. Of course, in our era of polarized parties and battles over the future of the federal courts, members of the Judiciary Committee also see advantages in staking out positions that may please interest groups and activists (Scherer, Bartels, and Steigerwalt 2008). The question-and-answer portion of the hearing affords committee members a venue for position taking, with the presumed payoffs for engagement increasing as the level of controversy surrounding a nominee increases.

How Hearings Serve Broader Purposes

Helping Ensure Quality Judges

If confirmation hearings are structured to serve senators' policy and electoral interests, do these proceedings also play a role in ensuring quality nominees are selected for the federal bench? Our evidence shows that individual scrutiny is not a primary purpose of lower court confirmation hearings for the vast majority of nominees. Because senators view noncontroversial nominees as "acceptable" by default (Scherer, Bartels, and Steigerwalt 2008) and receive vetting in the form of FBI background checks and a detailed committee questionnaire, there is little perceived need to individually vet these nominees during a hearing. Instead, most nominees receive a handful of fairly routine questions for which they may even have prepared answers. As we show in chapters 4 and 5, nominee-specific variables account for little variation in how many senators attend a nominee's hearing and in the quantity and type of questions posed by senators.

While hearings for typical nominees fit this pattern, when questioning controversial nominees, we find that senators do pose individualized queries designed in part to vet nominees' fitness for the bench. In chapter 7, we provide evidence that the most controversial nominees face highly individualized questions related to their backgrounds, previous experience, and past behavior. These controversial nominees are the exception rather than the rule when it comes to hearings for district and circuit court nominees.

As one Republican staffer commented, however, "for the average nominee the hearing does not play a big role, but it can." The prospect that a hearing *could* play a role in confirmation success is important. As one staffer told us, the mere presence of hearings may help ensure that primarily noncontroversial nominees are selected by the president. Indeed, an example from 2017 demonstrates how even a routine district court hearing has the potential to prove embarrassing for a presidential administration if a nominee is considered unqualified. In the hearing, Sen. John Kennedy (R-LA) used his time to question Matthew Petersen, a Trump nominee to the U.S. District Court for the District of Columbia, in a way that highlighted the Federal Elections Commission (FEC) commissioner's lack of judicial experience. In the exchange, which was reproduced in full on the *Washington Post*'s website (Blake 2017) and covered by such media outlets as the *New York Times* (Bromwich and Chokshi 2017), *USA Today* (Wolf 2017), and Fox News (Stirewalt 2017), Petersen admits to having never tried a civil, criminal, jury, or bench trial before Kennedy asks about his knowledge of a series of legal terms in the following exchange:

SENATOR KENNEDY: Yes, I've read your résumé. Just for the record, do you know what a motion in limine is?

MR. PETERSEN: I would probably not be able to give you a good definition right here at the table.

SENATOR KENNEDY: Do you know what the Younger abstention doctrine is?

MR. PETERSEN: I've heard of it, but I, again—

SENATOR KENNEDY: How about the Pullman abstention doctrine?

MR. PETERSEN: I—I—

SENATOR KENNEDY: Y'all see that a lot in federal court. (Ohlheiser 2017)

After the hearing, Sen. Sheldon Whitehouse (D-RI) tweeted out a video of the exchange that went "viral" (Ohlheiser 2017; Wolf 2017). As of August 2018, Senator Whitehouse's tweet had over 79,000 retweets and

130,000 likes, and the video of Senator Kennedy's questioning had over eight million views. Senator Kennedy, for his part, was later quoted as saying, "Just because you've seen 'My Cousin Vinny' doesn't qualify you to be a federal judge" (Savage 2017). In the end, Petersen withdrew his nomination, noting in a letter to President Trump that he did not want to be a "continued distraction from the important work of your administration and the Senate" (Savage 2017).

Although the level of attention to the Petersen-Kennedy exchange is exceptional, it highlights how hearings carry the potential to expose nominees who are either perceived as unqualified or ideologically extreme. Further, in chapter 7 we provide suggestive though not definitive evidence that nominees—both controversial and noncontroversial—who face more questions during their confirmation hearings are less likely to be confirmed. In the absence of hearings, the president and home-state senators may feel more empowered to select or recommend less qualified nominees, whether for ideological or personal reasons. Even if senators are not individually vetting most nominees at the hearing stage, then, it is possible that formal hearings help ensure qualified nominees make their way to the federal bench.

Providing Advice and Consent

The second important role these hearings can play is ensuring a robust role for the Senate in their constitutionally prescribed duty to advise and consent on judicial nominees. In this regard, the low levels of participation we find for most nominees could be problematic if it signals the Judiciary Committee's lack of engagement in the process. More specifically, it might suggest that committee members have informally ceded their duties to interest groups, who can monitor and identify controversial nominees in their stead (see, e.g., Scherer, Bartels, and Steigerwalt 2008). If so, this delegation could raise serious concerns about democratic accountability and an outsized influence by interest groups in the process.

Certainly, Judiciary Committee members do not seem enthusiastic to participate in the average noncontroversial hearing; as Senator Kyl told us, the attendees are those who drew the "short straw" for any given hearing. Hearing attendance, however, is only one measure of attention and vetting, and an incomplete one at that. While interest groups are constantly watching and researching nominees (and potential nominees), this activity is part of a swirl of information-gathering also generated by committee members, their staffs, and home-state senators.

Since we do not directly examine the consequences of interest group opposition itself but rather employ interest group opposition as an indicator of wider controversy, we are limited in our ability to speak to the potential for interest groups to exert too much influence over the confirmation process. As Senator Kyl also told us, however, interest groups were not solely responsible for labeling a nominee as controversial; instead, controversy tended to appear organically from several corners and, as Senator Kaufman mentioned, ultimately was widely agreed upon. This suggests that when interest groups choose to oppose a nomination, they contribute to and magnify concerns that typically exist elsewhere. Further, competing demands on time and other resources mean that interest groups play a public role in a minority of circuit court nominations and tend not to be involved in district court nominations, though it is often pivotal when interest groups do choose to oppose a nomination (see Scherer 2005; Scherer, Bartels, and Steigerwalt 2008; Steigerwalt 2010). More generally, the persistence of the compulsory confirmation hearing for all nominees, regardless of how noncontroversial the nominee, speaks to the Judiciary Committee's commitment to maintaining an active role in the advice and consent process.

Promoting Transparency and Accountability

Despite low levels of senator engagement and a lack of individualized scrutiny at most lower court confirmation hearings, we argue that the hearings play normatively important roles in the advice and consent process, including the advancement of the core democratic values of transparency and accountability. The literature on the role of Supreme Court confirmation hearings demonstrates how senators use these proceedings not as mere political props, but as a "democratic forum for the discussion and ratification of constitutional change" (Collins and Ringhand 2013, 2). Collins and Ringhand (2013) suggest that Supreme Court confirmation hearings offer an opportunity for senators to impart important information about public sentiments regarding the Constitution to nominees (e.g., discussing cases and issues seen as important to the public and asking nominees about their positions on key precedents). At the same time, they offer nominees the chance to interpret major Supreme Court decisions for senators and the public more generally. Wedeking and Farganis' (2014) findings that, contrary to conventional wisdom, Supreme Court nominees are not becoming more evasive in their responses at nomination hearings is consistent with the argument that hearings are a place where honest and substantive dialogue can happen between the nominees and the Senate Judiciary Committee.

These accounts suggest that Supreme Court confirmation hearings contribute to the larger debate over the nature and meaning of the Constitution independent of whether they are also serving to vet individual nominees. Of course, Supreme Court hearings receive extensive media coverage and are shown live on television and streamed online by major media outlets, which means the dialogue that takes place reaches a much wider audience than even the most contentious lower court confirmation hearing. Similarly, the high-profile nature of Supreme Court hearings means that senators are far more engaged and the questioning is far more exhaustive than the typical lower court hearing that involves a handful of questions from the few senators in attendance.

Despite the usually pro forma nature of hearings for lower court nominees, scholars have argued that they can provide democratic value. Ross (2001) and Shenkman (2012) note the potential for senators to use these hearings to communicate key information such as the importance of honoring precedent, judicial restraint, and an appropriate judicial temperament to nominees, although Shenkman (2012) and Walker (2012) express concerns that these topics are not the primary focus of the hearings in practice. Our evidence suggests that may be true at controversial nominees' hearings, where *Issues*-based questions are more prevalent, but that *Judicial Decision Making* questions tend to take the place of *Issues*-based questions at noncontroversial nominees' hearings. This category includes questions about adhering to precedent, judicial philosophy, temperament, and objectivity. Even when questions in this category are asked in general, mundane ways—e.g., "What is the role of precedent?"—it is a public opportunity for Judiciary Committee members to reinforce and remind themselves of the norms of judicial behavior and for nominees to voice their allegiance to these fundamental concepts of the judiciary. This reinforcement could be directed at several audiences, from committee members themselves, to other members of Congress more generally, to the nominee, to future nominees, and to the presidential administration. Again, while these hearings themselves are not individually salient events, the accumulated message over time is that these concepts are treasured and that those involved in the larger judicial nomination process must respect them.

We also find that issue-based questions are more common in times of divided government. This suggests that in times where the democratic mechanisms of elections create a Senate in partisan opposition to the president, this substantive opposition manifests in lower court confirmation hearings. In other words, our findings support the idea that these hearings are electorally responsive and that Judiciary Committee members use them to communicate with future judges about policy matters, though in ways that differ significantly from that of Supreme Court hearings and in ways that differ for controversial and noncontroversial nominees.

Reforms: Potential and Realized

Other commentators (e.g., Ross 2001; Shenkman 2012) note the potential for lower court confirmation hearings to serve a substantive purpose, but ultimately conclude that these hearings *do not* serve this substantive role in their current incarnations. Given this, Ross (2001) highlights some ideas for adjusting the hearing process to encourage more substantive questioning, such as delegating more substantive questioning to special counsels or, to deal with the potential for embarrassing nominees with difficult questions in front of their friends and families, moving certain portions of the questioning into a closed session (such as questions about judicial philosophy) or barring friends and family from attending the hearing altogether. Shenkman (2012) goes further and suggests eliminating standing hearings for district court nominees. If the Senate ever considers such proposals, our analyses suggest a handful of relevant considerations.

First, it is important to reiterate that the lack of controversy at the district court level may be precisely because of the existence of the compulsory hearings. In other words, by eliminating hearings for district court nominees, the president and like-party home-state senators may face fewer constraints in nominating ideologically extreme nominees or simply unqualified nominees.[1]

While Senate opponents would still notice these nominees—given that the hearings themselves do not tend to be the place where these things are uncovered—the controversy may not only increase, but may also play out in less transparent venues. As one former Democratic Judiciary Committee staffer during the Bush and Obama administrations noted, this transparency is a key benefit of the hearings: "If you care about the democratic role in the process, then this is, I think, a critical stepping stone . . . and a good check." Senator Kaufman expressed a similar sentiment:

> I think that it's important for lifetime appointments especially that there be this public question and answer for them. I think that's really important, and I think it's important especially at a time when there's so little faith in our institutions. . . . I do believe that one of the things the Congress provides is a place where at least people can't say, "Well it's all done in secret."

Moreover, while it is true that specifically scheduling a hearing does present an additional opportunity to slow things down (i.e., to push the hearing back as much as possible), eliminating the hearing would not necessarily eliminate the concomitant obstructive power. Senators interested in slowing down the process will find other means to do so, ones that are potentially less transparent than the current options. Indeed, the same former Democratic Judiciary Committee staffer who lauds the hearings for their transparent nature also noted that scheduling the hearings actually gives the committee guideposts and momentum to keep the process moving. The staffer said, "My view from inside was, unless you had those internal things to do, the process would just grind to a halt." While Judiciary Committee members could certainly learn a new process, the time and effort required to do so is not insubstantial and speaks to the larger path dependency of congressional procedure.

Second, it is important to note that there are some district court nominees who generate controversy and as a result face more intensive vetting at their hearings. While the vast majority of nominees opposed by interest groups are circuit court nominees, there are rare cases of opposition to district court nominees. A former staffer for a liberal advocacy group we interviewed mentioned the case of Bush nominee J. Leon Holmes, whose nomination was opposed by some liberal interest groups (People for the American Way 2004). And while there are stark differences between the average number of questions fielded by district court judges versus controversial circuit court nominees (6.9 versus 83.3), there are district court nominees who start to look like those controversial circuit nominees: Clinton nominee Frederica Massiah-Jackson, for example, was asked 85 questions, while Bush nominee Paul Cassell answered 73 questions. Many of these questions took on the same highly tailored form of questions posed to the controversial circuit nominees. While these controversial district nominees are uncommon, eliminating district court nominee hearings could endanger a key means for vetting them, which, in turn, could remove a key constraint on the president and home-state senators.

This is not to say that there is nothing that should or could be done to expedite the nomination and confirmation process. As Shenkman (2012) and many others have noted, senators obstruct this process for political purposes and policy gains. While this may be strategically useful, the empty judicial seats have real consequences for the speed at which cases can move through the courts, the workload of seated judges, and the legitimacy of the judiciary as a place to obtain swift and effective justice (see, e.g., Binder and Maltzman 2009, Binder and Wheeler 2011).

One type of proposal, creating a judicial fast track, attempts to address the increasing delay in filling seats on the federal bench (Binder and Maltzman 2009, 151–54). Under one such plan, each state would establish a bipartisan nominating commission with the presumption that these commissions will focus on the professional qualifications of potential nominees while de-emphasizing the role of partisanship and ideology, ideally agreeing on highly qualified potential nominees who are broadly acceptable (Binder and Maltzman 2009).[2]

If the president chooses to nominate one of the nominees recommended by the commission, that nominee would be guaranteed a faster route to consideration, which might include a maximum time until an up-or-down vote. Presidents could still choose a nominee that is not recommended by the commission; in such a case, that nominee would be subject to the existing nomination process. Another idea calls for classifying some judicial nominees as "privileged nominations"; if there were no objections, these nominations could then proceed directly to full Senate consideration without a full committee hearing. If a senator objected, specific nominees could be returned to the standard nomination process and receive a committee hearing (McMillion 2013).

The primary drawback to reforms in this vein, particularly the establishment of nominating commissions, is that it is possible that the ability of home-state senators to advise the president on judicial selections, which is a key component of the duty to advise and consent, might decrease in the early stages (Binder and Maltzman 2009). Others may object to the perceived diminished role and influence of the Judiciary Committee (McMillion 2013). These objections would make such a rules change politically difficult. In addition, depending on how these changes are instituted, they may face constitutional challenges (see, e.g., Bruhl 2011). But given the potential gains—speeding up the confirmation process, reducing caseload burdens for sitting judges, and providing quicker judicial resolution for litigants (see, e.g., Binder and Maltzman 2009)—proposals along these lines merit serious consideration. If such a proposal were implemented, the number of nominees deemed controversial might decrease, which in and of itself could move nominees through the confirmation process more quickly and increase the likelihood of confirmation (Binder and Maltzman 2009). For the hearings, this reduction in controversial nominees would limit the opportunity for senators to garner the benefits uniquely associated with hearings for these nominees and could, in turn, diminish the importance of hearings in the minds of senators. But the ability for home-state senators to claim credit through introductory remarks for a consensual, bipartisan nomination process would remain. Even given a lower number of controversial nominees, hearings would continue to provide an important venue for interbranch communication and policy discussions. In that case, the hearing's role as the sole public source of interbranch dialogue in the confirmation process is a key anchor to ensure the process remains deliberative and transparent.

While most reform proposals have not come to pass, there is one distinct change, the ramifications of which are still being explored. In November 2013, Senate Democrats "went nuclear" on executive and judicial nominees below the Supreme Court by reducing the threshold to invoke cloture from 60 to 51 (Berman 2017). Senate Republicans followed suit in April 2017 with respect to Neil Gorsuch's nomination to the Supreme Court. Democrats engaged in "the first partisan filibuster of a Supreme Court nominee" (Abramson 2017). Using this as a justification, Senate Republicans moved to change the rules so that only a simple majority—51 senators—were necessary to invoke cloture, rather than the existing 60 (Abramson 2017). Gorsuch was confirmed with 52 votes after Democrats moved to block the nomination (Totenberg 2017).

It is not yet clear what general implications this rules change brings. At least theoretically, with a significant means of obstruction eliminated, judicial nominees should face easier paths to confirmation. The consequences for hearings could go many ways: First, it could incentivize even more pro forma hearings if the minority party feels that a greater proportion of nominations will be foregone conclusions. Second, opposition party senators may see this rare public event as the only opportunity to make public declarations on objectionable nominees. One of our interviewees, a former Democratic Judiciary Committee and leadership staffer, predicts that removing the filibuster for judicial nominees could change the type of nominees and lead to less bipartisanship in the process. An analysis of the 113th Congress finds that the change did not lead to more ideologically extreme or less qualified nominees (Boyd, Lynch, and Madonna 2015). As the lack of a supermajority requirement for cloture on these nominees becomes ingrained over time, however, it is possible that we will see shifts in who the president nominates. Such a shift could manifest in more contentious hearings. A third option, of course, is that this rules change will not necessarily resonate in the hearings.

Preliminary evidence supports this third option. Using multiple measures of participation—including the number of questions the nominee fields and how many senators attended the hearing—data from lower court hearings immediately pre- and post-nuclear option generally suggest little change in how senators use these hearings, with some limited support for the idea that senators engage nominees *less* at these hearings (See appendix table A8.1). Overall, the results point to relatively minor changes in senator participation at the hearings post-nuclear option, leaving us with little reason to think the general patterns uncovered in this book have fundamentally changed in recent years.

More recent anecdotal evidence, however, may point to an erosion of hearing norms subsequent to the change in the filibuster rule. For example, on February 26, 2019, on a party-line vote, the Senate confirmed Trump nominee Eric Miller to the Ninth Circuit. This confirmation proceeded without a blue slip from either of the nominee's home-state senators (Carney 2019). This particular example also skirted the norms of the hearing process itself. Democrats were furious that the hearing was held during recess and, in contrast with Senate norms, not a single member of the opposition party was in attendance. Also rare was that members of Congress made a public issue of the hearing process. Sen. Patty Murray, one of the home-state senators, in a floor speech, said that this process is "a dangerous road for the Senate to go down. The hearing included less than five minutes of questioning—less questioning for a lifetime appointment than most students face for a book report in school" (Mascaro and Johnson 2019). While it is impossible to know if this incident was caused by the elimination of the filibuster in this situation—or even to know if this anecdote portends a pattern—it does point to the possibility that in times of unified government, we may witness the majority party blatantly treating the hearings as pro forma, as they did in this case, but also observe the minority party drawing indignant attention to that fact. In this case, then, we may see a newly salient role for lower court confirmation hearings, though a longer-term, systematic investigation of these post-nuclear-option hearings would be necessary before we draw too many conclusions.

In sum, then, in considering attempts to streamline the advice and consent process—by restricting the use of the filibuster or reducing or eliminating hearings, for example—these changes can only work if the restrictions are set high enough to prevent unnecessary obstruction. In setting that bar, however, those hearings necessary for controversial nominees may also be swept into the net. In all likelihood, Judiciary Committee members and other senators will not simply let these nominees through without a fight, thus moving the contention and controversy over these nominees out of the public eye and into less transparent venues. While these changes do not seem to have manifested immediately in the hearings in response to changes around the filibuster rules, it may simply be a matter of time before committee members adjust their behaviors to this new reality.

Concluding Thoughts

While a central contention of this book is that most lower court confirmation hearings provide policy and electoral benefits for senators, it is in fact vital not to underestimate these hearings as symbols of key components of democracy, in particular, transparency, accountability, and checks and balances among the branches. It is possible that most citizens would not lament, or even notice, moving the occasional controversy over lower court nominees out of the public eye. But the fact that the public rarely asserts itself in this particular process may be beside the point. Maintaining this accessible and public venue for discussion of nominees to lifetime seats on the federal bench facilitates the fundamental goal of having transparent, accountable institutions within government that hold each other in check.

Perhaps even more importantly, however, these hearings habituate Judiciary Committee members to these transparent practices. Supreme Court confirmation hearings are important and salient, but rare. Perhaps these less salient but frequent lower court confirmation hearings keep committee members in shape for these interbranch dialogues and frequently remind the committee members of the normative importance of this dialogue. The burden of proof, in this circumstance, rests with those advocating for change.

Moreover, the electoral and policy benefits provided to Judiciary Committee members, and senators more broadly, by these confirmation hearings suggest that senators would be reluctant to impose any significant changes to them. The committee members find them to be venues for pursuing electoral and policy goals, as these hearings are a stage to score points with interest groups when grilling controversial nominees, a rare public opportunity to share their policy views and perspective on the proper role of the judiciary, and an opportunity to gather policy information from future judges. For non-committee members, the chance to claim credit for the nomination of quality individuals provides an electoral benefit with little cost to the home-state senator. Because of these factors, it appears that the lower court confirmation hearing as we know it is here to stay.

APPENDIX

To explore whether the invocation of the nuclear option altered patterns of senator participation in confirmation hearings, we collected hearing transcripts for district and circuit court nominees for the 113th Congress (January 2013—January 2015). Of the 119 district and circuit court nomination hearings during this period, 54 occurred in the pre-nuclear-option period and 65 after the nuclear option was invoked, while maintaining continuity in the nominating president and party makeup of the Senate. Using multiple measures of participation—including the number of questions the nominee fields, the natural log of this value, and how many senators attended the hearing—the results generally suggest little change in how senators use these hearings, with some limited support for the hypothesis that senators engage nominees *less* at these hearings (Dancey, Nelson, Ringsmuth, and Solomon 2018). (See table A8.1.) In general, the results point to relatively minor changes in senator participation at the hearings after the nuclear option, leaving us with little reason to think the general patterns uncovered in this book have fundamentally changed in recent years.

TABLE A8.1. Average Senatorial Participation in Confirmation Hearings Pre- and Post-Nuclear Option—113th Congress (2013–14)

	District Court Nominees			**Circuit Court Nominees**		
Participation Measure	Pre-Nuclear	Post-Nuclear	*p*-value	Pre-Nuclear	Post-Nuclear	*p*-value
Total Questions	5.8	5.6	0.94	20.2	9.8	0.10
Democratic Questions	2.7	3.6	0.58	7.2	4.3	0.19
Republican Questions	3.2	2.0	0.07	13.0	5.5	0.15
Questions Logged	**1.6**	**1.2**	**0.04**	**2.8**	**2.2**	**0.04**
Senators Attending	2.2	1.9	0.44	3.6	2.5	0.26
N	40	59		13	6	

Note: p-values are from difference of mean t-tests. Bold indicates $p < 0.05$.

Appendix A

Interviews with Senators, Judiciary Committee Staffers, Senate Staffers, and Interest Group Staff

We conducted a series of interviews during February through June of 2016 with 14 individuals who currently or previously worked on some aspect of the judicial confirmation process. The interviewees included 9 current or former Senate staffers who either worked for the Judiciary Committee or worked for a senator on the committee (6 Democrats and 3 Republicans). One of the former Judiciary Committee staffers later worked on judicial confirmations for the Democratic leadership in the Senate. We also interviewed 3 staffers who handled judicial confirmations for senators not on the committee (1 Democrat and 2 Republicans). In addition to congressional staff, we interviewed one former and one current staff member for liberal advocacy groups that occasionally take positions on judicial nominees.

Finally, we interviewed two former senators who served on the Judiciary Committee and have substantial experience with the judicial confirmation process: Jon Kyl (R-AZ) and Ted Kaufman (D-DE). Senator Kyl served in the Senate from 1994 to 2012 and spent all 18 years on the Judiciary Committee. He also served in Republican Party leadership in the Senate from 2003 to 2012 as Republican Policy Committee chair (2003–7), conference chair (2007) and Republican Party whip (2007–12).

Senator Kaufman was appointed to fill the seat vacated by Sen. Joe Biden when Biden assumed the office of vice president in 2009. Kaufman represented Delaware in the Senate, and on the Judiciary Committee, from

2009 to 2010. He did not seek re-election in 2010. Along with his two years as senator from Delaware, Kaufman served on Senator Biden's staff from 1973 to 1995, including 19 years as Biden's chief of staff (1976–95). During that time, Biden served as both ranking member (1981–87) and chair (1987–95) of the Judiciary Committee.

We conducted the interviews using a semistructured format. Our conversations with participants covered a range of topics related to the judicial confirmation process, and the standard questions posed to staffers, interest group staffers, and senators covered three broad topics: (1) The role of confirmation hearings; (2) the factors that shape which senators attend and how a nominee is scrutinized; and (3) the relationship between nominee controversy and what takes place during the hearings. The interviews ran from roughly 30 minutes to 2 hours, with the two senator interviews lasting approximately 45 minutes each. The interviews were not recorded, with the exception of the two senator interviews.

Appendix B

Intercoder Reliability

To test the reliability of our coding scheme, an undergraduate coder independently coded a sample of transcripts. The coder began by coding a training set of 30 transcripts and worked with one of the authors to learn the coding system. The coder then coded a stratified random sample of 10 percent of noncontroversial nominee transcripts from each of the 10 Congresses (totaling 80 district court and 22 noncontroversial circuit court nominees). We focus on noncontroversial nominees for the purpose of intercoder reliability (ICR) tests since the majority of the analyses in the book focus exclusively on these nominees. Chapter 7 provides a more in-depth discussion of hearings for controversial nominees and how these hearings differ from hearings for noncontroversial nominees.

In general, there is some variation in intercoder reliability scores across categories and levels of analysis. Certain categories have low intercoder reliability levels due either to their catch-all nature (e.g., other) or low frequency (e.g., health). These categories are never analyzed separately in the book, however. Instead, our focus is mostly on the total number of questions asked, questions in the broader categories of *Issues*, *Qualifications*, or *Judicial Decision Making*, and the categories of rights for disadvantaged groups, privacy/abortion, crime/death penalty, and judicial philosophy. For these variables, we see strong correlations between our measures and the measures from the undergraduate coder as well as kappas that exceed 0.7 (and in many cases 0.8), with the few exceptions noted in the text below.

ICR for Individual Categories

The 102 transcripts coded by the undergraduate coder contained a total of 845 questions originally coded by the authors.[1] The intercoder reliability kappa statistic using all 25 categories at the question level was 0.64, with 67 percent agreement compared to 10 percent agreement expected by chance. There is no universally accepted "ideal" kappa score, although the literature variously characterizes kappa scores of 0.60 as evidence of "moderate" or "substantial" agreement (Viera and Garrett 2005; McHugh 2012). The kappas are higher at the question level for many of our individual categories. In total, out of 25 categories, 5 exceed a kappa of 0.8, 12 exceed 0.7, and 17 exceed 0.6. Table B.1 shows the full kappa scores for all categories.

TABLE B1. Intercoder Reliability for Individual Categories

877 questions coded by undergraduate compared to authors' codes

Category	Agreement (%)	Chance (%)	Kappa
Privacy/Abortion	100	98.9	1.00
Death Penalty	99.2	89.2	0.93
Domestic Commerce	99.7	97.2	0.88
Precedent	98.2	84.7	0.88
Group Affiliation	99.3	96.4	0.81
Disadvantaged Groups	98.6	93.4	0.79
Crime/Death Penalty[a]	93.4	71.5	0.77
Labor	99.7	98.5	0.77
Docket	98.5	93.9	0.76
Civil Rights Other	99.2	97.0	0.74
Judicial Philosophy	92.5	71.8	0.73
Conflict of Interest	99.2	97.2	0.72
Criminal Justice	93.7	79.7	0.69
Experience	90.0	71.0	0.66
Objectivity	97.2	92.2	0.63
Justiciability	98.9	97.1	0.61
Terrorism	99.4	98.5	0.61
Reversal Rate	99.8	99.5	0.50
Judicial Temperament	96.4	93.2	0.47
Other	91.0	84.7	0.41
Other Issue	98.4	98.2	0.12
Ethics	96.8	96.8	0
LGBT Rights	99.7	99.7	0
ABA Rating	99.4	99.4	0
Health	n/a	n/a	n/a
Environment	n/a	n/a	n/a
Indian Affairs	n/a	n/a	n/a

[a] This is the kappa statistic for the combined criminal justice/death penalty category that is used throughout the book. Separate kappas are also included for the individual criminal justice and death penalty categories.

Even though the analyses in the book tend not to use individual categories separately, we provide full kappa scores for the purposes of transparency and in case future researchers are interested in using any individual categories. Three categories—health, environment, and Indian affairs—did not appear in the intercoder reliability sample and therefore have "n/a" listed for their kappa scores. In addition, three categories—ethics, LGBT rights, and ABA rating—have kappas of 0, which reflects the fact that the authors and undergraduate coder did not agree on any of the questions that fell into these categories. The LGBT rights category is rarely mentioned, with the undergraduate coder identifying three questions and the authors identifying zero in the sample. The category list for the undergraduate coder mistakenly left out ABA rating, and the undergraduate coder put the five questions in this category into the experience category. In the analyses in the book, ABA rating and experience questions are combined into a broader *Qualifications* category (examined below), making this particular disagreement inconsequential for our analyses. The low kappa score for ethics questions is explained in more detail later in the appendix. Notably, none of the categories with n/a or 0 listed for their kappa scores are analyzed individually in the book.

For the most part, our analyses in the book do not rely on individual categories. The exception is figures 5.6 and 5.7, where we model whether or not a nominee received a question in one of four categories: rights for disadvantaged groups, privacy/abortion, criminal justice/death penalty, and judicial philosophy. All four of these categories have kappas of 0.73 or higher. The kappas are generally higher when we aggregate to the nominee level (i.e., did a nominee receive a question in a given category based on either the authors' or undergraduate coder's codes?). At the nominee level, the kappas are 0.83 for the disadvantaged groups category, 1.00 for the privacy/abortion category, 0.84 for the criminal justice/death penalty category, and 0.78 for judicial philosophy. Kappas exceeding 0.8 are typically considered evidence of strong agreement (see, e.g., Lombard, Snyder-Duch, and Bracken 2002; Viera and Garrett 2005; McHugh 2012).

ICR for Aggregated Categories

Most frequently in the book we explore total questions asked to nominees and the total number of questions that fall into three larger catego-

TABLE B2. Intercoder Reliability for Aggregated Categories

877 questions coded by undergraduate compared to authors' codes

Category	Agreement (%)	Chance (%)	Kappa
Judicial Decision Making	91.0	54.8	0.80
Issues	90.1	60.8	0.75
Qualifications	88.9	64.5	0.69
Ethics	96.7	94.1	0.44

ries: *Qualifications*, *Issues*, and *Judicial Decision Making and Philosophy*. At the question level, the kappas for whether a question is coded into one of three categories ranges from 0.69 for *Qualifications* questions to 0.80 for *Judicial Decision Making* questions (see table B2). *Ethics* questions have a much lower kappa score (0.44), but *Ethics* questions are not analyzed in detail in the book.

The lower kappa scores for the *Qualifications* and *Ethics* questions are mostly a function of one transcript (Terry Wooten), which contained 20 questions that the authors coded as *Ethics* and the undergraduate coder coded as *Qualifications*. These questions related to Wooten's time as a Senate Judiciary Committee staffer during the Clarence Thomas confirmation hearing and accusations that Wooten leaked classified information during that time (Savage 2001). Given the focus on the leaking of classified information, the authors view the *Ethics* codes as more appropriate. If questions for this nominee are excluded, the kappa for the *Qualifications* category increases to 0.74 and the kappa for the *Ethics* category increases to 0.72.

At the nominee level, we find a correlation of 0.994 between our measure of total questions asked of a nominee and the undergraduate's measure. Slight differences in the number of questions asked are attributable to differences in interpretation of whether a short aside by a senator qualifies as a question, or, more infrequently, a question missed by either the authors or by the undergraduate. Overall, we see nearly universal agreement on what was coded as a question.

Turning to total questions in the three broad categories explored in the book, the correlation between the number of questions we coded in each category and the number that the undergraduate coded in each category is 0.97 for *Issues*, 0.91 for *Judicial Decision Making and Philosophy*, and 0.76 for *Qualifications*. The correlation for the *Qualifications* category increases to 0.89 if the previously mentioned Wooten hearing is excluded.

Notes

CHAPTER 1

1. We refer to the interviews and comments made in them throughout the book. References to comments made by staffers, Senator Kyl, or Senator Kaufman are from the interviews we conducted unless otherwise noted.

CHAPTER 2

1. The U.S. Court of International Trade is also an Article III trial court with limited subject-matter jurisdiction but whose judges have lifetime appointments. Additionally, courts such as the U.S. Tax Court and U.S. Court of Appeals for Veterans' Claims draw their authority from Article I, and their judges hold office for a limited period of time. In the book, we focus on district and circuit court nominees.

2. Additionally, circuit courts may review cases from the Tax Court, and orders from some federal administrative agencies may bypass the district courts and be appealed straight to a circuit court (Baum 2013).

3. On rare occasions, at the discretion of the Judiciary Committee chair, someone other than the nominee (e.g., the American Bar Association) may be invited or allowed to testify. See Steigerwalt (2010, 27 note 5).

4. If a majority of the Judiciary Committee votes against a nomination, the committee may subsequently choose to vote to forward the nomination with the committee's negative recommendation or without a recommendation, allowing the full Senate to make the final determination about the fate of the nomination (Steigerwalt 2010, 27 note 6).

5. In the final chapter we discuss changes to the cloture threshold for lower court nominees in 2013.

6. See Steigerwalt (2010, 27 note 7).

7. The Senate is typically thought of as less specialized than the House (Fenno 1973), although that fact does not preclude specialization in the Senate.

8. Steigerwalt (2010) argues that a home-state senator's objection to a nomination is often not related to the nominee specifically, but rather is a response to institutional disputes or retaliation for the treatment of a previous nominee.

9. The Judiciary Committee chair has proceeded with a hearing despite the objections of home-state senators (see Binder and Maltzman 2009, 55 note 104; Steigerwalt 2010, 36 note 18).

10. The only exceptions to this rule were when a sitting senator, a former president (Sollenberger 2011, 105), an attorney general, or a secretary of war was nominated (Collins and Ringhand 2013, note 94). In these cases, referrals were not made and the Senate considered the nominations without going through the Judiciary Committee.

11. In the rare instance where a nominee was nominated for the same position by two presidents, we treat each president's nomination separately.

12. Throughout the book, all noted *p*-values are two-tailed, unless otherwise indicated.

13. Senate watchers often attribute this slowdown in hearings—and ultimately confirmations—to the Thurmond/Leahy Rule, which holds that the Senate should not consider judicial confirmations in the months preceding an election (Wheeler 2012). There is debate over whether this rule actually exists. It is unwritten and, therefore, not legally binding (Victor 2016). Due to its informality, it is impossible to say how close to elections the Thurmond/Leahy Rule should apply (Victor 2016). Perhaps unsurprisingly, opinions as to its usefulness and status as an institution tend to vary based on the party of the president and the party in power in the Senate.

14. More detailed descriptions of these variables and the sources of these data can be found in chapter 4. We also note that we ran both models for circuit court nominees with an additional variable controlling for interest group opposition. This variable is not statistically significant in either model, and including this variable does not alter the substantive findings of the other variables. Note: Two nominees are excluded from the analyses in table A2.1 since the ABA either did not list a rating in its report or because the nominee withdrew before the ABA provided a rating.

15. For conflicting accounts of the relationship between ABA ratings and confirmation see, e.g., Martinek, Kemper, and Van Winkle (2002); Stratmann and Garner (2004); Lott (2005); Scherer, Bartels, and Steigerwalt (2008); Binder and Maltzman (2009).

16. This was also noted in our interviews with staffers.

17. Data is from the CQ Press Electronic Library, CQ Press Congress Collection.

18. We use two-party presidential vote share from the CQ Press Election Library, CQ Press Congress Collection. For a list of senators in each Congress we rely on data from https://voteview.com (Lewis et al. 2019), and for committee assignment data we use Stewart and Woon (2017). Data also collected from the Biographical Directory of the United States Congress.

19. The pattern of relatively few senators who represent states where the other party's presidential candidate won is largely consistent from the 107th through the 112th Congresses.

20. Data from Vital Statistics on Congress, Table 8-8 (Brookings 2017). Downloaded June 2018.

21. All four senators served on the committee in the 115th Congress (2017–18). According to voteview.com, Lee and Cruz were the first and fourth most conserva-

tive senators in the 115th Congress, and Harris and Booker were the second and third most liberal senators.

22. These senators are Maria Cantwell (D-WA), Dianne Feinstein (D-CA), Amy Klobuchar (D-MN), and Carol Moseley-Braun (D-IL).

CHAPTER 3

1. We refer those interested in the determinants of interest group opposition to Scherer (2003, 2005) and Steigerwalt (2010). Their analyses indicate that the decision to oppose is based on nominee-specific factors (e.g., ideology and the presence of a detailed record), nomination-based factors (e.g., ideological balance of the circuit), interest group factors (e.g., single issue vs. broad interest groups), senator-based factors (e.g., support from home-state senators), and factors related to the political environment (e.g., presidential involvement in defending nomination). While we cannot capture many of these factors, we explored what characteristics distinguish nominees opposed by interest groups by running a logistic regression that predicts interest group opposition using the nominee-level and contextual factors examined in subsequent chapters (see chapter 4 for descriptions of these variables). This exploratory analysis includes all circuit nominees who received a confirmation hearing. The results reported in table A3.1 indicate that nominees who have a home-state senator from the president's opposition party are less likely to be opposed by interest groups, as are those nominated by Clinton compared to Bush. No other independent variable is statistically significant in this model.

2. We do find that the timing of documented interest group opposition is related to the amount of scrutiny nominees receive. Nominees for whom there is documented interest group opposition before the hearing face an average of 101 questions (median = 77) compared to an average of 46 questions (median = 26.5) for those where documented opposition occurred after the hearing. We see similar trends when we examine the number of senators attending the hearing. These differences provide suggestive evidence that the timing of interest group opposition matters for the level of senator engagement in hearings. This is the finding we would expect if interest group opposition incentivized greater senator participation at the hearing—presumably due to the greater perceived electoral payoff of position taking—and the measure of timing used here was a reliable indicator of when senators learned about interest group opposition. Although the observed differences give us increased confidence in the timing variable, there is ultimately no reliable way to ascertain when senators learned about interest group opposition. Given the evidence from interviews that senators tended to learn about opposition early in the process and that the measure does not capture the potential for informal signals of interest group opposition, we choose to treat the opposition variable as a dichotomous measure of opposition or not and assume senators learned about opposition before the hearing. To the extent that some nominees became controversial after their hearing, including them with the set of controversial nominees would likely lead us to underestimate the effect of prehearing controversy on levels of senator engagement at the hearing. At relevant sections in the book we make note of how the results do or do not change if nominees with documented interest group opposition after the hearing are treated differently.

3. Note that the type of participation examined in this section (asking at least one question) is reserved for members of the Judiciary Committee, which typically numbers between 18 and 20 senators per Congress.

4. See appendix B for information about intercoder reliability.

5. More specifically, 82 percent of all circuit court nominees and 56 percent of district court nominees received at least one judicial philosophy question.

6. The other issues category includes any questions about an issue-based policy or case that does not fit into the other substantive issue categories.

7. We do not examine the *Ethics* category in depth here since only 9 percent of district and 18 percent of all circuit court nominees are asked at least one *Ethics* question. Additionally, while the *Other* category occurs relatively more frequently, we lack theoretical expectations about its variation over time since it is a catch-all category for questions that do not directly fit into the other 24 categories.

8. The hearings in the 107th Congress (2001–02) all occurred after Sen. Jim Jeffords (I-VT) left the Republican Party and began caucusing with the Democrats, which gave Democrats control of the Senate. Additionally, no hearings occurred in 2002 after Republicans regained majority control in the Senate in November.

9. We consider a unique senator mention to happen the first time a specific senator mentions a case at a hearing, making the unit of analysis the senator-hearing. The most mentioned case during this time span was *Roe v. Wade*, which was mentioned in 49 nominees' hearings. *Roe* is, of course, a highly politicized case with significant electoral value. Since it is difficult to parse electoral and policy goals, we chose the next two commonly mentioned cases, which allows us to examine how senators treat questioning in the absence of overbearing electoral incentives.

CHAPTER 4

1. See http://www.americanbar.org/groups/committees/federal_judiciary/about_us.html

2. There is no uniform way of measuring ABA ratings in the literature. Binder and Maltzman (2002) use a three-category variable for ABA ratings (dummy variables for unanimously "well-qualified" nominees and a dummy variable for "qualified" nominees), while in later work they use a dummy variable to distinguish unanimously "well-qualified" nominees from all other nominees (see Primo, Binder, and Maltzman 2008; Binder and Maltzman 2009). Many researchers also treat the ABA ratings as a continuous variable ranging from 1 to 6 (e.g., Scherer, Bartels, and Steigerwalt 2008; Black, Madonna, and Owens 2014). Although we have tried the models with different versions of the ABA rating (including the 1–6 scale and a dummy variable only for "well-qualified" nominees), we find that to the extent there are differences based on ABA ratings it tends to be differences between the lowest-rated nominees (i.e., nominees who received at least a minority rating of "not qualified") and all other nominees. The three-category rating system best captures this dynamic.

3. To create the independent variables used in the analyses throughout the book we relied upon a variety of sources, including the Lower Federal Court Confirma-

tion Database (https://www.binghamton.edu/cdp/lfccd.html), created by Wendy L. Martinek on behalf of the Constitution Project's Courts Initiative, the Department of Justice website (https://www.justice.gov/archive/olp/nominations.htm), the Yale Law School Judicial Nominations website (http://judges.law.yale.edu), and the Federal Judicial Center website (https://www.fjc.gov/history/judges), as well as those noted explicitly in the text.

4. For the number of questions model, there is one observation for each circuit nominee. Since we are interested in the total scrutiny a nominee receives, the questions from both hearings are combined for nominees who received two hearings. There are a few two-hearing cases where contextual variables differ from one hearing to the next. In the case of opposition party senator, presidential election year, and divided government, we used the value from the nominee's first hearing. In the case of circuit balance, when a nominee with two hearings had two different values, we used the smaller of the two values.

Alternatively, the unit of analysis in the number of senators attending model is the nominee-hearing. Since senators have more than one opportunity to participate in a hearing for those with two hearings, we model the two hearings separately. This results in a different number of observations for the models predicting attendance and the models predicting total questions asked.

5. The assumption that the conditional mean equals the conditional variance is met for this model, which means a negative binomial regression reduces to a Poisson (Long 1997). For district court hearings, we cluster the standard errors by hearing date since most district court hearings involve more than one nominee. Given that the hearings involve more than one nominee, senators sometimes pose the same question to all nominees, but often individually question the nominees as well. Most hearings have only one circuit court nominee (either alone or with district court nominees), so we do not cluster by hearing date for circuit court nominees.

6. The conditional variance exceeds the conditional mean in this model, making a negative binomial regression appropriate. Predicted counts for district and circuit court nominees are calculated based on a nomination made by President Bush using median or modal values on all other variables.

7. These nominations all correspond to Article III positions, which come with a lifetime appointment. Specifically, we include nominees to the numbered circuits of the U.S. Courts of Appeals, the Court of Appeals for the District of Columbia Circuit, and the Court of Appeals for the Federal Circuit.

8. When we run the model without two outliers (Kavanaugh and Owen), the predicted number of questions changes slightly to 12.8 for noncontroversial nominees and 67.9 for controversial nominees ($p < 0.01$). Consistent with note 2 in chapter 3, if we include separate indicator variables for nominees opposed before and after the hearing (based on documented timing of opposition), we find that nominees opposed before the hearing receive more questions and have more senators at their hearings.

9. This interactive effect holds for both nominees opposed before and after the hearings based on our timing variable.

CHAPTER 5

1. A full list of the categories and their groupings can be found in table 3.1 (see chapter 3).

2. Though the geographic jurisdiction of circuit courts often includes multiple states, seats within a circuit are generally considered to be reserved for each of the states within the circuit. Given this designation, home-state senators are typically consulted by the administration regarding nominee selection. These senators' positions on the nominee carry weight during the confirmation process, though senators' influence is likely reduced on circuit court nominations compared to that of district court nominations (Binder and Maltzman 2009).

3. Since we are interested in the types of questions senators pose to nominees, in the relatively rare cases where a nominee receives two hearings, the questions from both hearings are combined.

4. Predicted probabilities are calculated from the models in figure 5.1 for a nominee with a middle rating from the ABA, no previous judicial experience, an opposition party senator, not from D.C. or Puerto Rico, nominated by Bill Clinton during a year in which there was no presidential election, and who faced five total questions at her hearing. These values correspond to the median or modal values in these categories.

5. The "Thurmond Rule," which has been claimed as an informal procedure by both parties, indicates that nominations should be halted the last several months prior to a presidential election (see Binder and Maltzman 2009, 87–89). Such a practice then suggests that only the least controversial nominees would be allowed to proceed during this time, perhaps to mollify objections that the Senate majority party is blocking all nominations.

6. The dependent variable here only includes judicial philosophy questions as laid out in the first row of table 3.1, in other words, questions that relate to the nominee's interpretive methods, role of judges, or separation of powers. This is in contrast to the broader *Judicial Philosophy and Decision Making* category we use earlier in the chapter. We chose this narrower category here because it most closely parallels the way judicial philosophy is discussed in Boyd, Collins, and Ringhand (2018), and it is more comparable to the other three more focused issue-specific variables in this section.

7. More specifically, ABA rating is now a dummy variable (1 = unanimously "well-qualified" rating; 0 = otherwise). Additionally, we have excluded the presidential election year and the D.C. Circuit variable, and we now compare Bush nominees with both Clinton and Obama nominees together.

8. While we also find a statistically significant coefficient that suggests those with prior judicial experience are more likely to be asked at least one question about rights for disadvantaged groups, the difference in predicted probabilities for those with judicial experience compared to those without is not itself statistically significant. Additionally, we have no strong theoretical basis to support this empirical result and we do not see a pattern that those with judicial experience are more likely to be scrutinized on either of the other two issues or in any of the earlier models, including the models of senatorial participation and the models of the number of questions asked in the broader categories.

9. While the coefficient in the privacy/abortion model is positive and statisti-

cally significant, the difference in the predicted probability is not statistically significant. The coefficient in the judicial philosophy model is not statistically significant.

10. Figure 5.7 also shows that senators are more likely to ask at least one criminal justice/death penalty question of Obama and Clinton nominees compared to Bush nominees. While this fits with earlier work arguing that conservative interest groups and party elites are particularly interested in this issue, which provides an incentive for Republican senators to raise these issues with Democratic nominees (Scherer 2005), the difference in predicted probabilities is not statistically significant.

11. There were a small number of repeat questions when a circuit court nominee and district court nominee shared a panel on the same day.

CHAPTER 6

1. The dataset is archived at https://github.com/lintool/GrimmerSenatePress Releases

2. Since there are two senators per state, each nominee equals two opportunities for a senator to participate. Because our focus is on home-state nominees here, we exclude the hearings for nominees from Puerto Rico, the District of Columbia, and the Federal Circuits.

3. Senators were more likely to provide introductory remarks at circuit court hearings than at district court hearings (93 percent of the time compared to 66 percent of the time). The difference in senator participation between the two types of hearings is statistically significant at $p < 0.01$. When looking at senator participation in any form, whether through introductory remarks, submissions for the *Record*, or participation in the question-and-answer portion of the hearing, home-state senators participate in circuit court hearings 93 percent of the time compared to 80 percent of the time at district court hearings ($p = 0.10$).

4. The list of contenders for president comes from the *New York Times*: https://www.nytimes.com/elections/2008/primaries/candidates/. The *New York Times* list also includes Evan Bayh, but Bayh had ended his bid for president in December 2006 (http://www.nytimes.com/2006/12/17/us/politics/17bayh.html) and Southwick's confirmation vote did not occur until late 2007. Sam Brownback dropped out in October 2007, which is shortly before the Southwick vote. Brownback, however, was a presidential candidate during debate over Southwick; therefore, despite ultimately dropping out of the race, he is included as a senator seeking his party's nomination for president.

5. The coefficient for presidential candidates remains positive and statistically significant at $p < 0.05$ if Sam Brownback is coded as not being a presidential candidate (see note 4).

6. We again use the presence of interest group opposition to capture controversy (see Scherer, Bartels, and Steigerwalt 2008; Steigerwalt 2010). See chapter 3 for details on this measure.

7. Beck (2018) offers an alternative method of estimating marginal effects using a constrained fixed effects model, although Monte Carlo simulations suggest that the difference between OLS and the constrained fixed effects logit models is minimal when the number of groups and observations per group is relatively large,

as it is in our case. We therefore adopt the fixed effects linear probability model. There are some changes in the statistical significance levels of the coefficients in a conditional fixed-effects logistic regression model. The most notable difference is that the interaction between chair/ranking member status and controversial circuit court nominees is not statistically significant in the conditional logit model (or in a random effects logit model). The interaction between presidential opposition and controversial circuit nominees is significant across all three specifications.

8. It is possible that the chair of the hearing does not ask a question while the ranking member does, which would mean that only the ranking member participated by our measure. This is a very rare occurrence in our dataset, however.

9. We coded senators as up for re-election when they were scheduled to run for re-election regardless of whether they actually ran that year or chose to retire. For Ted Kaufman, who was appointed in 2009 and did not run for the seat in 2010, we did not code him as up for re-election in 2010. We have replicated the models with a separate indicator for those senators who chose not to seek re-election, and the substantive effects of the re-election variable remain unchanged.

10. The results are substantively similar if we exclude from this model nominees whose documented interest group opposition occurred after the hearing.

CHAPTER 7

1. Press release archived at: http://freedomworks.org/content/groups-support-texas-supreme-court-priscilla-owen-nomination-fifth-circuit

2. Press release archived at: http://earthjustice.org/news/press/2003/senate-will-continue-debate-on-anti-environmental-judicial-nominee-owen

3. The extent of this vetting by interest groups is discussed in more detail in chapters 3 and 6.

4. See Scherer (2003, 2005) and Steigerwalt (2010) for more on the determinants of interest group opposition. We explored the characteristics that distinguish nominees opposed by interest groups within our data by running a logistic regression that predicts interest group opposition using the nominee-level and contextual factors examined throughout the book (see chapter 4 for descriptions of these variables). The results are reported in table A3.1 and discussed in note 1 of chapter 3.

5. A full list of the categories and their groupings can be found in table 3.1 (see chapter 3).

6. Three coders coded a subsample of identical questions to verify the intercoder reliability of this measure. Krippendorff's alpha was 0.73, which indicates a satisfactory level of agreement among the coders.

7. Unlike the other controversial nominees in this chapter, we could only find documented interest group opposition to Chatigny after his hearing.

8. This includes Clinton nominees Berzon, Paez, and Fletcher; Bush nominees Pickering, Sutton, and Myers; and Obama nominees Halligan, Hamilton, and Six.

CHAPTER 8

1. It is worth noting that there was not unanimous agreement on this point among the staffers we interviewed, with at least one suggesting that eliminating the hearings would likely not decrease the quality of the nominees.

2. Eighteen states currently have commissions, though there is variation in whether they have been explicitly created as bipartisan. Further, some additional states have similar, though less formal, mechanisms to make recommendations (National Center for State Courts 2018).

APPENDIX B

1. As discussed later, there were a few instances of disagreement between the authors and undergraduate coder regarding what qualified as a question. In total, there were 877 questions coded by the authors, undergraduate coder, or both.

References

Abramowitz, Alan I. 2012. "U.S. Senate Elections in a Polarized Era." In *The U.S. Senate: From Deliberation to Dysfunction*, edited by Burdett Loomis. Washington, DC: CQ Press.

Abramowitz, Alan I., and Steven Webster. 2016. "The Rise of Negative Partisanship and the Nationalization of U.S. Elections in the 21st Century." *Electoral Studies* 41: 12–22.

Abramson, Alana. 2017. "Republicans Just Used the 'Nuclear Option' to Confirm Neil Gorsuch. What's That?" *Time*, April 4. http://time.com/4723610/neil-gorsuch-supreme-court-nuclear-option-filibuster/

Abramson, Paul R., John H. Aldrich, and David W. Rohde. 1987. "Progressive Ambition Among United States Senators: 1972–1998." *Journal of Politics* 49 (1): 3–35.

Adler, E. Scott, and John D. Wilkerson. 2013. *Congress and the Politics of Problem Solving*. New York: Cambridge University Press.

Administrative Office of the Federal Courts. 2018a. "United States Courts of Appeals—Judicial Caseload Profile." Federal Court Management Statistics.

Administrative Office of the Federal Courts. 2018b. "United States District Courts—National Judicial Caseload Profile." Federal Court Management Statistics.

Ahmed, Saeed. 2006. "Senate OKs Batten for Federal Judgeship." *Atlanta Journal Constitution*, March 7. Retrieved from https://advance.lexis.com/api/document?collection=news&id=urn:contentItem:4JDT-NYN0-TX2J-42H0-00000-00&context=1516831

Asher, Herbert. 1974. "Committees and the Norm of Specialization." *The Annals of the American Academy of Political and Social Science* 411: 63–74.

Asmussen, Nicole. 2011. "Female and Minority Judicial Nominees: President's Delight and Senators' Dismay?" *Legislative Studies Quarterly* 36 (4): 591–619.

Barone, Michael. 2013. *Almanac of American Politics 2014*. Chicago: University of Chicago Press.

Barrett, Paul, and David Ingold. 2017. "One of the Biggest Reasons Republicans Stick by Trump." *Bloomberg*, July 10. https://www.bloomberg.com/news/features/2017-07-10/trump-begins-the-rightward-shift-of-america-s-courts

Bartels, Larry M. 2000. "Partisanship and Voting Behavior, 1952–1996." *American Journal of Political Science* 44 (1): 35–50.

Baum, Lawrence. 2013. *American Courts: Process and Policy*. Boston: Wadsworth, Cengage Learning.

Beck, Nathaniel. 2018. "Estimating Grouped Data Models with a Binary Dependent Variable and Fixed Effects: What Are the Issues?" At arxiv.org/abs/1809.06505. Accessed May 22, 2019.

Bell, Lauren Cohen. 2002a. "Senatorial Discourtesy: The Senate's Use of Delay to Shape the Federal Judiciary." *Political Research Quarterly* 55 (3): 589–607.

Bell, Lauren Cohen. 2002b. *Warring Factions: Interest Groups, Money, and the New Politics of Senate Confirmation*. Columbus: Ohio State University Press.

Berman, Russell. 2017. "How Democrats Paved the Way for the Confirmation of Trump's Cabinet." *The Atlantic*, January 20. https://www.theatlantic.com/politics/archive/2017/01/democrats-trump-cabinet-senate/513782/

Bernhard, William, and Tracy Sulkin. 2018. *Legislative Style*. Chicago: University of Chicago Press.

Berry, Jeffrey. 1997. *The Interest Group Society*. 3rd ed. New York: Longman.

Berry, William D., Matt Golder, and Daniel Milton. 2012. "Improving Tests of Theories Positing Interaction." *Journal of Politics* 74 (3): 653–71.

Binder, Sarah A. 2007. "Where Do Institutions Come From? Exploring the Origins of the Senate Blue Slip." *Studies in American Political Development* 21 (1): 1–15.

Binder, Sarah A., and Forrest Maltzman. 2002. "Senatorial Delay in Confirming Federal Judges, 1947–98." *American Journal of Political Science* 46: 190–99.

Binder, Sarah A., and Forrest Maltzman. 2009. *Advice & Dissent: The Struggle to Shape the Federal Judiciary*. Washington, DC: Brookings Institution Press.

Binder, Sarah A., and Steven S. Smith. 2001. *Politics or Principle? Filibustering in the United States Senate*. Washington, DC: Brookings Institution Press.

Binder, Sarah A., and Russell Wheeler. 2011. "Do Judicial Emergencies Matter? Nomination and Confirmation Delay during the 111th Congress." Brookings Institution (February 16).

Black, Ryan C., Anthony J. Madonna, and Ryan J. Owens. 2014. "Qualifications or Philosophy? The Use of Blue Slips in a Polarized Era." *Presidential Studies Quarterly* 44: 290–308.

Blake, Aaron. 2017. "That Painful Exchange between a Trump Judicial Pick and a GOP Senator, Annotated." *Washington Post*, December 15. https://www.washingtonpost.com/news/the-fix/wp/2017/12/15/that-painful-exchange-between-a-trump-judicial-pick-and-a-gop-senator-annotated/?utm_term=.248a2ee62f9d

Boyd, Christina L., Paul M. Collins Jr., and Lori A. Ringhand. 2018. "The Role of Nominee Gender and Race at Supreme Court Confirmation Hearings." *Law & Society Review* 52 (4): 871–901.

Boyd, Christina L., Lee Epstein, and Andrew D. Martin. 2010. "Untangling the Causal Effects of Sex on Judging." *American Journal of Political Science* 54: 389–411.

Boyd, Christina L., Michael S. Lynch, and Anthony Madonna. 2015. "Nuclear Fallout: Investigating the Effect of Senate Procedural Reform on Judicial Nominations." *The Forum* 13 (4): 623–41.

Brasher, Holly. 2006. "Listening to Hearings: Legislative Hearings and Legislative Outcomes." *American Politics Research* 34 (5): 583–604.

Bromwich, Jonah Engel, and Niraj Chokshi. 2017. "Trump Judicial Nominee Attracts Scorn After Flopping in Hearing." *New York Times*, December 15. https://www.nytimes.com/2017/12/15/us/politics/matthew-petersen-senator-kennedy.html

Brookings Institution. 2017. "Vital Statistics on Congress." https://www.brookings.edu/multi-chapter-report/vital-statistics-on-congress/

Bruhl, Aaron-Andrew P. 2011. "If the Judicial Confirmation Process Is Broken, Can a Statute Fix It?" *Nebraska Law Review* 85 (4): 960–1014.

Bullock, Charles S. 1985. "U.S. Senate Committee Assignments: Preferences, Motivations, and Success." *American Journal of Political Science* 29 (4): 789–808.

Burden, Barry C. 2002. "United States Senators as Presidential Candidates." *Political Science Quarterly* 117 (1): 81–102.

Burden, Barry C. 2007. *Personal Roots of Representation*. Princeton: Princeton University Press.

Carnes, Nicholas. 2013. *White-Collar Government: The Hidden Role of Class in Economic Policy Making*. Chicago: University of Chicago Press.

Carney, Jordain. 2019. "Senate Confirms Trump Court Pick Despite Missing Two 'Blue Slips.'" *The Hill*, February 26. https://thehill.com/homenews/senate/431717-senate-confirms-trump-court-nominee-despite-missing-two-blue-slips

Christophersen, James. 2013. "Obama's Empathy Rule: Alive and Well in the Second Term." *National Review*, April 9. http://www.nationalreview.com/bench-memos/345108/obamas-empathy-rule-alive-and-well-second-term-james-christophersen

Clark, Tom S., Jeffrey R. Lax, and Douglas Rice. 2015. "Measuring the Political Salience of Supreme Court Cases." *Journal of Law and Courts* 3: 37–65.

Collins, Paul M. Jr., and Lori A. Ringhand. 2013. *Supreme Court Confirmation Hearings and Constitutional Change*. New York: Cambridge University Press.

Collins, Paul M. Jr., and Lori A. Ringhand. 2016. "The Institutionalization of Supreme Court Confirmation Hearings." *Law & Social Inquiry* 41 (1): 126–51.

Dancey, Logan, Kjersten R. Nelson, and Eve M. Ringsmuth. 2011. "'Strict Scrutiny?' The Content of Senate Judicial Confirmation Hearings during the George W. Bush Administration." *Judicature* 95 (3): 126–35.

Dancey, Logan, Kjersten R. Nelson, and Eve M. Ringsmuth. 2014. "Individual Scrutiny or Politics as Usual? Senatorial Assessment of U.S. District Court Nominees." *American Politics Research* 42 (5): 784–814.

Dancey, Logan, Kjersten R. Nelson, Eve M. Ringsmuth, and Emma Solomon. 2018. "Invoking Precedent: Discussion of Supreme Court Decisions at Circuit Court Confirmation Hearings." *American Politics Research*. https://doi.org/10.1177/1532673X18788041

Dewar, Helen. 2003. "Polarized Politics, Confirmation Chaos; Retribution Appears Evident in Nominations Since the Late 1980s." *Washington Post*, May 11, A05.

Diermeier, Daniel, and Timothy J. Feddersen. 2000. "Information and Congressional Hearings." *American Journal of Political Science* 44 (1): 51–65.

Doyle, Michael. 2011. "Federal Appeals Court Nominee Liu Faces Senate Vote."

McClatchy Newspapers, May 18. http://www.mcclatchydc.com/news/politics-government/article24633889.html

Duffin, Diane L. 2003. "Explaining Participation in Congressional Oversight Hearings." *American Politics Research* 31 (5): 455–84.

Eastland, James O. 1962. "The Senate Judiciary Committee." *Mississippi Law Journal* 33 (May): 360–65.

Egan, Patrick J. 2013. *Partisan Priorities: How Issue Ownership Drives and Distorts American Politics*. New York: Cambridge University Press.

Evans, C. Lawrence. 1991. "Participation and Policy Making in Senate Committees." *Political Science Quarterly* 106 (3): 479–98.

Evans, C. Lawrence. 1997. *Leadership in Committee: A Comparative Analysis of Leadership Behavior in the U.S. Senate*. Ann Arbor: University of Michigan Press.

Farganis, Dion, and Justin Wedeking. 2014. *Supreme Court Confirmation Hearings in the U.S. Senate*. Ann Arbor: University of Michigan Press.

Fenno, Richard. 1973. *Home Style: House Members in Their Districts*. Boston: Little, Brown.

Fenno, Richard. 1977. "U.S. House Members in Their Constituencies." *American Political Science Review* 71: 883–917.

Fiorina, Morris P. 1989. *Congress: Keystone of the Washington Establishment*. New Haven: Yale University Press.

Fraser, Eric M., David K. Kessler, Matthew J. B. Lawrence, and Stephen A. Calhoun. 2013. "The Jurisdiction of the D.C. Circuit." *Cornell Journal of Law and Public Policy* 23: 131–55.

Francisco, Brian. 2018. "Local Attorney Holly Brady Fields Senators' Questions at Judicial Confirmation Hearing." *The Journal Gazette*, June 6. http://www.journalgazette.net/news/local/20180606/local-attorney-holly-brady-fields-senators-questions-at-judicial-confirmation-hearing

Frisch, Scott A., and Sean Q. Kelly. 2004. "Self-Selection Reconsidered: House Committee Assignment Requests and Constituency Characteristics." *Political Research Quarterly* 57 (2): 325–36.

Frisch, Scott A., and Sean Q. Kelly. 2006. "Committee Assignment Politics in the U.S. Senate: Democratic Leaders and Democratic Committee Assignments, 1953–1994." *Congress & the Presidency* 33 (1): 1–23.

Galston, William A. 2012. *Reforming Institutions: The Next President Should Not Miss This Moment to Make Government Work*. Brookings Institution. https://www.brookings.edu/research/reforming-institutionsthe-next-president-should-not-miss-this-moment-to-make-government-work/

Gamble, Katrina L. 2007. "Black Political Representation: An Examination of Legislative Activity within U.S. House Committees." *Legislative Studies Quarterly* 32 (3): 421–47.

Gilbert, Meghan. 2006. "U.S. Senate Confirms Zouhary: Unanimous Vote Sends Judge to Federal Bench." *Toledo Blade*, March 17. Retrieved from https://advance.lexis.com/api/document?collection=news&id=urn:contentItem:4JH1-7200-TW9S-2300-00000-00&context=1516831

Gilligan, Thomas W., and Keith Krehbiel. 1990. "Organization of Informative Committees by a Rational Legislature." *American Journal of Political Science* 34 (2): 531–64.

Goldman, Sheldon. 1997. *Picking Federal Judges: Lower Court Selection from Roosevelt through Reagan*. New Haven: Yale University Press.
Greenhouse, Linda. 1995. "The Nation: Gavel Rousers; Farewell to the Old Order in the Court." *New York Times*, July 2. https://www.nytimes.com/1995/07/02/weekinreview/the-nation-gavel-rousers-farewell-to-the-old-order-in-the-court.html
Greenhouse, Linda. 2000. "Battle on Federalism." *New York Times*, May 17. https://www.nytimes.com/2000/05/17/us/battle-on-federalism.html
Grimmer, Justin. 2010. "A Bayesian Hierarchical Topic Model for Political Texts: Measuring Expressed Agendas in Senate Press Releases." *Political Analysis* 18 (1): 1–35.
Grimmer, Justin. 2013. *Representational Style: What Legislators Say and Why It Matters*. New York: Cambridge University Press.
Grimmer, Justin, Sean Westwood, and Solomon Messing. 2014. *The Impression of Influence: Legislator Communication, Representation, and Democratic Accountability*. Princeton: Princeton University Press.
Haire, Susan B., and Laura P. Moyer. 2015. *Diversity Matters: Judicial Policy Making in the U.S. Court of Appeals*. Charlottesville: University of Virginia Press.
Hall, Richard L. 1987. "Participation and Purpose in Committee Decision Making." *American Political Science Review* 81: 105–28.
Hefling, Kimberly. 2017. "Thousands Flood Senate Phone Lines Seeking to Halt Confirmation of Devos." *Politico*, January 26. http://www.politico.com/story/2017/01/betsy-devos-confirmation-senate-phone-lines-234216
Holian, David. B. 2004. "He's Stealing My Issues! Clinton's Crime Rhetoric and the Dynamics of Issue Ownership." *Political Behavior* 26: 95–124.
Huitt, Ralph K. 1954. "The Congressional Committee: A Case Study." *American Political Science Review* 48 (2): 340–65.
Huddy, Leonie, and Nayda Terkildsen. 1993. "Gender Stereotypes and the Perception of Male and Female Candidates." *American Journal of Political Science* 37: 119–47.
Hulse, Dean. 2017. "Unity Was Emerging on Sentencing. Then Came Jeff Sessions." *New York Times*, May 14. https://www.nytimes.com/2017/05/14/us/politics/jeff-sessions-criminal-sentencing.html
Ives, Kathleen O'Connor. 2006. "Out of the Loop: Female Federal District Court Candidates Disadvantaged by a Nomination Process Imbued with Favoritism." *Texas Journal of Women and the Law* 16: 103–27.
Jacobsmeier, Matthew L. 2015. "From Black and White to Left and Right: Race, Perception of Candidates' Ideologies, and Voting Behavior in U.S. House Elections." *Political Behavior* 37. http://link.springer.com/article/10.1007/s11109-014-9283-3
Jacobson, Gary C. 2015. "It's Nothing Personal: The Decline of the Incumbency Advantage in U.S. House Elections." *Journal of Politics* 77 (3): 861–73.
Kastellec, Jonathan P. 2011a. "Hierarchical and Collegial Politics on the U.S. Courts of Appeals." *Journal of Politics* 73: 345–61.
Kastellec, Jonathan P. 2011b. "Panel Composition and Voting on the U.S. Courts of Appeals Over Time." *Political Research Quarterly* 62: 377–91.
Kastellec, Jonathan P. 2013. "Racial Diversity and Judicial Influence on Appellate Courts." *American Journal of Political Science* 57: 167–83.

Koch, Jeffrey W. 2000. "Do Citizens Apply Gender Stereotypes to Infer Candidates' Ideological Orientations?" *Journal of Politics* 62: 414–29.

Krehbiel, Keith. 1991. *Information and Legislative Organization*. Ann Arbor: University of Michigan Press.

Lapinski, John, Matt Levendusky, Ken Winneg, and Kathleen Hall Jamieson. 2016. "What Do Citizens Want from Their Member of Congress?" *Political Research Quarterly* 69 (3): 535–45.

LeRose, Kelsie. 2018. "Tom Kleeh Considered for District Judge for Northern District." *The Journal*, April 26. http://www.journal-news.net/news/local-news/2018/04/tom-kleeh-confirmed-as-district-judge-for-northern-district/

Lewis, Andrew R. 2014. "Staffing the Front Line of the Culture War: Constituency Religious Effects on Assignment to the Senate Judiciary Committee." *Congress & the Presidency* 41 (2): 167–89.

Lewis, Jeffrey B., Keith Poole, Howard Rosenthal, Adam Boche, Aaron Rudkin, and Luke Sonnet. 2019. *Voteview: Congressional Roll-Call Votes Database*. https://voteview.com/

Lombard, Matthew, Jennifer Snyder-Duch, and Cheryl Campanella Bracken. 2002. "Content Analysis in Mass Communication: Assessment and Reporting of Intercoder Reliability." *Human Communication Research* 28 (4): 587–604.

Long, J. Scott. 1997. *Regression Models for Categorical and Limited Dependent Variables. Advanced Quantitative Techniques in the Social Sciences Number* 7. Thousand Oaks, CA: Sage Publications.

Lott, John R. Jr. 2005. "The Judicial Confirmation Process: The Difficulty with Being Smart." *Journal of Empirical Legal Studies* 2 (3): 407–47.

Lott, John R. Jr. 2006. "Pulling Rank." *New York Times*, January 25 (final ed.), A21.

Mahony, Edmund. 2018. "U.S. Judge Nominee Has Senate Hearing." *Hartford Courant*, March 7. http://www.courant.com/news/connecticut/hc-dooley-hearing-20180307-story.html

Martin, Elaine, and Barry Pyle. 2005. "State High Courts and Divorce: The Impact of Judicial Gender." *University of Toledo Law Review* 36: 923–48.

Martinek, Wendy L., Mark Kemper, and Steven R. Van Winkle. 2002. "To Advise and Consent: The Senate and Lower Federal Court Nominations, 1977–1998." *Journal of Politics* 64 (2): 337–61.

Mascaro, Lisa, and Gene Johnson. 2019. "Senate Confirms Circuit Court Nominee Over Dem Objections." *Associated Press*, February 26. https://www.apnews.com/77281f9c37dc42b9bd1c3fe7fdb22ecf

Mayhew, David. 1974. *Congress: The Electoral Connection*. New Haven: Yale University Press.

McCubbins, Mathew D., and Thomas Schwartz. 1984. "Congressional Oversight Overlooked: Police Patrols versus Fire Alarms." *American Journal of Political Science* 28 (1): 165–79.

McDermott, Monica L. 1998. "Race and Gender Cues in Low-Information Elections." *Political Research Quarterly* 51 (4): 895–918.

McHugh, Mary L. 2012. "Interrater Reliability: The Kappa Statistic." *Biochemia Medica* 22 (2): 276–82.

McMillion, Barry J. 2013. "Length of Time from Nomination to Confirmation for U.S. Circuit and District Court Nominees: Overview and Policy Options to Shorten the Process." Congressional Research Service Report. November 20.

Minta, Michael D. 2009. "Legislative Oversight and the Substantive Representation of Black and Latino Interests in Congress." *Legislative Studies Quarterly* 34 (2): 193–218.

Munger, Michael C., and Gary M. Torrent. 1993. "Committee Power and Value in the U.S. Senate: Implications for Policy." *Journal of Public Administration Research and Theory* 3 (1): 46–65.

National Center for State Courts. 2018. "Federal Judicial Selection." http://www.judicialselection.us/federal_judicial_selection/federal_judicial_nominating_commissions.cfm?state=&st=California. Accessed on August 27, 2018.

NBC News. 2005. "Confirmation Vote for Embattled Nominee Expected Wednesday." http://www.nbcnews.com/id/7962734/ns/politics/t/confirmation-vote-for-embattled-nominee-expected-wednesday/#.WMrYpWfavIU

Nemacheck, Christine L. 2007. *Strategic Selection: Presidential Nomination of Supreme Court Justices from Herbert Hoover through George W. Bush*. Charlottesville: University of Virginia Press.

Ohlheiser, Abby. 2017. "A Trump Judicial Nominee Starred in a 'Must Watch' Viral Video. In 2017, Does That Matter?" *Washington Post*, December 15.https://www.washingtonpost.com/news/the-intersect/wp/2017/12/15/a-trump-judicial-nominee-starred-in-a-must-watch-viral-video-in-2017-does-that-matter/?utm_term=.3a0754da75d3

Ostberg, C. L., and Matthew Wetstein. 2007. *Attitudinal Decision Making in the Supreme Court of Canada*. Vancouver: University of British Columbia Press.

Park, Ju Yeon. 2017. "A Lab Experiment on Committee Hearings: Preferences, Power, and a Quest for Information." *Legislative Studies Quarterly* 42 (1): 3–31.

People for the American Way. 2004. "Leon Holmes Should Not be Confirmed to Federal Bench." http://www.pfaw.org/press-releases/leon-holmes-should-not-be-confirmed-to-federal-bench/. Accessed on August 24, 2018.

Peresie, Jennifer L. 2005. "Female Judges Matter: Gender and Collegial Decision-making in the Federal Appellate Courts." *Yale Law Journal* 114: 1759–90.

Petrocik, John R. 1996. "Issue Ownership in Presidential Elections, With a 1980 Case Study." *American Journal of Political Science* 40: 825–50.

Primo, David M., Sarah A. Binder, and Forrest Maltzman. 2008. "Who Consents? Competing Pivots in Federal Judicial Selection." *American Journal of Political Science* 52: 471–89.

Ross, William. 2001. "The Questioning of Lower Federal Court Nominees at Senate Confirmation Hearings." *William & Mary Bill of Rights Journal* 10 (1): 119–76.

Rutkus, Denis Steven. 2016. "The Appointment Process for U.S. Circuit and District Court Nominations: An Overview." Congressional Research Service Report. June 17.

Sanbonmatsu, Kira. 2002. "Gender Stereotypes and Vote Choice." *American Journal of Political Science* 46 (January): 20–34.

Savage, Charlie. 2017. "Poor Vetting Sinks Trump's Nominees for Federal Judge." *New York Times*, December 18. https://www.nytimes.com/2017/12/18/us/politics/matthew-petersen-judge-nominee-withdraws-trump.html

Savage, David G. 2001. "Anita Hill Writer Says Judge Leaked FBI Files." *Los Angeles Times*, August 25.

Scherer, Nancy. 2003. "The Judicial Confirmation Process: Mobilizing Elites, Mobilizing Masses." *Judicature* 86: 240–50.

Scherer, Nancy. 2004. "Blacks on the Bench." *Political Science Quarterly* 119: 655–72.

Scherer, Nancy. 2005. *Scoring Points: Politicians, Activists, and the Lower Federal Court Appointment Process*. Palo Alto, CA: Stanford University Press.

Scherer, Nancy, Brandon L. Bartels, and Amy Steigerwalt. 2008. "Sounding the Fire Alarm: The Role of Interest Groups in the Lower Federal Court Confirmation Process." *Journal of Politics* 70 (4): 1026–39.

Schneider, Monica C., and Angela L. Bos. 2011. "An Exploration of the Content of Stereotypes of Black Politicians." *Political Psychology* 32: 205–32.

Segal, Jeffrey A., Harold J. Spaeth, and Sara C. Benesh. 2005. *The Supreme Court in the American Legal System*. New York: Cambridge University Press.

Senate Rule XXXI. United States Senate. Available at https://www.rules.senate.gov/rules-of-the-senate

Sen, Maya. 2014. "How Judicial Qualifications Ratings May Disadvantage Minority and Female Candidates." *Journal of Law and Courts* 2: 33–65.

Shenkman, Michael L. 2012. "Decoupling District from Circuit Judge Nominations: A Proposal to Put Trial Bench Confirmations on Track." *Arkansas Law Review* 65: 217–315.

Shottenkirk, Jerry. 2006. "Oklahoma Attorney Holmes Passes Judiciary Committee Test." *Journal Record Legislative Report*, July 14. Retrieved from https://advance.lexis.com/api/document?collection=news&id=urn:contentItem:4KDG-KY00-TX2H-22JV-00000-00&context=1516831

Sievert, Joel, and Seth C. McKee. 2018. "Nationalization in U.S. Senate and Gubernatorial Elections." *American Politics Research*. https://doi.org/10.1177/1532673X18792694

Sinclair, Barbara. 1989. *The Transformation of the U.S. Senate*. Baltimore: Johns Hopkins University Press.

Sinclair, Barbara. 2012. "The New World of U.S. Senators." In *Congress Reconsidered: Tenth Edition*, edited by Lawrence C. Dodd and Bruce I. Oppenheimer. Washington, DC: Congressional Quarterly Press.

Smelcer, Susan Navarro, Amy Steigerwalt, and Richard L. Vining Jr. 2012. "Bias and the Bar: Evaluating the ABA Ratings of Federal Judicial Nominees." *Political Research Quarterly* 65: 827–40.

Smith, Steven S., and Christopher J. Deering. 1984. *Committees in Congress*. Washington, DC: Congressional Quarterly Press.

Sollenberger, Mitchel A. 2010. "The Blue Slip: A Theory of Unified and Divided Government, 1979–2009." *Congress & the Presidency* 37: 125–56.

Sollenberger, Mitchel. 2011. *Judicial Appointments and Democratic Controls*. Durham, NC: Carolina Academic Press.

Solowiej, Lisa A., Wendy L. Martinek, and Thomas L. Brunell. 2005. "The Impact of Party in the Confirmation of Minority and Female Federal Court Nominees." *Party Politics* 11 (5): 557–77.

Spaeth, Harold J., Lee Epstein, Andrew D. Martin, Jeffrey A. Segal, Theodore J. Ruger, and Sara C. Benesh. 2018 Supreme Court Database, Version 2018 Release 02. URL: http://Supremecourtdatabase.org

Steigerwalt, Amy. 2010. *Battle Over the Bench: Senators, Interest Groups and Lower Court Confirmations*. Charlottesville: University of Virginia Press.

Stewart, Charles III, and Jonathan Woon. 2017. Congressional Committee Assignments, 103rd to 112th Congresses, 1993–2011: Senate.

Stirewalt, Chris. 2017. "Senator Kennedy and the Case of the Nervous Nominee." *Foxnews.com*, Dec. 15. http://www.foxnews.com/politics/2017/12/15/senator-kennedy-and-case-nervous-nominee.html

Stout, David. 2007. "Judge Opposed by Democrats Confirmed." *New York Times*, October 24.

Stratmann, Thomas, and Jared Garner. 2004. "Judicial Selection: Politics, Biases, and Constituency Demands." *Public Choice* 118: 251–70.

Swers, Michele L. 2013. *Women in the Club: Gender and Policy Making in the Senate*. Chicago: University of Chicago Press.

Swers, Michele L. 2016. "Pursuing Women's Interests in Partisan Times: Explaining Gender Differences in Legislative Activity on Health, Education, and Women's Health Issues." *Journal of Women, Politics, & Policy* 37: 249–73.

Tobias, Carl W. 2016. "Fixing the Federal Judicial Selection Process." *Emory Law Journal* 65: 2051–59.

Toronto Star. 2005. "U.S. Senate in Vicious Showdown Over Judges." *Toronto Star*, May 21, A20.

Totenberg, Nina. 2017. "Senate Invokes 'Nuclear Option' to Ease Gorsuch Nomination." *National Public Radio*, April 6: https://www.npr.org/2017/04/06/522903426/senate-invokes-nuclear-option-to-ease-gorsuch-nomination

Treul, Sarah A. 2009. "Ambition and Party Loyalty in the U.S. Senate." *American Politics Research* 37 (3): 449–64.

Truman, David B. 1951. *The Governmental Process: Political Interests and Public Opinion*. New York: Alfred A. Knopf.

"United States v. Lopez." *Oyez*, 19 June 2018. www.oyez.org/cases/1994/93-1260

"United States v. Morrison." *Oyez*, 19 June 2018. www.oyez.org/cases/1999/99-5

U.S. Census. 2011–2012. "Population of Wisconsin: Census 2010 and 2000 Interactive Map, Demographics, Statistics, Quick Facts." Retrieved from http://censusviewer.com/state/WI

Viera, Anthony J., and Joanne M. Garrett. 2005. "Understanding Interobserver Agreement: The Kappa Statistic." *Family Medicine* 37 (5): 360–63.

Victor, Daniel. 2016. "What Is the 'Thurmond Rule'?." *New York Times*, February 13. https://www.nytimes.com/live/supreme-court-justice-antonin-scalia-dies-at-79/what-is-the-thurmond-rule/

Walker, John M. Jr. 2012. "The Unfortunate Politicization of Judicial Confirmation Hearings." *The Atlantic*, July 9. http://www.theatlantic.com/national/archive/2012/07/the-unfortunate-politicization-of-judicial-confirmation-hearings/259445/

Watson, George, and John Stookey. 1988. "Supreme Court Confirmation Hearings: A View from the Senate." *Judicature* 71 (4): 186–96.

Westergren, Sarah. 2004. "Gender Effects in the Courts of Appeals Revisited: The Data Since 1994." *Georgetown Law Journal* 92: 689–708.

Wheeler, Russell. 2012. "Judicial Confirmations: What Thurmond Rule?" *Issues in*

Governance Studies 45 (March). http://www.brookings.edu/~/media/research/files/papers/2012/3/judicial-wheeler/03_judicial_wheeler.pdf

Wolf, Richard. 2017. "Court Nominee Matthew Petersen Withdraws after 'Two Worst Minutes' on TV and Viral Video." *USA Today*, December 18. https://www.usatoday.com/story/news/politics/2017/12/18/court-nominee-matthew-petersen-withdraws-after-two-worst-minutes-tv-and-viral-video/962019001/

Index

Note: Page numbers in italics refer to tables or figures.